Every Vote Matters

The Power Of Your Voice, From Student Elections To The Supreme Court

Judge Tom Jacobs
Natalie Jacobs

16pt

Copyright Page from the Original Book

Copyright © 2016 by Thomas A. Jacobs, J.D., and Natalie C. Jacobs, J.D.

All rights reserved under International and Pan-American Copyright Conventions. Unless otherwise noted, no part of this book may be reproduced, stored in a retrieval system, or transmitted in any form or by any means, electronic, mechanical, photocopying, recording, or otherwise, without express written permission of the publisher, except for brief quotations or critical reviews. For more information, go to www.freespirit.com/permissions.

Free Spirit, Free Spirit Publishing, and associated logos are trademarks and/or registered trademarks of Free Spirit Publishing Inc. A complete listing of our logos and trademarks is available at www.freespirit.com.

Library of Congress Cataloging-in-Publication Data
Jacobs, Thomas A., author.
 Every vote matters : the power of your voice, from student elections to the Supreme Court / by Tom Jacobs and Natalie Jacobs.
     pages cm
 Includes bibliographical references and index.
  1. Law—United States—Juvenile literature. I. Jacobs, Natalie, author. II. Title.
KF387.J33 2016
342.7308'5—dc23

2015032349

Free Spirit Publishing does not have control over or assume responsibility for author or third-party websites and their content. At the time of this book's publication, all facts and figures cited within are the most current available. All telephone numbers, addresses, and website URLs are accurate and active; all publications, organizations, websites, and other resources exist as described in this book; and all have been verified as of October 2015. If you find an error or believe that a resource listed here is not as described, please contact Free Spirit Publishing. Parents, teachers, and other adults: We strongly urge you to monitor children's use of the Internet.

Photo credits: page 28 © Albund | Dreamstime.com, page 38 © Alakoo | Dreamstime.com, page 48 © Flynt | Dreamstime.com, page 57 © Scott Kelsey | Dreamstime.com, page 68 © Clewisleake | Dreamstime.com, page 79 © Chonlawut Brahmasakha | Dreamstime.com, page 89 © Rolandm | Dreamstime.com, page 99 © Fotovika | Dreamstime.com, page 108 © Gemenacom | Dreamstime.com, page 119 © Darya Petrenko | Dreamstime.com, page 128 © Jorge Salcedo | Dreamstime.com, page 138 © Saksit Choeiklin | Dreamstime.com, page 148 © Hxdbzxy | Dreamstime.com, page 158 © L Hill | Dreamstime.com, page 170 © Roman Milert | Dreamstime.com

Reading Level High School–Adult; Interest Level Ages 13 & up; Fountas & Pinnell Guided Reading Level Z+

Edited by Cathy Broberg and Alison Behnke
Cover and interior design by Colleen Rollins

Free Spirit Publishing Inc.
6325 Sandburg Road, Suite 100
Golden Valley, MN 55427-3674
(612) 338-2068
help4kids@freespirit.com
www.freespirit.com

Free Spirit offers competitive pricing.
Contact edsales@freespirit.com for pricing information on
multiple quantity purchases.

TABLE OF CONTENTS

DEDICATION	ii
ACKNOWLEDGMENTS	iii
Foreword	v
Introduction	viii
PART 1: The Supreme Court, the Law, and the Power of One Vote	1
PART 2: 5–4 Supreme Court Cases—How Do They Affect Your Life?	32
CASE 1: Evan Miller v. Alabama(2012)	32
CASE 2: United States v. Antoine Jones(2012)	50
CASE 3: Camreta v. Greene(2011)	67
CASE 4: Morse v. Joseph Frederick(2007)	82
CASE 5: McCreary County v. American Civil Liberties Union (ACLU)(2005)	101
CASE 6: Board of Education v. Lindsay Earls(2002)	120
CASE 7: Boy Scouts of America v. James Dale (2000)	137
CASE 8: Texas v. Gregory Lee Johnson (1989)	153
CASE 9: Island Trees School District v. Steven Pico(1982)	169
CASE 10: Plyler v. Doe(1982)	189
CASE 11: Regents of the University of California v. Allan Bakke (1978)	204
CASE 12: Ingraham v. Wright(1977)	222
CASE 13: Goss v. Dwight Lopez(1975)	239
CASE 14: Hazel Palmer v. Thompson(1971)	256
CASE 15: Ernesto Miranda v. Arizona(1966)	277
Additional Supreme Court 5–4 Decisions	294
A Final Word	319
How to Do Legal Research	325
Glossary of Terms	328
Notes	337
About the Authors	352
Index	359

"We are in urgent need of effective civic education, and *Every Vote Matters* is an excellent contribution that deserves wide readership."
—Rob Richie, executive director, FairVote

DEDICATION

Every Vote Matters is dedicated to my grandchildren in the hope that Kali, Taylor, Austin, Parker, Chase, Natalia, Tiago, Levi, Hannah, Paige, Felix, Jackson, Hudson, and Tomas will engage in a positive manner, travel, and contribute to our world in any way they choose.
—Tom

To my precious little ones, Paige and Felix, may you grow with courage and strength to use your voice and to allow it to be heard.
—Natalie

ACKNOWLEDGMENTS

We'd like to thank the many people who helped us with this book at various stages over three years of research and writing. Our deepest appreciation goes out to each of you. No project can succeed without the support and encouragement of others. In no particular order, they include:

Anne Lee Johnson, Lucie Jacobs, Harry and Linda Jacobs, Mike Olson, Colin Poe, Professor Ann Beeson, Sharon Dennis, Jeffrey Jacobs, Nicholas Lowinger, Julie and Nick Karnes, Steven Schwartz, Shayne Caffrey, Meera Kumar, Clint Bolick, James Sutton, Peyton Gallovich, Heather Smith, Vanessa Levy, Mike and Lana Malone, Dave and Audrey Aungst, Chris Nasrallah, Professor Rick Pildes, Frank LoMonte, Mary Beth Tinker, Jilly Dos Santos, Alex Jacobs, James Dale, Jess Bravin, Clayton Pilcher, and Jon Davis Wiley.

A note of appreciation is also extended to the Coconino County, Arizona, law librarian, Gretchen Hornberger, and the staff at the Flagstaff Public Library for their assistance throughout this endeavor.

We were also fortunate to have the wisdom and guidance of editors Cathy Broberg and Alison Behnke. Thank you both for your keen eyes and superb editing skills. Acquisitions editor, Meg Bratsch, supported and nurtured this book since 2011. Thank you, Meg, for the encouragement and creative suggestions. Judy Galbraith and her staff at Free Spirit Publishing supported this project early on. We are grateful to Free Spirit for allowing us to stimulate interest and participation by all skeptics on the subject of voting.

"Happiness—it lies in the joy of achievement, in the thrill of creative effort."
—Vincent van Gogh

Foreword

Judge Tom Jacobs is an encourager. He also cares deeply about young people and the quality, direction, and impact of their lives. The degree of his encouragement and caring fill every page of this book, *Every Vote Matters: The Power of Your Voice, from Student Elections to the Supreme Court,* by Tom and his daughter Natalie.

Tom and Natalie discuss many instances and circumstances where a single opinion—one solitary vote—dramatically changed an outcome. In turn, that change continues to affect the lives of many every day. Indeed, the impact of one vote is often more powerful and long lasting than most people realize.

You may have heard this tired excuse for not voting: "Why should I bother? It's not going to matter anyway." But that simply isn't true. Regardless of the question or the candidate, your opinion matters, because *you* matter. Besides, no matter your age or circumstance, the skills of civic responsibility grow stronger *only* when they are used. So vote when there's opportunity. It *does* make a difference.

What If You Couldn't Vote?

Few of us will ever face a situation where, as much as we would like to register our opinion, voting would be impossible. But if that *were* the situation, how might it affect you? That's a good question—one that deserves a bit of thought.

That was precisely the circumstance of a friend of mine who was a Navy pilot. During the Vietnam Conflict his aircraft was shot down over North Vietnam, and he became a prisoner of war (POW) for over seven years in the dreaded Hoa Lo Prison, better known as the Hanoi Hilton.

As a POW, he was unable to vote in the elections back home, but he continued to exercise the character of citizenship. "Even with the torture and the deplorable conditions there," he told me, "I was acutely aware of what was right and what was wrong, and that I *knew* the difference." He was finally freed in 1973, and I'm pretty sure he's never passed up a ballot box since. He even ran for a seat in the U.S. Senate in his home state of Hawaii.

Honoring Those Who Paid the Price

As I reflect on the rights and responsibilities that come with living in the United States, I realize that my first lesson in American citizenship came early: I was born during what historians call the Battle of the Bulge, the biggest and most costly battle involving U.S. forces in WWII Europe. These troops, desperately low on food, ammunition, and cold-weather clothing, were surrounded and subjected to a terrifying, nonstop shelling by the enemy's biggest guns. Yet they did not retreat or surrender. They held their ground with courage and fortitude. In doing so, they hastened the end of an ugly war.

It was many years later before I really understood that these soldiers took a stand for me—then just a tiny baby in Texas—as much as for anyone else. I wish I could say that since then I've honored their sacrifice in my actions every day. What I can say is that, with this book, Tom and Natalie Jacobs have restoked a fire in me, and I intend to *keep* that fire lit from now on. I wish for you that same experience.

James D. Sutton, Ed.D.
Psychologist and host of The Changing Behavior Network

Introduction

> **Statement:** My one vote won't make any difference, so why should I bother to register and vote?
>
> **Response:** Never doubt the power of your voice and your vote. The president of the United States can be elected by *one* vote! And once elected, the president nominates Supreme Court justices, who can sit on the Court for life and who decide cases important to all Americans—sometimes by *one* vote. Elections at all levels and ballot propositions can also succeed or fail due to just *one* vote.

Imagine having the power to cast your vote to help determine answers to society's toughest questions, the most complicated and controversial issues of the day: crime and punishment, religion, same-sex marriage, healthcare, affirmative action, and many more concerns. That is exactly the task before the nine justices on the U.S. Supreme Court. Each year, these justices hear and decide approximately eighty cases that affect every American of every age. Perhaps on the Court more than in any other setting, the power of one vote has a lasting and an extensive reach. Indeed, since majority rules in the nation's highest Court, that one vote can result in a 5–4 decision, giving immense power and responsibility to each Supreme Court justice.

Yet all citizens of the United States, once they reach age eighteen, also have the power to cast votes on issues and candidates that affect their lives and the world around them. From voting for local and state officials, to voting for ballot measures such as **referendums** or **initiatives,** to casting a vote in presidential elections, we each have the opportunity to voice our opinions when we go to the polls. And while you may not have a direct say when it comes to the larger issues that the Supreme Court grapples with, you do have some influence over who *does* have a vote.

Every four years, the president of the United States is either elected or reelected. One of his or her many duties and responsibilities is to nominate justices to the United States Supreme Court when openings arise. Then the president's nominations must be confirmed by majority support in the U.S. Senate. The 100 senators have an opportunity to question the nominee, which can take a few days or even weeks, depending on the candidate and the issues raised. (And by the way, some justices have received Senate confirmation by just one vote.)

IN OTHER WORDS

"The shift of a single vote would sharply alter the court's philosophical balance, on a host of issues that touch the lives of every American."

—Clint Bolick, Goldwater Institute

This means that when you cast a vote for president or for your state's two senators, you are potentially affecting the makeup of the Supreme Court, since presidents typically nominate—and senators typically confirm—justices who share their views on important issues. In this way, every vote in presidential and senate elections counts not only toward deciding who sits in the Oval Office and Senate chambers, but also toward deciding who sits in the highest court of the land for many years (or even decades) and makes decisions about the fundamental constitutional rights of all Americans.

Did You Know?

In the 2012 Supreme Court term, twenty-three decisions—nearly one-third of the Court's cases—resulted in a 5–4 vote. In the 2013 term, ten out of the sixty-seven cases heard were decided by one vote. And in the 2014 term, the Court ruled 5–4 in nineteen out of seventy-six cases.

While many Court decisions are unanimous, some contentious issues have divided the Court. In these cases, one vote makes all the difference. Since 1946, more than 1,000 Supreme Court cases have been decided by a single vote. The lead cases in each chapter of this book all resulted in these 5–4 decisions, and all affect teenagers and children as well as adults. Had one vote gone the other way in these cases, your world might have been quite different. In this book, we'll look at some of these cases and the thorny issues they involved, including:

- whether your school can suspend or expel you without explaining why or giving you a chance to be heard
- your rights in the **juvenile** justice system
- the authority of police to track your location without a search warrant
- whether kids and teens over eight years old can be sentenced to prison for life without parole
- the right for same-sex couples to marry under federal law
- whether religious messages and symbols can be displayed in public schools
- in the college admission process, the right to consider an applicant's race in an attempt to build a diverse student body

Other 5–4 cases in this book focus on issues such as drug testing students at school, excluding gay leaders in the Boy Scouts, flag burning, censorship at school, and your rights as a student on and off campus.

IN OTHER WORDS

> **Former Justice William Brennan once asked his law clerks, "What's the most important law at the Supreme Court?" His answer: "Five! The law of five! With five votes, you can do anything around here."**

As you will read in this book, a single vote by one Supreme Court justice—or by one electoral college member, or one U.S. Senator—has the power to affect the lives of millions. Similarly, the vote of every citizen counts, whether in a school, city, state, or national election. Even before you're old enough to vote in state and national elections, your opinion matters and you can make a difference. As a teenager, you can get involved in the election process in several ways. If your school holds class elections, you can vote in these elections, support a candidate, or run for an office yourself. You can also listen to the issues discussed during the elections for student body offices. You have the right to vote, and your vote may help decide what changes or improvements your school's new student leaders make. You can also make your voice heard in the clubs you join or sports you play. Club officers and team captains have responsibilities that build skills for future pursuits. When you participate in these opportunities, you make your voice heard, and you lay the foundations of a lifelong habit of engagement and action that you can be proud of.

> ### Did You Know?
> In the 2014 **midterm elections,** only 37 percent of eligible voters cast ballots—the lowest turnout rate since World War II.

As an adult, your vote becomes a powerful way to voice your opinion. Voting is often called a privilege and a right, and it's essential to a thriving democracy as a way to share your opinions and ideals. After reading this book, you'll have a better understanding of why it's so important to have a say in matters that impact your life and you'll see how you can make a difference. Your opinion counts. Silence is nonproductive. How will you use your voice?

About This Book

This book is divided into two parts. Part I discusses the history of the Supreme Court, how it works, and its role in our nation as the highest court in the judicial system. We'll also look at the election process in the United States, talk about the process of voting and how to register to vote, and discuss why your vote makes a difference. You'll learn about key events in the history of voting in the United States. Whether this information is new to you or you read it as a refresher, it will help you understand the cases that follow.

Part II presents fifteen Supreme Court cases that were decided by a vote of 5–4. Each case begins with the key issue and the facts of the case. Then the Court's ruling is revealed, along with the reasoning the justices used to reach this decision. Related cases are presented next, illustrating the ongoing debate over these issues in courtrooms across the country. Some of these related cases were Supreme Court cases, while others were heard in lower courts at the federal or state level. The decisions in some, but not all, of these cases came down to one vote. (The case names and year can be found at the end of each related case; full citations for these cases appear in the Notes section at the end of the book.)

At the end of each chapter, you'll find discussion starters or suggestions for taking action on the issues that interest you. Each chapter closes with a list of resources.

> ## IN OTHER WORDS
> "Nobody will ever deprive the American people of the right to vote except the American people themselves and the only way they could do this is by not voting."
> —President Franklin Roosevelt

The cases you read about in this book may spur further questions in your mind. If you want to learn more about the cases and why the U.S. Supreme Court (or a lower court) ruled the way it did, check out the section called "How to Do Legal Research" at the back of the book. You'll find lots of tips for doing your own investigation into legal decisions.

In addition, in reviewing the cases discussed in the book, you'll come across certain legal terms that may be new to you. Terms in **bold** are included in the glossary at the end of the book.

We're always interested in hearing from teens about their experiences and questions. If you'd like to get in touch with us, you can reach us through our website, AsktheJudge.info. You can also email us at help4kids@freespirit.com, or contact us in care of:
Free Spirit Publishing
6325 Sandburg Road, Suite 100
Golden Valley, MN 55427-3674

We look forward to hearing from you!

Tom Jacobs, J.D., and Natalie Jacobs, J.D.

PART I

The Supreme Court, the Law, and the Power of One Vote

The U.S. Supreme Court: What Does It Do and Why Is It Important?

In 1789, Congress passed the Judiciary Act, which established the U.S. Supreme Court as the highest court in the land. The act determined that the Court would be composed of a Chief Justice and five associate justices. In the Court's first eighty years, its size changed a number of times, but since 1869, nine justices have been on the Court (eight associate justices and one Chief Justice). The U.S. Constitution (Article II, Section 2) gives the president the power—with the Senate's consent—to appoint judges to the Supreme Court when seats are open.

The Supreme Court heads the judicial branch of the federal government. The three branches of government—the judicial, executive, and legislative branches—provide checks and balances on each other's actions and authority. The Supreme Court's job is to interpret the Constitution and review lower court cases. The Court also has the power to declare an act of Congress unconstitutional.

Local laws and ordinances, as well as state and federal statutes, govern the actions of all U.S. citizens and others who live in the United States. Rights and responsibilities stem from the U.S. Constitution and its amendments, particularly the first ten, which are referred to as the Bill of Rights. It is the job of the Supreme Court to interpret these founding documents while taking into account legal precedent (how earlier courts have ruled on similar issues), as well as considering current national consensus (what most citizens think about an issue).

Did You Know?

When the Supreme Court first met in 1790, the justices had little to do as they had no cases to consider. So they traveled the country conducting trials in lower court cases.

The Supreme Court meets each year in Washington, D.C., from the first Monday in October to the end of June. Arguments are open to the public, but the limited seating is offered on a first-come, first-served basis.

The Court receives about 10,000 petitions for **certiorari** (review) each year. At least four justices must agree to accept a case, and only 1 percent (75 to 80 cases) are accepted each term and set for oral argument. During oral argument, each side has thirty to sixty minutes to present its position. During this process, the justices frequently interrupt the lawyers' arguments to ask questions.

The Supreme Court decides what cases it will hear based on national importance and pressing legal issues of the day. The Court hears specific types of cases—for example, ones that involve disputes between states, and cases from lower federal courts that conflict with each other. It also interprets federal laws and treaties. The most common types of case it hears involve constitutional questions in civil and criminal matters. If an issue involving a federal constitutional right exists, the case may proceed to the federal courts for resolution. Otherwise, state courts are the proper **jurisdiction** to settle disputes.

IN OTHER WORDS

"The most fundamental principle of constitutional adjudication is not to face constitutional questions but to avoid them, if at all possible."

—Justice Felix Frankfurter, **concurring opinion** in *U.S. v. Lovett* (1946)

Each year, the Court is petitioned to consider issues including a woman's right to choose, gun control, LGBTQ rights, campaign finance laws, voting rights, equal opportunity hiring practices, income equality, and other issues important to all Americans.

One area of law the Court is reluctant to hear is family law cases, or what's often called "domestic relations." The Court has held this view since at least 1890 when the justices wrote in *In re Burrus,* "The whole subject of the domestic relations of husband and wife, parent and child, belongs to the laws of the States and not to the laws of the United States."

The Court recognizes the importance of the decision to hear or not hear a case. In the 1936 case *U.S. v. Butler,* Justice Harlan Stone wrote that "the only check upon our own exercise of power is our own sense of self-restraint." And in 1982 Chief Justice William Rehnquist wrote that the Court had a "long considered practice not to decide abstract, hypothetical or contingent questions, or to decide any constitutional question in advance of the necessity for its decision." *(Island Trees School District v. Pico)*

(For more information about how the Court selects cases for review, see case 3: *Camreta v. Greene.*)

Although the justices do not consider evidence or arguments from anyone who is not involved in the case before them, they do pay attention to issues and trends of national concern. Sometimes, they allow organizations to file "friend of court briefs," called **amicus briefs,** in high-profile cases. For example, when the Court legalized same-sex marriage in 2015 in *Obergefell v. Hodges,* more than 100 amicus briefs were filed with the Court. These are written arguments presenting organizations' positions on an issue before the court.

Talk, Think, and Take Action

- If you feel strongly about an issue that is currently before the Supreme Court, make your views known. One way to do this is by contacting a national group or foundation that has taken a stand on the issue as well and is preparing an amicus brief. Express your views to such a group, so it can consider your position while preparing its amicus brief for the Court.
- What do you think of the petitioning process and the method the Court uses for deciding which cases to hear? Do you think these practices could be improved in any way? If so, how?
- Justices on the U.S. Supreme Court need to be educated in law, though they do not need to be law school graduates. What are your thoughts about this? Do you think there should be official requirements for a Supreme Court justice? If so, what do you think would best prepare someone for this important

position? If you see yourself taking a seat on the Court someday, what education and career path do you plan on pursuing?

• The first African-American justice appointed to the Supreme Court was Thurgood Marshall, who served from 1967 to 1991. Justice Sandra Day O'Connor was the first woman on the Court, serving from 1981 to 2006. And in 2009, Sonia Sotomayor became the first Hispanic Supreme Court justice; she is still on the Court. Do you think it's ideal for the makeup of the Court to be diverse? If so, in what ways do you think it should be diverse? How do you think issues are viewed differently by people with different backgrounds?

• New Supreme Court justices are a bit like freshmen in high school: They have not yet earned all the privileges that come with being an upperclassman. On the Court, the duties of the newest justice may include taking notes, speaking last during conferences when the justices gather to discuss a case, and answering the door if someone knocks during a conference. Unlike being a freshman in high school, however, the most recently appointed justice continues carrying out these duties for more than one year in most cases. He or she does so until the next justice is appointed—which has been as long as ten years. What do you think of this ranking system? Although being a "freshman" justice has disadvantages, what do you think some advantages might be of being in this position on the Court?

- If you're interested in the thought process, analysis, and discussion that go into judicial decision making, you may be able to get a taste while you're still in high school by volunteering with a local teen court. Teen courts offer an alternative disciplinary program in the school setting and a way for minor juvenile offenses to be diverted away from, or stay out of, the justice system. To learn more about teen court and volunteer opportunities available near you, contact your local juvenile justice department or check out globalyouthjustice.org for a list of such programs around the country.

The Election Process

The president of the United States is elected through a combination of the popular vote (votes by ordinary citizens) and the electoral vote (votes by congressional delegates). Each state is allotted a certain number of electoral votes that varies depending on the number of representatives the state has in Congress. So each state receives two votes for its two Senators, plus the number of members the state has in the House of Representatives. (The District of Columbia has three electoral votes.) The number of representatives for each state is based on the state's population according to the U.S. Census taken every ten years. For example, Florida has two senators, plus twenty-seven members in the House of Representatives. Therefore, Florida had twenty-nine electoral votes in the 2012 presidential election. In all states but Maine and Nebraska (which award electoral votes based on voting within its congressional districts), electoral votes are pledged to the candidate who receives the greatest number of popular votes in that state. In order to win the presidential election, a candidate needs 270 electoral votes.

Did You Know?

• George Washington was the only U.S. president in history elected unanimously by the Electoral College. In 1789 and 1792, he won the popular vote in each state, thereby giving him all of the electoral votes.

• In 1800, Thomas Jefferson was elected president by one vote in the House of Representatives over Aaron Burr who became vice president.

• In 1876, Rutherford B. Hayes became the nineteenth president after defeating Samuel Tilden by one electoral vote. If the popular vote in any number of states had gone the other way by just *one* citizen's vote, the electoral votes might have been distributed differently, leading to a different outcome.

IN OTHER WORDS

"Do you really want to have no say in policies that determine whether or not you have a job, what you pay for college, whether climate change ever gets addressed or even acknowledged? Voting is critical, but it is just one step in the broad spectrum of engagement required to advance real change, whatever your goals and ideology. For democracy to flourish, we need people to do it all—vote, volunteer, and raise some righteous hell."
—Professor Ann Beeson, University of Texas

In 2000, George W. Bush was elected the forty-third president by a margin of just five electoral votes. The popular vote in Florida was so close that Bush's opponent, Al Gore, requested a recount. The Florida Supreme Court ordered a manual recount of the votes. Then Bush asked the Supreme Court to get involved and stop the recount. Because the Florida court had, in essence, created new election law by ordering certain counties to conduct the recount, the Supreme Court found the recount plan unconstitutional. The Court stopped the recount by a vote of 5–4. As a result, Florida's twenty-five electoral votes went to Bush, giving him the White House by an electoral vote of 271 to 266. If the Court had decided to allow the recount to continue, U.S. presidential history might look different today.

Did You Know?

By a majority vote, senators approve or disapprove nominated Supreme Court justices. In 1861, Jeremiah S. Black was rejected by one vote. On the other hand, Stanley Matthews was confirmed by one vote in 1881. One hundred years later, Sandra Day O'Connor was confirmed as the first woman on the Court by a vote of 99–0 in 1981.

Talk, Think, and Take Action

• In what ways do you think the United States might be different if the Supreme Court had not intervened in the 2000 election?

• Think about some ways you participate in the election process. Whether you're of voting age or not, there are many ways you can make a difference in elections. Student council and class offices are a great way to learn through on-the-job efforts. You can also write a letter, email, or tweet to let politicians and candidates know your thoughts on issues that are important to you. Or you could volunteer to work on their campaign; get involved with the Young Democrats, Young Republicans, Green Party, or other organizations; or take part in get-out-the-vote efforts.

• If you aren't old enough to vote yet, think about how you *would* vote if you had the opportunity and what factors would go into that decision. What are some ways you could learn more about a proposition being brought to vote? How would you study the candidates so you can be certain that your vote reflects your beliefs and values?

• What do you think are the best ways for candidates to communicate their plans and beliefs? Debates, interviews, written campaign literature? What about campaign commercials and "robo-calls"? You've probably heard of mudslinging campaigns. Do you think focusing on the faults or negative qualities of an opponent is beneficial in any way? If so, in what ways? Does it help voters better understand a candidate's position, or lead to a better turnout at the polls?

• If you're interested in lowering the voting age or expanding voting rights in general, consider getting involved with organizations like FairVote and National Youth Rights Association.

See their websites at FairVote.org and YouthRights.org.

- What do you think of celebrity endorsements of candidates? (Endorsements mean a person is making his or her support of the candidate public and possibly donating to the campaign.) In what ways do you think such endorsements can help—or hurt—candidates?

Who Gets to Vote?

The right to vote enjoyed by most Americans is the result of decades of struggle. Yet, of the 197 million registered voters in the United States, only 55 percent actually went to the polls and voted in the 2012 presidential election. Among young voters, only 11 percent of eighteen- to twenty-four-year-olds voted in that election. And the average voter turnout is consistently lower for state and local elections than for presidential elections.

Generally, any citizen of the United States who is at least eighteen years old may vote in local, state, and national elections. Congress and the states determine the qualifications to vote. Some states allow seventeen-year-olds to vote in primaries and caucuses. Other factors—including residency requirements, criminal history, and homelessness—vary from state to state. Contact your local elections office for information. Remember, many states require voters to register before Election Day.

> ## IN OTHER WORDS
> **"One who does not vote has no right to complain."**
> —Louis L'Amour, American author

Do you believe the government plays an important role in your life? If you answered yes, most people agree with you. Yet millions of eligible voters do not vote when the time comes. Why is that? A survey conducted just before the 2012 election indicated that people feel they are too busy, are not excited about the candidates, have a lack of trust in leaders, or believe that their votes don't matter and that nothing gets done regardless of who wins an election.

> ## IN OTHER WORDS
> "This generation's teens feel less confident in the power of the vote. They have become disillusioned with the promise of political change and prefer to dedicate their time to volunteering. However, lasting change cannot be made without engaging in both voting and volunteering."
> —Meera, 17

Yet voting is your way to make a difference and have a say in important issues that matter in your life. Otherwise, others will decide for you—and you won't always agree with the outcome. In the United States, voters benefit from 200 years of voting history, during which the rules about who could and who could not vote were established, expanded, and improved. Today, local, state, and federal election laws that regulate voting are generally aimed at encouraging inclusion and participation, and guaranteeing all eligible U.S. citizens the right to vote. See the timeline in section entitled "A Timeline of Issues Affecting Voting in the United States" for an overview of how U.S. voting rights have evolved over time.

A Timeline of Issues Affecting Voting in the United States

IN OTHER WORDS

"What's our excuse today for not voting?"
—President Barack Obama

1805	York, an African-American slave, and Sacagawea, a Shoshone teenager, are permitted to vote with the Lewis and Clark expedition members on where they should spend the winter on the Pacific coast.

1857	The Supreme Court decides the Dred Scott case, declaring that slaves are property and have "no rights which the white man was bound to respect." The Constitution does not recognize black people as persons in the eyes of the law.
1863	President Lincoln issues the Emancipation Proclamation, an executive order that frees slaves in ten states and becomes one factor in the Civil War (1861–1865).
1865	The Thirteenth Amendment outlawing slavery is ratified: "Neither slavery nor involuntary servitude, except as a punishment for crime whereof the party shall have been duly convicted, shall exist within the United States, or any place subject to their jurisdiction."
1868	The Fourteenth Amendment is ratified, guaranteeing all U.S. citizens equal protection and due process of law.
1870	The Fifteenth Amendment is ratified, guaranteeing the right to vote for all men regardless of race: "The right of citizens of the United States to vote shall not be denied or abridged by the United States or by any State on account of race, color, or previous condition of servitude." Also in this year, Wyoming becomes the first state to allow women to vote.
1872	Women's suffragist Susan B. Anthony is fined $100 for voting in the presidential election.
1920	The Nineteenth Amendment is ratified, guaranteeing all women the right to vote: "The right of citizens of the United States to vote shall not be denied or abridged by the United States or by any State on account of sex."
1963	In his State of the Union address, President John F. Kennedy says that "the most precious and powerful right in the world, the right to vote is not to be denied to any citizen on grounds of his race or color ... all those who are willing to vote should always be permitted."

1964	The Twenty-Fourth Amendment is ratified, prohibiting poll or other taxes as a requirement to vote and thereby removing poverty as a barrier to voting.
1965	President Lyndon Johnson signs the Voting Rights Act, eliminating obstacles and racial discrimination in voter registration, such as literacy tests.
1971	The Twenty-Sixth Amendment is ratified, lowering the voting age from 21 to 18 in federal and state elections.
1993	Congress passes the National Voter Registration Act (Motor Voter Law), authorizing voter registration at the Department of Motor Vehicles when applying for or renewing a driver's license.
2013	The Supreme Court instructs Congress to rewrite the formula used to determine which parts of the country need federal approval to change their voting procedures. This approval was a critical part of the Voting Rights Act of 1965. (See section entitled "SHOULD RESTRICTIONS PLACED ON CERTAIN VOTING DISTRICTS FORTY YEARS AGO TO REDUCE DISCRIMINATION REMAIN IN PLACE?" for Shelby County, Alabama v. Holder).
2015	"Georgia representative John Lewis introduced the Voter Empowerment Act (H.R. 12) into Congress. It calls for public websites for voter registration, same-day registration, and help for those with disabilities. The bill is still under consideration.

IN OTHER WORDS

"The vote is the most powerful instrument ever devised by man for breaking down injustice and destroying the terrible walls which imprison men because they are different from other men."

—President Lyndon Johnson

Barriers to Voting

Although Congress passed the Voting Rights Act fifty years ago, obstacles to voting continue to appear in new forms. While poll taxes and literacy tests have been outlawed, recent voter identification laws in some states make it harder for some eligible voters to cast their ballots. For a variety of reasons, millions of Americans don't have government ID cards. For instance, low income, transportation and mobility challenges, or childcare expenses can contribute to the challenges in obtaining the required documents.

IN OTHER WORDS

"**By voting we can always stand and say 'I gave my opinion. I did my job.'**"
—Peyton, 17

Did You Know?

In 1975 the Voting Rights Act was amended to require ballots in languages other than English—including Spanish as well as in Asian, Native American, and Alaskan Native languages—in areas with large minority groups. See www.justice.gov for details.

Proponents of these laws argue that they are designed to prevent fraud by requiring voters to show a government-issued ID before casting a ballot. They say the laws improve the public's view of the electoral process and guarantee that the system is fair and trustworthy. Others see the push for voter ID laws as an attempt to **disenfranchise** minorities, people living in poverty, and college students. Opponents of these laws describe the proposed statutes as voter suppression laws.

In 1979, the Supreme Court ruled that college students have the right to vote in the state where they attend school. However, some states' voter ID laws exclude student ID cards from their lists of acceptable forms of identification, even though these may be the only way some students can document where they live. In addition, students without transportation may find it difficult to get to the polls unless the school has a polling place on campus. Students may also vote in their home precincts using absentee ballots.

> **"You think your vote doesn't matter? Then why are they trying so hard to take it away from you?"**
> —Heather Smith, president of RocktheVote.com

A remaining barrier that some view as acceptable involves adult criminals. Most states prohibit convicted felons from voting until their civil rights are restored after they serve their sentence or by court order.

See RocktheVote.com for individual state requirements.

Did You Know?

• In 1840, abolitionist (someone who supported or advocated for the end of slavery in the United States) and former slave Frederick Douglass walked to the town hall of the city where he lived in Massachusetts and paid a local tax of $1.50 to register to vote. At the time, several states allowed freed slaves to vote.

• Today, more than thirty U.S. states have laws that require government-issued identification in order to vote or that restrict early voting and same-day registration and voting. For example, Texas does not accept student photo IDs or IDs from federally recognized Native American tribes. An attempt to strike down the Texas law failed in 2014. For more information, see *Veasey v. Perry* (2014).

• Wisconsin law requires voters to show photo identification before casting a ballot. In 2015, the Supreme Court declined without

> comment to review this law, leaving it in place. (Frank v. Walker)

Should Voting Be Mandatory?

This question has been debated for decades. Those who support such a requirement argue that good citizenship means taking responsibility for the many rights Americans enjoy, including voting. They say that by participating in democracy on Election Day, citizens encourage leaders to pay attention to their views on vital issues.

Opponents of mandatory voting believe it would be better to encourage people to go to the polls in other ways, such as by holding open primaries where independent voters can vote in the primary of their choice and by making elections publically funded instead of relying on outside donations. Law professor Rick Pildes of New York University commented, "Rather than trying to force people to vote, we ought to focus on getting rid of unnecessary barriers to voting—many of which affect young people the most—and we ought to do much more to get those who aren't voting to realize that what government does has powerful effects on their lives."

Around the world, almost three dozen countries do have some form of mandatory voting. In Australia, for example, voting is compulsory and those who do not vote must pay a small fine. Since this law passed in 1924, more than 90 percent of citizens turn out to vote and most Australians view voting as a civic responsibility. Likewise, compulsory voting in Belgium resulted in voter turnout of 89 percent in 2014.

Should the Voting Age Be Lowered?

In the United States, eighteen-year-olds were granted the right to vote in 1971 with the passage of the Twenty-Sixth Amendment. This gave over ten million more Americans a say at election time. Previously, the voting age in most states had been twenty-one.

The National Youth Rights Association has been trying to lower the voting age to sixteen for years. However, only a few places have lowered the age, and only for local elections. In Maryland, for example, Takoma Park was the first city to lower the voting age to sixteen in local elections. In the November 2013 election, 59 teens voted (out of 119 who had registered). Hyattsville, Maryland, followed suit for local elections in 2015. In addition, thirteen states allow seventeen-year-olds to vote in primary elections if they will turn eighteen before the general election in November. On the other hand, an attempt to lower the voting age to sixteen in Brattleboro, Vermont, failed in 2015.

Did You Know?

Consider these stories of young politicians.

- In 2011, twelve-year-old DeQuan Isom of North Carolina announced his plans to run for president. The Constitution requires candidates to be thirty-five years old. For DeQuan, that will be in 2034. In the meantime, DeQuan filed with the Federal Election Commission and is raising money for his campaign.
- Bobby Tufts was three years old when he was elected mayor of Dorset, Minnesota, in 2012. The town of two dozen people stages an unofficial election each year as part of a local fundraiser—ballots cost $1 and the winner is drawn from a hat. Tufts was reelected to the ceremonial position in 2013.
- In 2014, nineteen-year-old high school senior Morgan Baskin ran for mayor of Toronto, Canada's largest city. Morgan asserted that "YOUth matter, not only because we are the future but because we are also part of today." Morgan finished fifth in a field of over sixty candidates.

IN OTHER WORDS

> **"The greatest weapon, perhaps, in the modern world is the power of the ballot."**
> —W.E.B. Dubois, journalist, educator, and civil rights activist

Supporters of lower voting ages argue that allowing older teens to vote would encourage politicians to pay attention to issues important to many young people, including education and the environment.

Did You Know?

- A few countries have lowered the national voting age to sixteen, including Brazil, Argentina, Nicaragua, and Austria. In some parts of Germany and Switzerland, sixteen-year-olds are allowed to vote in local elections.
- In 2014, Scotland's independence from the United Kingdom was on the ballot. Because of the importance of the referendum to young people and their futures, the voting age was temporarily lowered to sixteen. While many teens did go to the polls, the measure nonetheless failed.
- In 2014, many high school and college students took to the streets in Hong Kong to protest the Chinese communist government's refusal to allow free elections or an open

choice of candidates. (Currently, rather than simply being nominated, candidates for office are screened by a committee dominated by people loyal to China's leaders.) Protest leader eighteen-year-old Joshua Wong commented, "If students don't stand in the front line, who will?"

Registering to Vote

Although you may be under eighteen, the time will come when you become an adult and can register to vote. Even before then, however, you can familiarize yourself with the voting process and the responsibilities of active participation in our democracy.

Did You Know?

• In Colorado, sixteen- and seventeen-year-olds can preregister to vote at the Department of Motor Vehicles when they take their driving tests. When they turn eighteen, their names automatically transfer to the voting rolls.

• In 2012, the state of Washington became the first state to allow registration through a Facebook account.

• In 2015, Oregon became the first state to automatically register everyone eighteen and

> older who comes to a Department of Motor Vehicles office.

In the United States, a person must be a citizen either by birth or **naturalization** to register to vote in state and federal elections. It is illegal to falsely claim citizenship in order to register to vote.

Each state has its own election laws governing voter registration. Generally, you can't register until you're a certain age. At that point, registration usually involves a few simple steps, which are spelled out on www.RegisterToVote.org. Click on your state, complete a short online form, print it out, and mail it to your local elections office. In some states, you can register to vote online. You can also go to your local elections office or county recorder for information and a voter registration form. You can choose, if you wish, to register with a political party. Or, if you register as an Independent, you can choose which primary (Democrat or Republican) you want to vote in.

IN OTHER WORDS

"When I am eighteen, I will be sure to vote because I want to make a difference, no matter how big or small, in my country and state."
—Vanessa, 14

First-time voters are required to show proof of identification. That may include a current and valid photo ID such as a driver's license, state-issued ID card, a tribal ID card or enrollment number, or passport. Further proof may include a current utility bill, bank statement, or government check that shows your name and address. Depending on where you live, you may also need to show an ID card each time you go to the polls to vote.

If you know in advance that you'll be away from your voting precinct on Election Day, you can arrange for an absentee ballot. That means you can vote early, usually by mail but sometimes in person. Your local election officials can help with this. Military members can complete the Federal Post Card Application available at www.fvap.gov. This is the Federal Voting Assistance Program that's designed for service men and women and citizen voters who are abroad.

Did You Know?

Some public high schools hold voter registration days.

Another way to participate in democracy is to contribute money to campaigns. Under campaign finance rules, minors may contribute to a candidate or political party but it must be their decision and their money. In 2007, over

1,000 teenagers added $2 million to the electoral process.

Talk, Think, and Take Action

- Does your high school sponsor a voter registration day on campus? If not, consider getting together with your friends and classmates to push for one. Talk with your principal and local elections office about this.
- Would you vote if the age was lowered to sixteen? What would you do to learn about the different candidates and the issues?
- Do you think voting should be mandatory? Why or why not?
- In addition to voting, you can make a difference in your community by recognizing a need and taking action. Consider the following young people who did just that.

* Julia Bluhm was a fourteen-year-old in Maine when she succeeded in fighting airbrushed photos of girls in *Seventeen* magazine. In 2012, through her online petition, she gathered signatures from over 80,000 people who were against altered images and led a protest in front of the magazine's New York headquarters. Soon after, the magazine announced they would not digitally alter the shapes of models' faces or bodies, and would depict healthier body images for its readers.

* Research shows that sleep directly affects learning and overall health. After she heard that her school was considering moving up their start time, sixteen-year-old Jilly Dos Santos of Rock Bridge High School in Missouri created a Facebook page, Twitter account, and online petition to help the public better understand the benefits of starting school later in the morning. After she spoke before the local school board in 2013, they decided to change the first bell from 7:50a.m. to 8:55a.m. for high school students.

* Laurie Wolff was a thirteen-year-old in Nevada when she decided to take action because some of her friends received failing grades for refusing to do animal dissections in class. She gathered signatures and testified before the Las Vegas School Board. She urged them to allow students who were against dissecting animals to have the option to do virtual dissections instead. The board adopted a policy for such alternatives in 2002.

* Close to 1,000 students in Massachusetts campaigned to protest discrimination against gay and lesbian students in public schools. They attended rallies, spoke at legislative hearings and public forums, met with lawmakers, and started a letter-writing campaign. Their efforts led to the passage of the country's first Gay and Lesbian Student Rights Law in 1993.

* By age fourteen, Jazz Jennings was already an influential voice for transgender kids. She explained that she was a girl trapped in a

boy's body and knew this from the time she was just two years old. She has written a children's book about her experiences and has been honored by a number of organizations and media outlets for her activism and courageous voice. She uses social media to connect with her followers and advocate for transgender youth rights, and appeared in a cable TV show that premiered in 2015 called *I Am Jazz.*

* Currently, states and local authorities set their own election and voting laws. Proponents of a right-to-vote amendment to the U.S. Constitution believe that such an amendment is necessary to ensure equal voting rights for all, and that all votes are counted fairly. What do you think about this issue? For more information about it, see FairVote's Promote Our Vote Project at PromoteOurVote.com.

Further Reading and Resources

Ben's Guide to the U.S. Government
BensGuide.gpo.gov
Created by the Government Publishing Office, this site provides an illustrated review of the branches of government, how laws are made, the election process, and more for children and teens.

CanIVote.org
www.CanIVote.org
This site allows you to verify your eligibility to vote as well as locate your polling place, determine if you need to bring identification to your polls, and learn about the candidates.

FairVote
www.fairvote.org
FairVote is a nonprofit, nonpartisan organization that advocates for fair representation, fair elections, and fair access to the polls.

OurTime.org
www.OurTime.org
This nationwide nonprofit organization works to increase voter participation by young people. It also advocates for the interests of young Americans on issues including voting reform, college affordability, equal rights, and job creation.

Oyez Project
www.oyez.org
This archive created by the Chicago-Kent College of Law provides summaries of cases and audio of Supreme Court arguments.

Real Kids, Real Stories, Real Change: Courageous Actions Around the World by Garth Sundem (Minneapolis: Free Spirit Publishing, 2010).

Rock the Vote
www.RocktheVote.com
This organization uses innovating ways—including pop culture, music, and technology—to help increase voter registration and political involvement by young people.

SCOTUSblog
www.scotusblog.com

This Supreme Court of the United States blog offers one- to two-sentence summaries of Court decisions.

Taking Back the Vote: Getting American Youth Involved in Our Democracy by Jane Eisner (Boston: Beacon Press, 2004).

VolunTEEN Nation
www.volunteennation.org

This organization, led by teens and young adults, helps maximize the power of young people to make a difference in their communities. The site offers a database of volunteer opportunities for teens, information about service-related grants and scholarships, and blogs about serving others.

Your Voice Your Vote: Teens Can Make a Big Impact in Politics—Even Before They're Old Enough to Vote by Diane Webber (e-document 2008).

Youth Activism Project
www.YouthActivismProject.org

This nonpartisan youth development organization promotes civic engagement and provides advice to help young people create proposals and develop solutions for problems they care about.

PART 2

5–4 Supreme Court Cases—How Do They Affect Your Life?

CASE 1

Evan Miller v. Alabama (2012)

Key Issue: Prison Terms for Young People

Can a **juvenile** be sent to prison for life without the possibility of earning release on parole?

As we grow up, we generally face more severe consequences for our mistakes. A lie told by a four-year-old may bring a timeout, whereas a fifteen-year-old caught in a lie may be grounded or face another form of discipline from a parent or caregiver. When teens make mistakes that are crimes and the police and court system become involved, the consequences reach another level entirely.

Is it best to treat young people differently from adults when setting sentences for crimes? Should kids and teens always be given a chance to change and reform when they break the law, even when they commit violent crimes? Is it a violation of the Eighth Amendment—that is, is it a form of cruel and unusual punishment—to set mandatory life sentences for certain violent crimes for minors? These are some of the questions the Supreme Court agreed to consider when it took up the *Evan Miller v. Alabama* case in 2012. The results of this case would be decided by one vote.

Facts of the Case

Evan Miller grew up in Alabama with a mother who was addicted to drugs and a stepfather who physically abused him. He also moved in and out of foster care during his turbulent childhood and attempted suicide four times—the first time when he was just six years old. Miller had run-ins with the law early on, but they involved fairly minimal offenses such as **truancy** and **criminal mischief.** This changed when he was fourteen.

Did You Know?

Mandatory sentencing is when a trial judge or jury has no **discretion** when sentencing the offender. They must automatically impose whatever sentence state law requires.

In July 2003, Miller and a friend spent an evening at a neighbor's house drinking and using drugs with him. Later that night, the boys beat the fifty-two-year-old neighbor with a baseball bat and set his house on fire. The man died. Miller was charged with murder in the course of arson and was tried as an adult. A jury found him guilty and he was sentenced to life without the possibility of parole, as state law required for a murder conviction. Miller's sixteen-year-old friend received a lighter sentence (life with the possibility of parole) in return for testifying against Miller.

> ## IN OTHER WORDS
>
> **"Excessive bail shall not be required, nor excessive fines imposed, nor cruel and unusual punishments inflicted."**
> —Eighth Amendment to the U.S. Constitution

When the Supreme Court agreed to review the *Miller* case, it consolidated it with another case from Arkansas that raised the same basic question. This case (*Jackson v. Hobbs*, 2012) involved Kuntrell Jackson, who was fourteen when he and two older friends went to a video store to commit a robbery in November 1999. On the way to the store, Jackson saw that one of his friends had a sawed-off shotgun under his coat. Jackson stayed outside the store during most of the robbery. When he went in, he saw his friend demanding money from the clerk. When she refused, the boy shot and killed her. Jackson was charged as an adult and convicted by a jury of **felony murder** and aggravated robbery. Under Arkansas state law, the trial judge was barred from considering Jackson's age or his limited role in the crime, and had no choice but to sentence him to prison for life without the possibility of parole.

Did You Know?

In 2012, there were nearly 2,500 inmates in the United States serving life sentences without the possibility of parole for crimes committed while under the age of eighteen.

Both Evan Miller and Kuntrell Jackson lost their appeals in state court and took their cases to the U.S. Supreme Court. They claimed their sentences violated the Eighth Amendment by being excessive considering their ages at the time of the murders.

The Court's Ruling and Reasoning

As the Supreme Court reviewed the *Miller* case, it considered earlier decisions on sentencing juvenile offenders. In particular, the justices studied two other cases: *Roper v. Simmons* (2005) and *Graham v. Florida* (2010). Both of those Supreme Court cases concluded that children are constitutionally different from adults for sentencing purposes. In *Roper,* the Court ruled that the Eighth Amendment protects people from "excessive sanctions." The Court also quoted an earlier case, saying that "'punishment for crime should be graduated and proportioned' to both the offender and the offense." The specifics of the *Roper* case are discussed under Related Cases.

The Court in the *Graham* case ruled that mandatory life sentences for young people who did not commit murder are forbidden as violations of the Eighth Amendment. In the *Graham* decision, the Court compared a sentence of life without parole for a juvenile to the death penalty and noted, "Youth is more than a chronological fact. It is a time of immaturity, irresponsibility, impetuousness and recklessness." In *Graham,* the Court agreed that it is increasingly clear that adolescent brains are fundamentally different from the brains of adults and are not yet fully mature. In particular, it said the "parts of the brain involved in behavior control" are still being developed and this is especially evident when it comes to impulse control, planning ahead, and avoiding risk. Therefore, the Court concluded, adolescents are less likely than adults to consider potential punishment when they commit crimes. Further, the *Graham* Court said, "Life without parole ... reflects an irrevocable judgment about an offender's value and place in society" that is at odds with the potential for young people to change or be rehabilitated. Consequently, the Court found that "an offender's age is relevant to the Eighth Amendment" and that "youth matters" when it comes to sentencing.

The Court in *Miller* determined that mandatory sentencing ignored three hallmarks of youth: impulsive behavior, immaturity, and difficulty considering risks and consequences. In addition, the Court's decision, written by Justice Elena Kagan, noted that a child's actions are less likely than an adult's to be evidence of problems or personality traits that are beyond **rehabilitation.** It concluded that mandatory life without parole violates the Eighth Amendment and is therefore unconstitutional. Instead, the Court ordered that trial courts carry out individualized sentencing, after they consider relevant information about the juvenile. A minor could still receive life without parole, but the Court commented that it would be "uncommon."

Did You Know?

As a result of the *Miller* decision, in some states inmates who were under eighteen when they committed their crimes, such as Jeffrey

> Ragland of Iowa, became eligible for parole. Ragland was seventeen when he was convicted of first degree felony murder for his role in the killing of a nineteen-year-old man in 1986. He was given a life sentence without the possibility of parole. After *Miller*, he was resentenced to twenty-five years with the possibility of parole. Ragland was denied parole when he first applied in 2013, but he can now reapply every year. (As of June 2015, he remains in custody.)

Four justices dissented (disagreed with the majority) in *Miller*. They argued that states should have the right to decide this issue and that a broad application to all defendants under eighteen weakened lawmakers' authority. The dissent also suggested that the majority opinion opened the door to prohibiting the entire practice of trying juveniles as adults.

The Court Speaks

"We think appropriate occasions for sentencing juveniles to this harshest possible penalty will be uncommon." In writing this comment, Justice Elena Kagan noted the "great difficulty" in distinguishing at age fourteen between the immature juvenile offender and "the rare juvenile offender whose crime reflects irreparable corruption." In her view, a sentencing judge needs to look at all of the juvenile's circumstances before depriving him or her of any chance of eventually being released from prison.

What If...?

If the court had denied Evan Miller's appeal, it would have left in place laws about mandatory sentencing that applied to minors in twenty-eight states—and 2,500 people who committed crimes as teenagers would still be spending the rest of their lives in prison. It would also have disregarded recent scientific findings about the development of the adolescent brain that tell us the prefrontal cortex—the part of the brain that controls rational thinking and impulsivity—does not fully develop until about age twenty-five. The United States would have more young people in prison without any hope of release even if they matured and became rehabilitated.

In the Supreme Court's 2015–2016 term, it will hear the case of *Henry Montgomery v. Louisiana* to determine if the *Miller* decision applies retroactively to cases of juveniles incarcerated before June 25, 2012, the date of the *Miller* decision. The Supreme Court did not address whether their decision was retroactive.

That leaves the issue to the individual states. In *Ragland,* Iowa said it was retroactive, while in *Montgomery,* Louisiana said it wasn't.

Related Cases

Did you know that the criminal laws of each state also apply to teens? There aren't two sets of criminal laws—one for adults and another for those under eighteen. For example, if teens break into someone's house and steal money, they will be charged with burglary and theft under the same laws that cover adults. However, their cases will be handled in the juvenile justice system rather than in the adult system. The goal of juvenile court is to rehabilitate young people by requiring them to face certain consequences for their wrongdoings and to provide services that will help them make better choices in the future. The purpose of the adult criminal system is punishment and community safety.

In the cases that follow, you'll read about some of the issues teens in the juvenile justice system have faced. Although the percentage of American teens in trouble with the law is small, the decisions in these cases are important. Discrimination in sentencing, the death penalty, and the possibility of prosecuting a minor in adult court are considered.

CAN MINORS BE SENTENCED TO DEATH?

Stanford v. Kentucky **(1989) and** *Roper v. Simmons* **(2005)**

Kevin Stanford was seventeen in 1981 when a jury convicted him of murder, robbery, receiving stolen property, and sodomy. He was sentenced to death under Kentucky state law. He appealed the sentence as a violation of the Eighth Amendment's protection against cruel and unusual punishment. In 1989, the Supreme Court voted 5–4 against Stanford's plea, ruling that capital punishment for sixteen- and seventeen-year-old juveniles was constitutional. However, in 2003, Kentucky governor Paul Patton **commuted** Stanford's sentence to life in prison without parole.

Sixteen years later, the Court took up this issue again in a case involving Christopher Simmons. Simmons was seventeen when he developed a plan to rob and kill someone. He convinced a friend, Charles Benjamin, to help him, arguing that they could get away with it because they were underage. The two boys broke into a woman's home and tied her up, then stole her van and took her to a nearby park. They wrapped her head in a towel and duct tape, and threw her off a bridge into a river where she drowned. Simmons was tried as an adult, convicted of murder, and, as recommended by the jury, sentenced to death. (Benjamin was sentenced to life in prison.)

> ## IN OTHER WORDS
>
> "The age of eighteen is the point where society draws the line for many purposes between childhood and adulthood. It is, we conclude, the age at which the line for death eligibility ought to rest."
> —Justice Anthony Kennedy, *Roper v. Simmons* (2005)

In considering this appeal, the Supreme Court examined the rationale used in earlier decisions on this issue, along with current national opinion about executing minors. In a 5–4 decision, they ruled that the death penalty for juveniles was unconstitutional. The Court commented that, when compared to adults, minors "are more vulnerable to negative influences and outside pressures including from their family and peers; they have limited control over their own environment and lack the ability to extricate themselves from horrific, crime-producing settings."

IS THE DEATH PENALTY APPLIED MORE OFTEN TO MINORITY DEFENDANTS THAN TO NON-MINORITIES?

Furman v. Georgia **(1972)**

William Henry Furman, a twenty-six-year-old African-American man who lived in Georgia, broke into a home at about 2a.m. Upstairs, five children and their parents slept. When Furman heard noises on the stairs, he pulled out his gun but then decided to leave rather than confront anyone. On his way out, Furman tripped and fell to the floor. The gun went off, killing the family's twenty-nine-year-old father.

Furman was convicted of murder and sentenced to death. He appealed, arguing that his conviction violated the Eighth and Fourteenth Amendments. The Supreme Court ruled 5–4 that the death penalty in this case was unconstitutional because it had historically been applied in an arbitrary manner, often indicating a racial bias against black defendants. year national **moratorium** on capital punishment that gave the states and Congress time to rethink their laws and ensure that the death penalty would not be administered in a discriminatory or arbitrary way.

> **Did You Know?**
>
> According to the Death Penalty Information Center, the number of people sentenced to death each year in the United States peaked in 1996 with 315. In 2013, the number dropped to 80. Executions also declined from a high of 98 in 1999 to 39 in 2013.

Following the *Furman* decision, thirty-four states passed new, more specific death penalty statutes that would prevent discriminatory practices. Furman was paroled and later convicted of another burglary. In 2004, he was sentenced to twenty years in prison.

CAN MINORS BE TRIED AS ADULTS?

Kent v. United States (1966)

Morris Kent was sixteen when he was arrested and charged with burglary, robbery, and rape. Without holding a hearing to listen to arguments by Kent's attorney or conducting a thorough investigation, the trial judge sent Kent's case to adult court. There he was convicted and sentenced to prison for thirty to ninety years. Kent appealed the ruling and said the case should not have been moved to adult court without granting him **due process.** The Supreme Court ruled in his favor, agreeing that sending a juvenile to the adult criminal system is a "critically important" decision—one that must be based on due process including a thorough investigation, hearing, and stated reasons for the trial court's decision. The case was sent back to the juvenile court for reconsideration.

> ### Talk, Think, and Take Action
>
> • What do you think about the **dissenting opinion** in *Evan Miller v. Alabama?* Do you think the issue should be left to the states to decide? Why or why not?
>
> • What is your opinion about criminal justice and the different kinds of sentences given to juveniles and adults? Do you agree that defendants under eighteen should be tried and sentenced as adults in some instances? If so, how young do you think is too young for a person to be tried as an adult? What do you think about the death penalty in the United States? Should it be abolished for adults? If not, do you believe it should be used for eighteen- and nineteen-year-olds, who are legally adults but whose brains are not fully mature?
>
> • If you feel passionate about social justice and criminal law, give some thought to joining a local or national organization that advocates for change. Your input and participation are valuable. Check out www.change.org, an online

petition platform. Browse their petitions tagged under "criminal justice." You can sign the ones you support and learn about getting more involved. You can also start your own online petition to effect change on issues important to you.

• You can also get involved with your school's teen court program. Take a look at www.pcteencourt.com as an example. If your school doesn't have its own teen court, consider starting one.

• If you are interested in law and the legal system, consider joining a mock trial program. Take a look at the website www.nationalmocktrial.org for information about the annual mock trial competition and getting a team together at your school if one doesn't already exist.

• Did you know that death by a firing squad is still a legal method of execution in the state of Utah? Many people feel that this is inhumane and outdated, but in recent years there have also been serious problems with the lethal injection method of executing people. In these "botched" executions by injection, the procedure has taken far longer than expected, resulting in extreme pain and suffering for the person sentenced to death. What are your thoughts on this? If you believe in the death penalty, what do you think would be a more humane way to execute someone who has

> been sentenced to death? Some people feel this issue is a reason to move away from the death penalty. What are your thoughts on this issue?

Closing Comments

You can see that, if just one justice had voted the other way in *Evan Miller v. Alabama*, the course of history would be different. Thousands of young people might have served life terms with no hope of release even if they matured, changed, and were fully rehabilitated, or even if they were minor players in the actual crimes. Similarly, all of the related cases in this chapter came very close to being decided the opposite way. If that had happened, you could be tried as an adult without a chance to argue against it, or remain in prison for life regardless of the circumstances or your age at the time of the crime.

Further Reading and Resources

Primary Case: *Miller v. Alabama*, 132 S.Ct. 2455 (2012).

50 Ways to Love Your Country: How to Find Your Political Voice and Become a Catalyst for

Change by MoveOn.org (Makawao, HI: Inner Ocean Publishing, 2004).

"Justice for Girls: Are We Making Progress?" by Francine T. Sherman, 59 *UCLA Law Review* 1584 (August 2012).

"Juvenile Lifers and Judicial Overreach: A Curmudgeonly Meditation on *Miller v. Alabama*" by Frank O. Bowman III, 78 *Missouri Law Review* 1015 (Fall 2013).

The Teenage Brain: A Neuroscientist Survival Guide to Raising Adolescents and Young Adults by Frances E. Jensen (New York: Harper, 2015).

50
CASE 2
United States v. Antoine Jones (2012)

Key Issue: Search and Seizure in the Digital Age
Can police gather information about you by attaching a tracking device to your car?

Have you ever heard someone say, "Big brother is watching you"? This phrase comes from the novel *Nineteen Eighty-Four* written by George Orwell in 1948, a book that some say warned against the dangers of unchecked government surveillance. (The concept was used as the basis for the reality TV show *Big Brother.*) Today's technology makes it possible for the government—or even your parents—to track your movements, listen to your phone conversations, and watch you on hidden cameras. The question is, just because we can do these things, *should* we? This case examines whether the Fourth Amendment right to privacy limits the way the government can use a global-positioning system (GPS) to conduct investigations.

Facts of the Case

Antoine Jones, a nightclub owner in Washington, D.C., was suspected of trafficking drugs. The FBI and the local police department worked together on investigating Jones. They obtained a search warrant that allowed them to place a GPS device on Jones's car to track his movements, but the judge issued the warrant with some limitations: (1) the device had to be installed within ten days, and (2) it could only be placed on Jones's car in the District of Columbia. However, that's not what happened. The police attached the GPS tracker to the underside of Jones's Jeep on the *eleventh* day after receiving the warrant—and they did so in the state of Maryland. The GPS device then collected information over a twenty-eight-day period, and the resulting evidence led to an **indictment** charging Jones with conspiracy to distribute and possess cocaine. Convicted by a jury, Jones was sentenced to prison for life. He appealed, arguing that his Fourth Amendment rights were violated by the way the tracking device was used.

The Court's Ruling and Reasoning

The Supreme Court began its analysis of the case by holding that the Fourth Amendment protects the right of everyone "to be secure in their persons, houses, papers, and effects (personal belongings) against unreasonable searches and seizures." They determined that a car or truck is an "effect" covered by the Fourth Amendment. This means that the government's installation of a GPS device on a suspect's vehicle (private property) constitutes a search.

The Court's opinion, written by Justice Antonin Scalia, quoted from an English case dating back to 1765 *(Entick v. Carrington)*. The cited

English law held that individual property is so sacred that anyone who sets foot on his neighbor's property without permission is a trespasser. The Fourth Amendment recognizes a person's "reasonable expectation of privacy." To uphold this amendment, the Court said, any new methods of investigating and gathering information must follow accepted standards and not physically intrude on areas or property that are constitutionally protected—and these may change as technology advances. For example, in 2014 the Court unanimously ruled that a warrant is needed before the police can search a cell phone taken during an arrest (see *Riley v. California* in Related Cases).

Regarding *Jones,* the Court stated, "We have no doubt that such a physical intrusion would have been considered a 'search' within the meaning of the Fourth Amendment when it was adopted." The police, however, violated the terms and scope of the search warrant. Consequently, the Court reviewed the case as if no warrant had existed. Since the government gathered evidence that led to Jones's conviction without a valid search warrant or his consent, the conviction was reversed and Jones became a free man.

IN OTHER WORDS

"The overriding function of the Fourth Amendment is to protect personal

> privacy and dignity against unwarranted intrusion by the State."
> —Justice William Brennan, *Schmerber v. California* (1966)

Although the Court's decision was unanimous—it voted 9–0 that the Fourth Amendment had been violated—the justices were split 5–4 on the reasons for declaring the search unconstitutional. It is not uncommon for the justices to agree unanimously on a decision but disagree with the underlying reasons for the decision. They are at liberty to vote as they see fit and explain their position in either a concurring or dissenting opinion.

The five justices in the majority found that attaching the GPS to the car had been an act of trespassing because it went beyond the time and geographical limits allowed in the warrant, and therefore amounted to an illegal search. The other four justices reached the same decision in the case, but their reasoning was slightly different. These four justices paid special attention to Jones's right not only to protection from illegal searches of his physical property, but also from intrusions on his privacy. The justices held that Jones's reasonable privacy expectations were violated by the long-term monitoring of his car's movements.

The Court Speaks

In her **concurring opinion,** Justice Sonia Sotomayor wrote, "GPS monitoring generates a precise, comprehensive record of a person's public movements that reflects a wealth of detail about her familial, political, professional, religious and sexual associations."

Justice Sotomayor recognized the Fourth Amendment's goal to curb or limit biased use of police power. The government can benefit from GPS monitoring that is done through lawful surveillance techniques. However, extended surveillance to collect data that reveals private aspects of a person's life is susceptible to abuse, Sotomayor reasoned.

What If...?

If the Supreme Court had ruled the other way in this case, our expectation of privacy would be more limited. Justice Sonia Sotomayor's concurring opinion in this case expressed concern about the many aspects of life that could be tracked if law enforcement officials were allowed to randomly place monitoring devices on anyone's private property. Her comments quoting a 2009 earlier case *(People v. Weaver)* summarized the potential consequences of unlimited investigation:

> Disclosed in GPS data will be trips to the psychiatrist, the plastic surgeon, the abortion clinic, the AIDS treatment center, the strip club, the criminal defense attorney, the by-the-hour motel, the union meeting, the mosque, synagogue or church, the gay bar and on and on. The Government can store such records and efficiently mine them for information years into the future.

Sotomayor reasoned that, if the Court had allowed this warrantless invasion of privacy, there would be no limit to government eavesdropping or collection of evidence.

Related Cases

The search of a person by a police officer or school official may involve a simple pat down for weapons (usually by the police), or a more invasive strip search for weapons or drugs. Whether the search is legal depends on many factors including age, consent, officer safety, and whether the legal standards of **probable cause** or **reasonable suspicion** exist.

The Fourth Amendment's protections regarding search and seizure apply to minors but to a limited degree. For example, parents have a right to search your bedroom and possessions and confiscate anything they object to. They do not need to get a search warrant. The police, however, must follow certain procedures before conducting a search, with or without a search warrant.

The following cases consider other ways that your privacy may be limited, or not, when the police and school officials are investigating wrongdoings.

IS IT LEGAL TO SEARCH A CELL PHONE WITHOUT A WARRANT?

Riley v. California (2014)

In a victory for greater privacy rights, the Supreme Court ruled unanimously in *Riley v. California* that police generally must obtain a search warrant before going through a cell phone taken during an arrest. In rare cases, a warrantless search may be justified if officer safety or the destruction of evidence is threatened.

Although this case focused on criminal investigations, the reasoning of the justices—supported by the principles of the Fourth Amendment—may apply to students and school searches. School authorities need what is called "reasonable suspicion" that either a school rule or a law has been broken before searching a student's personal property, such as a backpack, car, or locker. The rationale of *Riley* may also be applied to a student's cell phone or tablet at school.

IS AN ANONYMOUS TIP ENOUGH TO STOP AND DETAIN SOMEONE?

Navarette v. California (2014)

An anonymous 911 tip led to a traffic stop of two brothers. The caller, who was run off the road, gave a description of the truck and license plate number. Thirty pounds of marijuana were found in the bed of the truck and the brothers were convicted of drug trafficking. In a 5–4 decision, the Supreme Court ruled that a tipster's call may provide enough reasonable suspicion to justify stopping and searching a driver or pedestrian.

CAN A SCHOOL OFFICIAL SEARCH A STUDENT BASED ON SUSPICIOUS BEHAVIOR?

State v. Alaniz (2012)

Christian Alaniz Jr. was an eighteen-year-old student in North Dakota when a school resource officer observed him acting suspiciously. Alaniz was questioned by the officer and the school's assistant principal. When asked if he had anything on him, Alaniz emptied his pockets of a glass pipe and synthetic marijuana. He was charged with felony possession of a controlled substance and drug paraphernalia. Alaniz pleaded guilty but challenged the search as unconstitutional. The court upheld the search, concluding that his observed behavior supported reasonable suspicion that he was in possession of drugs. They said the search was not excessively intrusive nor was he physically searched.

HOW MUCH SUSPICION IS NEEDED FOR A STUDENT'S PERSONAL BELONGINGS TO BE SEARCHED AT SCHOOL?

New Jersey v. T.L.O. (1985)

T.L.O. (Terry) was a fourteen-year-old girl caught smoking in a bathroom at her high school. She was taken to the principal's office where she was questioned. When the assistant principal asked T.L.O. for her purse, she handed it over. He opened it and found cigarette rolling papers, single dollar bills, a bag of marijuana, and a list of names of students who owed her money. The school turned the matter over to the police, and T.L.O. was charged with possessing marijuana and found guilty.

T.L.O. challenged the search as unconstitutional, but the Supreme Court upheld it as reasonable under the circumstances. Once again, the question hinged on the presence of "reasonable suspicion," which is required to make a school search (locker, backpack, desk, etc.) lawful. The known facts at the time of T.L.O.'s search constituted reasonable suspicion that a law or school rule had been broken.

CAN SCHOOL OFFICIALS STRIP SEARCH STUDENTS SUSPECTED OF POSSESSING CONTRABAND?

Safford Unified School District v. Redding (2009)

A student at Safford Middle School in Arizona reported that her thirteen-year-old classmate Savana Redding had ibuprofen at school, a violation of school policy. The eighth-grade honors student was then taken to the office where, in the presence of two female staff members, she was told to remove her outer clothes and pull her underwear out for inspection. No ibuprofen or other "contraband" were found through the search.

> ### Did You Know?
>
> In 2013, the Supreme Court split 5–4 in three search cases. They ruled that a search warrant was needed to draw blood from a DUI suspect except in the rarest of cases; that a warrant was not needed to take a DNA cheek swab (a twenty-first-century version of fingerprinting) from a suspect arrested for a violent or sexual offense; and that a search warrant supported by probable cause is needed before taking drug-sniffing dogs on to a suspect's property, including the front porch. (*Missouri v. McNeely*, *Maryland v. King*, and *Florida v. Jardines*)

Savana and her mother sued the school officials, alleging an unlawful and unreasonable search. The Supreme Court agreed and ruled that the search violated the Fourth Amendment. By a 7–2 margin, they voted in Savana's favor and said that efforts by school officials to discover and remove contraband must be "reasonably related to the objectives of the search and not excessively intrusive in light of the age and sex of the student and the nature of the infraction."

Remember, in *T.L.O.* the Supreme Court established that the "probable cause" standard that law enforcement must follow when conducting a search does not apply to school officials. Rather than the higher "probable cause" standard, authorities need only "reasonable suspicion" to carry out a search at school. The Supreme Court allowed Savana to proceed with her lawsuit against the school. The school district **settled** the case for $250,000 plus Savana's legal expenses.

Talk, Think, and Take Action

• What do you think about privacy and the government's role in your life? Do you think the National Security Agency (NSA), for example, should be allowed to monitor your text messages and phone calls? Should local, state, and federal agencies be permitted to freely track your movement and communications? If you have a strong opinion about privacy rights or the responsibility of the government to keep people safe, consider sharing your thoughts with your representatives. You can email or write any politician about issues that concern you, even if you aren't old enough to vote yet. To find their contact information, simply search for their name online.

• Have you read your school's student handbook lately? What does it say, if anything, about school searches on and off campus? What can you do if you disagree with any of the rules? How would you go about approaching school officials to discuss controversial issues or suggest changes? Try to find out if there is a procedure for petitioning the school to create a new rule or change an existing one.

• School searches of cell phones and other electronic devices happen frequently in schools across the country. If you believe that a teacher, principal, or other school official has violated your rights concerning your devices, talk to a parent or other adult about it. If you feel that the school policies on these devices is invading students' privacy, make an appointment with your principal, attend a school meeting, discuss the issue with your friends and classmates, and gain support for the changes you'd like to see.

• The fact that the police were able to get a search warrant in the *Jones* case means that they had probable cause to believe Jones was trafficking drugs. However, the Court ruled that the police acted almost as though there were no warrant at all, since they did not follow the terms granted by the judge who signed off on the warrant. Therefore, Jones's conviction was reversed.

What are your thoughts and feelings about the legal principles here? How do you feel about a possibly guilty man having his conviction reversed because the police didn't

> follow the exact terms of the warrant? If the police have strong evidence against someone, how important do you think these technicalities should be?

Closing Comments

There is a fine line between your right to privacy and the government's right to know. Law enforcement is charged with protecting the public and, at the same time, respecting the rights of citizens as outlined under the Constitution and Bill of Rights. Search and seizure laws depend on warrants issued by neutral judicial officers whose duty is to authorize limited searches based on known facts presented by the police. When searches are challenged in court and found to be illegal, key evidence may be excluded from the trial.

> ### IN OTHER WORDS
>
> "The right to be let alone—the most comprehensive of rights and the right most valued by civilized men."
> —Justice Louis Brandeis, *Olmstead v. United States* (1928)

A shift in the 5–4 votes in some of these cases may have meant more restrictions on conducting searches for some authorities and fewer restrictions for others: the police could have the freedom to track your whereabouts without any oversight and for unlimited periods; your principal could have a much more difficult time carrying out searches for weapons or drugs, and consequently have trouble maintaining a safe campus for everyone; and a teacher or administrator might need very little evidence to order or conduct a strip search of a student.

With more and more students bringing digital devices to school, educators and courts alike have struggled with the proper way to respond. "Reasonable suspicion" remains the test to support a search at school by school officials. However, this determination is often challenged by students, parents, and criminal defense attorneys if formal charges are filed.

Further Reading and Resources

Primary Case: *United States v. Antoine Jones*, 132 S.Ct. 945 (2012).

"A Check-in on Privacy After *United States v. Jones*: Current Fourth Amendment Jurisprudence in the Context of Location-Based Applications and Services" by Kathryn Nobuko Horwath, 40 *Hastings Constitutional Law Quarterly* 925 (Summer 2013).

"The Mosaic Theory of the Fourth Amendment" by Orin S. Kerr, 111 *Michigan Law Review* 311 (December, 2012).

The Search and Seizure Handbook by David M. Waksman (Upper Saddle River, NJ: Prentice Hall, 2009).

CASE 3

Camreta v. Greene (2011)

Key Issue: Accepting or Rejecting a Case for Review

Will the Supreme Court consider a case that is "stale"—that is, one that is no longer current or no longer has a direct effect on the parties involved?

When the announcement comes that a Supreme Court decision will be released, ears turn to the radio and eyes begin scanning the headlines. Indeed, many people eagerly await the high court's ruling on thorny issues—even knowing that those decisions may later be reversed, and that they will probably not permanently resolve the deepest controversies. So does the individual case really matter, or is it more important that the Supreme Court provide a precedent to guide lower courts on a specific constitutional issue?

This case provides an example of the broad authority of the Supreme Court. Before the Court could consider the main issue in *Camreta*—whether an interview with a child is a "search"—the justices first needed to determine if the case was properly before them. In other words, was the case "ripe for review"? Had all of the rules governing appeals been followed, and was the issue before the court "alive"—that is, would the Court's decision still affect the parties involved in the lawsuit?

Facts of the Case

S.G. was a nine-year-old student at an elementary school in Oregon. A child welfare worker and deputy sheriff interviewed her at school about allegations that her father had sexually abused her. They talked to her even though they did not have a warrant or her parents' permission to conduct the interview. During the interview, S.G. eventually said that she had been abused by her father. He stood trial for the abuse, but the jury failed to reach a verdict and the charges were later dismissed.

S.G.'s mother sued the state, the caseworker, and the deputy sheriff for conducting an illegal interview of her daughter, arguing that the Fourth Amendment was violated because the child was removed from class and interviewed with neither her parents' permission nor a warrant to do so. The Fourth Amendment protects citizens from "unreasonable searches." A lower federal court gave the caseworker and deputy **immunity** (protection), stating that the law was not clear regarding their possible liability in this situation and so they could not be subject to financial damages. With this ruling, the defendants in effect won the case. However, the court also ruled that their warrantless interview violated the Constitution, and that unless officials had a parent's consent, they needed to get a warrant before interviewing a child at school about possible abuse or neglect. Even though the caseworker and deputy had been granted immunity in this particular case, they wanted to know for future situations whether their interview of S.G. was indeed unlawful and violated the Fourth Amendment. They appealed to the Supreme Court to find an answer to this question. The Court agreed to consider the case.

> **Did You Know?**
>
> The third article of the Constitution gives the Supreme Court the power to review a legal dispute when someone with a personal stake in the outcome presents a current controversy to the court.

The Court's Ruling and Reasoning

With this case, the Court needed to decide two separate issues. The first question was whether the defendants had a right to have the Court review their case even though a lower court had given them immunity. If so, the second issue before the court would be whether the defendants' interview of S.G. had been an unreasonable search according to the Fourth Amendment and therefore illegal. The "search" in this case was the interview itself—gathering information by questioning a possible witness. Since a lower court had ruled that the search violated the Fourth Amendment, clarification on the issue by the Supreme Court would have helped guide future investigations by law enforcement and child welfare agencies nationwide.

The Supreme Court noted that its justices are authorized by the Constitution to settle legal disputes where the parties have a personal stake in the outcome. That interest must exist at the time of the incident and throughout the lawsuit. In this case, they determined that, even though they had been given immunity, the child protection worker and the sheriff still had a stake in the Fourth Amendment issue of the case. But when the justices reviewed S.G.'s continuing interest in the case, the majority found that she no longer had a stake in the outcome because she had moved out of state and was almost eighteen. Essentially, she no longer needed protection from questioning in a school setting, so the case was moot—it had become stale over the passage of time.

Did You Know?

Michael Newdow challenged the recitation of the Pledge of Allegiance each morning at his daughter's elementary school. He and the girl's mother were divorced. Since Newdow's ex-wife had legal custody of the child, the Court found that Newdow did not have **standing** to sue on his daughter's behalf, and they dismissed the case. *Elk Grove Unified School District v. Newdow (2004)*

Camreta v. Greene is an example of the freedom the Supreme Court has in deciding issues brought before them. Although the Court granted the petition for review, after hearing oral argument on the issues, they ruled 7–2 that the case shouldn't be before them. Concerning how S.G. was interviewed, the justices ruled 5–4 that since they didn't have a "live" case, they could not review the Fourth Amendment claim of an illegal search. However, the Court did **vacate** (set aside) the lower court's ruling on this case: that the in-school interview was unconstitutional and that authorities needed to obtain a warrant before interviewing a child in school.

The Court Speaks

"That choice [of whether to review a case] will be governed by the ordinary principles informing our decision whether to grant certiorari—a 'power [we] ... sparingly exercis[e].'" (Justice Elena Kagan's comment on this matter includes a quotation from *Forsyth v. Hammond*, an 1897 Supreme Court decision.)

IN OTHER WORDS

The Supreme Court has "unqualified power to grant certiorari upon the petition of any party."
—Justice Elena Kagan, *Camreta v. Green* (2011)

The Court's long history of selecting cases to review is based on the importance of the issue involved, the necessity of avoiding conflict in lower federal courts, and how an issue affects the nation's interests.

What If...?

If the Supreme Court had not vacated the lower court's ruling, all law enforcement and child welfare agencies in the Ninth Circuit (nine western states) would have needed to change the way they investigate cases of abuse. Before interviewing any reported cases of abuse or neglect with victims who were minors, they would be required to obtain a search warrant. Such a policy change could potentially affect the way investigators collect evidence of wrongdoing in child abuse cases.

Related Cases

The Fifth Amendment talks about self-incrimination and your right to remain silent. This means that when faced with an interrogation by the police, you don't have to talk or provide them with evidence that may be used against you. It's best in this situation to have a parent or **guardian** with you. For example, there may be a time when the police or other officials (such as social workers from a state agency) want to talk with you. You may not be in trouble but may know something that's important to an investigation. Feel free to ask for your parent to be present. Some states require that juveniles who are given the **Miranda warnings** by the police are also told that they have a right to have their parents present. If you make this request before being questioned, you're not hindering the officials' investigation. You're simply protecting your right to have your parents with you to give you support and advice. The following related cases involved teens who were being interviewed or interrogated.

DOES A MINOR HAVE THE RIGHT TO SPEAK WITH A PARENT BEFORE BEING INTERVIEWED BY POLICE?

In re Andre M. (2004)

In 2002, after a fist fight was reported at his school, sixteen-year-old Andre was sent to the principal's office and was interviewed by the police. Shortly afterward, his mother arrived at the school but was not allowed to see her son. Then, police discovered a sawed-off shotgun in the trunk of another student's car and, suspecting it belonged to Andre, interviewed him again—without his mother being present. He admitted to possessing the weapon and was convicted and placed on **probation** for one year.

Courts have held that when a juvenile's parents are present but the police refuse to let them speak with their child, the juvenile's statements appear to be involuntary. Because the police excluded Andre's mother from sitting in on the interrogation without giving a reason, Andre's confession should not have been used as evidence against him. His conviction was reversed.

WHAT ABOUT AN INTERVIEW OR INTERROGATION BY A TEACHER?

Ohio v. Clark, 135 S.Ct. 2173 (2015)

A preschool teacher in Ohio noticed that a three-year-old boy (referred to in the case as L.P.) in her class had injuries. The bruises and other marks looked like they had been made by hitting the child with a belt. When the teacher questioned L.P., the boy said he was abused by his mother's boyfriend.

At trial, evidence would show that L.P. had been whipped, hit, bitten, and grabbed with enough force to leave lasting marks. The trial court allowed the teacher to testify about what L.P. had told her, and the court denied the defendant's request to cross-examine the child. The defendant was convicted and sentenced to prison. Although the Confrontation Clause included in the Sixth Amendment grants a person the right to confront his accuser, it does not apply to young children who are determined incompetent to testify at trial due to their age. The trial court, in this case, found L.P. incompetent to testify.

IN OTHER WORDS

"The schoolroom is the first opportunity most citizens have to experience the power of government.... The values they learn there, they take with them in life."

—Justice John Paul Stevens, *New Jersey v. T.L.O.* (1985)

The defendant appealed the conviction, and his case eventually moved to the Supreme Court. There, the justices ruled 9–0 that teachers are required by law to report suspected incidences of child abuse. That does not make teachers or any other mandatory reporter of abuse an agent of law enforcement, and therefore they are not required to issue *Miranda* warnings to students they question. The boy's statements to his teacher were ruled admissible. In his majority opinion, Justice Samuel Alito wrote, "statements by very young children will rarely, if ever, implicate the Confrontation Clause."

WHAT HAPPENS IF POLICE INTERROGATE A MINOR WHO HAS LIED ABOUT HIS AGE?

Stone v. Farley (1995)

Lorenzo Stone was seventeen when he and four others went to a bar in Gary, Indiana, to commit a robbery. Two of the men, but not Stone, had handguns and told everyone in the bar to get down on the floor. One customer drew his weapon in self-defense and was shot and killed. When Stone was arrested, he lied about his age—he told the police he was nineteen so he would be placed in an adult holding area where he could smoke. Throughout interviews that included a confession to the crime, Stone continued to say that he was nineteen. The police checked their records and found that Stone had reported being nineteen in four previous arrests. Consequently, he remained in the adult system for prosecution.

Stone then asked the trial court to suppress his confession, since he was really seventeen years old and hadn't been afforded his rights as a juvenile, including having a parent present when he was interrogated. The court denied his request since it was his "own self-serving statements" that led to his treatment as an adult. His conviction for first degree murder under the **felony murder rule** and life sentence were **affirmed.**

Talk, Think, and Take Action

• Have you ever been questioned at school by the principal or other school official? How about by the police or a social worker? What do you know about your rights in such a situation? What do you think would happen if you refused to answer questions or provide information about yourself or your classmates? Spend some time researching what your rights are in this situation.

• What would you do if a teacher or coach demanded that you provide your password to Facebook, Twitter, or Instagram? Do you know whether or not you would be required to do so? What does your school policy say about digital devices and social media? If your school does not have a written policy on this, how could you and your fellow students work on getting one put in place?

• Have you read your school's student handbook or code of conduct? If so, what does it say about interviews with the principal or other administrators? Can you ask that your parents be present? Can you refuse to answer any questions? If you are familiar with your school's policies, what do you think about them? In what ways do you think they might be improved? Do you think most other students in your school are familiar with these policies? If not, how could you spread the word and help your classmates be more informed about how to protect their rights?

• Keep in mind that anything you tell a school administrator, school resource officer, or police officer while at school may be used against you in a school discipline case, in a criminal case, or both. If you are interested in your rights and this subject, then find your school and/or school district's policy on interviews and questioning of students. In most school districts, anyone has the right and ability to help create or revise a school policy. As a student, you can start the conversation, begin the process of examining policies, educate the community on a relevant topic, and advocate for change. Building awareness and support for an issue that affects students is a great way to create or revise school policies on an issue, including the way that students may be questioned on campus.

Closing Comments

The Supreme Court has the freedom to select which cases it will hear each term. To hear a case, four justices must vote in favor of doing so. When voting on whether to grant certiorari, each justice has the opportunity to write a statement regarding the vote. If the required four votes are not met, a justice may explain in writing why he or she feels the case should be considered by the Court. On the other hand, any justice who voted against hearing the case can explain his or her position.

Besides agreeing to hear cases that are still relevant to the people involved, the Court will occasionally revisit an issue depending on current research and changing societal views. For example, in 1973, abortion was legalized in *Roe v. Wade*. The Court continues to hear cases challenging different aspects of the abortion process. Likewise, the Court has revisited the death penalty as applied to adults and juveniles, as well as voting rights and other contentious issues affecting the rights and responsibilities of Americans.

Further Reading and Resources

Primary Case: *Camreta v. Greene*, 131 S.Ct. 2020 (2011).

"Fourth Amendment Implications of Interviewing Suspected Victims of Abuse in School" by Jennifer Kwapisz, 86 *Saint John's Law Review* 963 (Fall 2012).

"Guidelines on Investigatory Interviewing of Children: What Is the Consensus in the Scientific Community?" by Hollida Wakefield, 24 *American Journal of Forensic Psychology* 57 (2006).

The Illustrated Guide to Criminal Procedure by Nathaniel Burney (CreateSpace Independent Publishing Platform, 2014).

"Letting the Fox Guard the Hen House: Why the Fourth Amendment Should Not Be Applied to Interviews of Children in Child Abuse Cases" by Rachael Yourtz, 40 *Hastings Constitutional Law Quarterly* 653 (Spring 2013).

CASE 4

Morse v. Joseph Frederick (2007)

Key Issue: Student Free Speech and Expression

Does the First Amendment right to free speech prohibit public schools from disciplining students for speech that promotes the use of illegal drugs?

Are your constitutional rights limited in certain settings, such as school? Or do you always retain your rights, such as the right to free speech, no matter the situation? When the Supreme Court agreed to hear *Morse v. Joseph Frederick,* it was not the first time the Court had considered the issue of student expression. The 1969 landmark case of *Tinker v. Des Moines* focused on a rule limiting students' right to free expression in school. In this case, a group of students and adults in Des Moines, Iowa, planned to stage a silent protest against the Vietnam War in 1965 by wearing black armbands. The local school district feared this would cause a disruption and passed a rule against wearing armbands at school. Students would be asked to remove them or be sent home and suspended if they refused to do so. Mary Beth Tinker was thirteen years old at the time. She, her three siblings, and one other student wore the armbands to school and were sent home when they refused to take them off. The Tinkers sued the school district, claiming that the rule violated their free speech. After four years of litigation, the case was decided in their favor by the Supreme Court.

The Supreme Court in *Tinker* was considered a victory for free speech and famously held that students and teachers do not "shed their constitutional rights to freedom of speech or expression at the schoolhouse gate." It concluded that students have a right to free speech in school as long as it does not disrupt the school environment or violate the rights of other students. The question before the Court in *Morse v. Joseph Frederick* was whether such a disruption—often called the *Tinker* disruption test—was the *only* acceptable reason for limiting student speech.

Facts of the Case

In January 2002, the Olympic Torch Relay was scheduled to pass through Juneau, Alaska, on its way to the start of the Winter Games in Salt Lake City, Utah. Runners would carry the torch along a street in front of the Juneau-Douglas High School while school was in session. The school's principal, Deborah Morse, decided to let students watch the event as an approved class activity. The students were allowed to stand on both sides of the street while being supervised by teachers and staff.

IN OTHER WORDS

Justice Clarence Thomas wrote in this case that "Through the legal doctrine of *in loco parentis*, courts [have historically] upheld the right of schools to discipline students, to enforce rules, and to maintain order" while they acted in the place of parents during the school day.

> *In loco parentis* is Latin for "in the place of a parent."

Joseph Frederick was an eighteen-year-old senior who, with his friends, watched the event on the street across from the school. When the torchbearers passed by, Frederick and his friends held up a fourteen-foot banner that read "BONG HiTS 4 JESUS." The large banner was plainly visible to other students and observers, including the media.

Principal Morse saw the banner. After identifying Frederick as the owner, she told him to take it down. When he refused, Morse took the banner from him and sent him to her office. There she explained that the message encouraged illegal drug use, specifically marijuana use, in violation of school policy. Frederick received a ten-day suspension. After appeal to the school superintendent, Frederick ended up with an eight-day suspension.

Frederick filed a civil rights lawsuit claiming the school violated his First Amendment rights to free speech. Further, he claimed that the sign did not promote drug use and "that the words were just nonsense meant to attract television cameras."

The Court's Ruling and Reasoning

The First Amendment is designed, in part, to protect political speech. However, Joseph Frederick did not argue that his banner put forth a political or religious message. In fact, he offered no further explanation of the banner's text other than it was "meaningless and funny." He just wanted to get on television.

As the justices deliberated, they reviewed the history of public education in America and its role in society. The Court noted that the rights of students must be viewed in light of the special characteristics of the public school environment. Deterring drug use by schoolchildren is an "important—indeed, perhaps compelling—interest." In this case, the majority of the justices felt that maintaining a drug-free environment at school was of utmost importance. So, schools may regulate some speech by students during the school day even though the government could not censor similar speech outside the school setting. Schools may "take steps to safeguard those entrusted to their care from speech that can reasonably be regarded as encouraging illegal drug use." The Court ruled against Frederick.

Chief Justice John Roberts wrote the majority opinion. He concluded with the following statement:

> *School principals have a difficult job, and a vitally important one. When Frederick suddenly and unexpectedly unfurled his banner, Morse had to decide to act—or not act—on the spot. It was reasonable for her to conclude that the banner promoted illegal drug use—in violation of established school policy—and that failing to act would send a powerful message to the students in her charge, including Frederick, about how serious the school was about the dangers of illegal drug use. The First Amendment does not require schools to tolerate at school events student expression that contributes to those dangers.*

IN OTHER WORDS

"No one wishes to substitute courts for school boards, or to turn the judge's chambers into the principal's office."
—Justice Stephen G. Breyer, *Morse v. Frederick* (2007)

The Court's ruling created a third exception to the *Tinker* disruption standard regarding the regulation of student speech. Schools could now censor drug-related speech, obscene speech

(*Bethel School District v. Fraser*, 1986), and unacceptable content in student productions including plays, yearbooks, and a school newspaper (*Hazelwood School District v. Kuhlmeier*, 1988). Courts have long struggled with defining what's obscene and what passes as acceptable expression. For instance, in 1964, Justice Potter Stewart commented that, although he was unable to define obscenity or hardcore pornography, "I know it when I see it" (*Jacobellis v. Ohio*, 1964). Since there is no strict formula to apply in these cases, they are evaluated individually based on content and intended audience.

The Court Speaks

Justice Stephen Breyer wrote on this case, "Most students ... do not shed their brains at the schoolhouse gate, and most students know dumb advocacy when they see it."

Justice John Paul Stevens dissented, however, commenting that Frederick's banner was "a nonsense message, not advocacy." He questioned whether it would actually persuade any student to change his or her behavior. He went on, "Even if advocacy could somehow be wedged into Frederick's obtuse reference to marijuana, that advocacy was at best subtle and ambiguous."

What If...?

One vote made the difference between Joseph Frederick's suspension and being allowed to wave his banner without consequences. But that doesn't mean the justices were separated into two distinctly different viewpoints. Besides the majority opinion, written by Chief Justice John G. Roberts, there were four additional opinions written in this case: two concurring opinions, one opinion that concurred with the judgment overall but dissented in part, and one dissenting opinion.

Although Justice Clarence Thomas agreed that the principal was not personally liable, he went further than the majority ruling on the issue of student rights. He wrote: "In my view, the history of public education suggests that the First Amendment, as originally understood, does not protect student speech in public schools." If four other justices held the same beliefs as Justice Thomas, students' right to free speech at school may have been greatly reduced.

Did You Know?

> In the Court's written decision, the justices referred to Frederick's banner as cryptic, curious, ambiguous, ridiculous, obscure, silly, quixotic, stupid, gibberish, dumb, obtuse, and nonsensical. The "BONG HiTS 4 JESUS" banner is now displayed at the Newseum in Washington, D.C.

On the other hand, Justice Stevens wrote in his dissent that he felt there was no justification to discipline Frederick "for his attempt to make an ambiguous statement to a television audience simply because it contained an oblique reference to drugs. The First Amendment demands more, indeed, much more." If four other justices agreed with Justice Stevens, instead of just three, the door may have been opened to greater freedoms of expressions for students at schools. While this might stimulate a lively dialogue about various issues in schools across the country, such a decision could also present challenges for teachers and administrators as they attempt to teach students and maintain order.

Justice Thomas also stated that, given the opportunity, he would reverse *Tinker*—the decades old "disruption test" regarding student free speech. Does that surprise you? Imagine how your life as a student would be different without these First Amendment speech protections.

Related Cases

Schools are able to monitor and control many aspects of students' lives on campus. For instance, most public and private K–12 schools in the United States have zero-tolerance policies when it comes to drugs and weapons on campus and at school events. Bullying, whether in person or online (cyberbullying), is also covered by many schools' policies—including their rules on digital speech. Students may be suspended or expelled for violating these rules. Criminal charges and civil lawsuits are also possible consequences.

As it stands, schools have quite a bit of direction from the Supreme Court regarding student expression—*except* when it comes to online or digital speech. A key question is whether a school can discipline a student for off-campus digital speech (text, Instagram, Twitter, and so on). How far does the school's authority reach—into your room, your iPad during spring break, or cell phone during the summer? All of the following related cases deal with students' digital speech made outside of school.

CAN A STUDENT BE SUSPENDED FOR ENCOURAGING OTHERS TO CYBERBULLY A CLASSMATE?

Kowalski v. Berkeley County Schools (2012)

Kara Kowalski, a senior in West Virginia, started a social networking page called "S.A.S.H." It quickly became a vehicle for spreading mean-spirited and hateful comments against a classmate, and Kowalski invited others to post their thoughts about this classmate. Kowalski was suspended for five days and banned from extracurricular activities for a semester. In response, she sued the school district and administrators, claiming that the discipline violated her First Amendment right to free speech and her Fourteenth Amendment right to due process. The court ruled in favor of the school, since her deeds inflicted harm on the targeted classmate and disrupted the school environment.

DOES THE FIRST AMENDMENT PROTECT STUDENTS' ONLINE EXPRESSIONS MADE OFF CAMPUS?

Layshock v. Hermitage School District (2012)

Two students at different schools in Pennsylvania created fake profiles of their principals on a social networking website. Justin Layshock, a high school senior, wrote online that his principal was a "big steroid freak" and similar juvenile comments. He added a photo of the principal taken from the school's website. Justin was suspended for ten days for being disrespectful and using a school photo without permission. He and his parents sued the school, claiming his speech was protected under the First Amendment. The court agreed, stating that school officials were not "censors of the World Wide Web."

Jill Snyder, an eighth grader, created a lewd parody of her principal on her home computer and made inappropriate comments about his sex life. She was also suspended for ten days and, with her parents, filed suit. The federal court ruled in Jill's favor, stating that the school cannot punish a student for profanity away from school and during nonschool hours.

The school districts in Justin's and Jill's cases appealed to the Supreme Court. Kara Kowalski also petitioned the Supreme Court for review. The Court, without statement or explanation, denied each petition. As a result, the lower courts' decisions were left in place.

It is important to note that by the time the Supreme Court decided not to review these cases, the students had already served their suspension and returned to school. Because of the time involved in challenging a disciplinary action at school or appealing a court decision (criminal or civil), the punishment is often completed by the student or affected person before the final decision in the case is reached. However, if successful on appeal, their record may be cleared of the incident.

Talk, Think, and Take Action

• What do you think Joseph Frederick's banner meant? Do you see it as a message promoting the use of marijuana? If its meaning is unclear, was the principal right or wrong in disciplining him? Why? Now that recreational marijuana is legal in some states, including Alaska where this incident took place, what—if any—difference do you think that would make in the outcome of the case if it went to Court today?

• Do you agree with Justice Thomas's view that the First Amendment does not apply to students, or with Justice Stevens's argument that Frederick's banner was protected speech under the First Amendment? Where do you draw the line between offensive speech and protected speech? What kind of limits on your speech or expression do you think are appropriate at school? What about off-campus? Do you agree with the *Tinker* disruption test? Why or why not?

- Do you think adults have more or less freedom than students to express themselves? Think of instances when someone in the public eye had an email, a tweet, or a text message backfire and go viral. Consider the idea that just because you have a legal right to say something doesn't mean it's always a good decision to exercise that right. It's wise to be cautious before posting or sending any message or photo, and it's important to remember that being free to express yourself isn't the same as being free from consequences in your personal or professional life. Talk to your friends about what advice you might give younger kids about protecting themselves and making smart decisions when using social media. Consider writing an opinion piece on this topic for a blog or the local paper.
- Think about the related case involving bullying. How much do you know about the policies at your school on this topic? If you witness bullying at school, how willing would you be to report it? What factors would likely be involved in your decision to come forward as opposed to remaining silent or looking the other way? Do you know if you can report bullying anonymously in your school? Do you and your friends take bullying seriously? What do you think it means to stand up for someone who is being bullied? How can you

stand up for someone else and still keep yourself safe?

• What can you do to make the world a kinder place? How could you start in your school or neighborhood? How can you spread your message to others? Teens across the country have created accounts on Twitter and other social media sites to spread positive messages about classmates in an effort to combat cyberbullying. Check out @OsseoNice Things, for example, to see how a few words can make a person's day.

• Do you (or does anyone you know) have a vanity license plate on a car? If so, do you think the message on the plate speaks for the government that issued it, or just for the driver (or owner) of the car? How are messages on a license plate different from messages on a bumper sticker? Could the government restrict your speech if you wanted, for example, to display the Confederate flag (which is deeply controversial because of its connections to slavery in the United States) on a license plate? The Supreme Court considered this issue in 2015. They ruled 5–4 that since license plates are government property, a state can prohibit messages it finds objectionable. What do you think about this, and how do you think it should be decided what is "objectionable"? What about a religious message, or a stand on a controversial topic?

How much control, if any, do you think the government should have on materials that they produce?

- What do you see as differences and similarities between saying something to someone's face and writing it on social media or in a text message? Do you know whether you can be sued or prosecuted for digital speech? Consider the case of Gregory Elonis. He was twenty-eight years old when he posted a Facebook rant against his estranged wife and against FBI agents. He also threatened to take his fury out on a kindergarten class. In 2015, his case was considered by the Supreme Court. Elonis's defense hinged on his right to free speech, and he argued that his online rants did not constitute true or actual threats. The Court ruled that "wrongdoing must be conscious to be criminal." They returned the case to the lower court to determine if Elonis had intended to cause harm (*Elonis v. United States*, 2015).
- Laws regarding the criminalization of marijuana have changed significantly in the past few years. Numerous states now have new medical marijuana laws, and some states have also legalized marijuana for personal or recreational use. Do you believe that the passage of these laws makes marijuana more available to teens who are not medical card holders? In what ways, if any, do you think

these new laws will affect use among young people? What are your state's laws concerning the possession and use of medical marijuana for both adults and minors?

Closing Comments

IN OTHER WORDS

"**Not every defiant act by a high school student is constitutionally protected speech.**"

—U.S. district judge Santiago E. Campos, *Bivens v. Albuquerque Public Schools* (1995)

The cases in this chapter show that the government can place some limits on your freedom to act and speak. School is an environment where teachers and administrators step in momentarily in your parents' absence to see that you are safe and allowed to mature in a healthy setting. As Chief Justice Warren Burger wrote in the 1986 Supreme Court's opinion in *Fraser*, the First Amendment rights of students in public schools "are not automatically coextensive with [the same as] the rights of adults in other settings, and must be applied in light of the special circumstances of the school environment." Furthermore, the Court stated in *Hazelwood* that "a school need not tolerate student speech that is inconsistent with its basic educational mission."

Since the Court has yet to consider a student online speech case, this surely isn't the final word on the subject of student expression.

Further Reading and Resources

Primary Case: *Morse v. Frederick*, 127 S.Ct. 2618 (2007).

Let the Students Speak: A History of the Fight for Free Expression in American Schools by David L. Hudson (Boston: Beacon Press, 2011).

"*Morse v. Frederick:* Did the Supreme Court Weaken or Strengthen Student Freedom of Expression?" by David Schimmel, 226 *West's Education Law Reporter* 557 (January 24, 2008).

"Recent Developments in Education Law: Regulating Student Speech in Cyberspace" by James C. Hanks, 43 *Urban Lawyer* 723 (Summer 2011).

"Recognizing the Public Schools' Authority to Discipline Students' Off-Campus Cyberbullying of Classmates" by Douglas E. Abrams, 37 *New England Journal on Criminal and Civil Confinement* 181 (Summer 2011).

"School Speech in the Internet Age: Do Students Shed Their Rights When They Pick Up a Mouse?" by Michael J. O'Connor, 11 *University* of *Pennsylvania Journal of Constitutional Law* 459 (2009).

The Struggle for Student Rights: Tinker v. Des Moines *and the 1960s* by John W. Johnson (Lawrence: University Press of Kansas, 1997).

CASE 5

McCreary County v. American Civil Liberties Union (ACLU)(2005)

Key Issue: Freedom of Religion in Government Buildings

Does a display of the Bible's Ten Commandments in public buildings violate the First Amendment?

The United States was founded on the principle of religious freedom. The First Amendment gives us the right to practice the religion of our choice, or to practice no religion at all. There is no official religion for the country, and the government is not to favor one religion over another—they are to remain neutral in matters of religion. This has been called the separation of church and state, and although the Constitution does not include those exact words, the First Amendment essentially guarantees this separation in what is called the Establishment

Clause. The Establishment Clause mandates **neutrality** and prohibits favoring one religion over another, or religion over non-religion. The Establishment Clause applies to all states and their political subdivisions, including cities, counties, and school districts. Here's what it says:

"Congress shall make no law respecting an establishment of religion, or prohibiting the free exercise thereof."

But this clause has been interpreted in different ways over the years, and we still see aspects of religion in some government settings. For example, your school may have a prayer or Bible group that meets before classes begin; you may have heard prayers before a presidential inauguration or other public ceremony; or you may have noticed that the words "In God We Trust" appear on all U.S. currency. The blurred lines on this issue, and the strong feelings involved, point to the difficulty in weighing what is really at stake when it comes to the government and action that may be connected to religion—or action that may be at least viewed that way. Indeed, the separation between church and state is not as clear as some would like and others would prefer the separation to be less precise. The day that the decision of this case was issued, a similar case *(Van Orden v. Perry)* was resolved as well—with an opposite ruling. The power of one vote was ever clear in these two cases.

> **IN OTHER WORDS**
>
> **"The religion of every man must be left to the conviction and conscience of every man."**
> —President James Madison

Facts of the Case

In 1999, a copy of the Ten Commandments was posted in two county courthouses in Kentucky. When challenged as a violation of the First Amendment, the displays were modified by adding historical documents that were foundational to American government, and which also had specific references to Christianity. In McCreary County, the Commandments were posted in a "very high traffic area of the courthouse." In Pulaski County, the Commandments were hung in a ceremony presided over by a judge and his pastor and included references to a "divine God." The displays were visible to all citizens who had business in the courthouse. The American Civil Liberties Union (ACLU) challenged both displays as an unconstitutional endorsement of religion.

The Court's Ruling and Reasoning

When considering a case under the Establishment Clause, the Supreme Court looks to "purpose"—whether the act is meant to be secular (non-religious), or is meant to promote or advance a particular religion.

In the 1971 case of *Lemon v. Kurtzman*, the Court developed a test for analyzing whether the two religion clauses of the First Amendment had been violated. For any law or government act (including those by public schools) to comply with the Establishment Clause, it must:
- have a non-religious purpose
- not promote or inhibit the practice of religion
- not foster "an excessive government entanglement with religion"

Applying this test to the facts in *McCreary*, the Court found no valid secular or educational purpose for posting the Ten Commandments in a public building. In a 5–4 decision the Court ruled that they violated the First Amendment and were unconstitutional. The Commandments needed to be removed from these courthouse displays. The majority of justices stated that the Commandments are a distinctly religious document believed to be sacred by many in the Christian and Jewish faiths. Consequently, the displays presented a predominantly religious purpose—to advance religion.

In a concurring opinion, Justice Sandra Day O'Connor wrote that "the purpose of the display was relevant, because an unmistakable message of endorsement of religion had been conveyed to the reasonable observer." She further pointed out that "under the Establishment Clause detail is key.... The question is what viewers may fairly understand to be the purpose of the display.... Free people are entitled to free and diverse thoughts, which government ought neither to constrain nor to direct."

The Court's ruling, however, did not prohibit using a sacred text as part of a government display on law or history. But in this case the justices considered the changed displays in McCreary County as secondary to the main religious objective of the displays. The decision in *Lemon* requires that the secular purpose of a display be genuine. The revisions made to the courthouse display of the Ten Commandments were reviewed, and the way that the display had evolved was also considered. The Court found enough evidence to conclude that the county's purpose was to emphasize and celebrate the Commandment's religious message, in violation of the First Amendment.

> ### Did You Know?
>
> Location and intent make a difference when it comes to religious symbols. In the case whose decision was announced the same day as *McCreary*, the display of a Ten Commandments monument on the grounds of the Texas state capitol was challenged. The Court ruled 5–4 that the monument's placement was acceptable. In this case, *Van Orden v. Perry*, the Court held that, although religious, the Ten Commandments had an undeniable historical meaning and, as such, did not offend the Establishment Clause.

Four justices disagreed with the majority, stating that U.S. history supports the displays challenged in *McCreary*. Justice Antonin Scalia wrote for the dissenters that he acknowledges the prohibition against government favoring one religion over another. He stated, "That is indeed a valid principle where public aid or assistance to religion is concerned ... or where the free exercise of religion is at issue ... but it necessarily applies in a more limited sense to public acknowledgment of the Creator."

The Court Speaks

"When the government acts with a predominant purpose of advancing religion, it violates the Establishment Clause value of official religious neutrality." Justice Souter wrote the majority decision in this case, emphasizing the need for government neutrality in all matters regarding religion. He commented that liberty and social stability demand a religious tolerance that respects the views of all citizens.

What If...?

If the Court had ruled in favor of allowing displays of the Ten Commandments in public buildings, the displays would have remained posted in the Kentucky courthouses, leading some to believe that these counties favored people who believed in the Commandments over those who did not. As the Court held, "liberty and social stability demand a tolerance that respects the religious views of all citizens." Remember, the key word and principle in these cases is "neutrality." Separation of church and state depends on a neutral government when it comes to religion.

Related Cases

The rights laid out in the First Amendment (speech, expression, religion, and association) are debated at all levels of education across the country. For example, when it comes to wearing a religious symbol to school, the First Amendment applies. Students and administrators may not see eye to eye on school dress codes, but court orders and decisions come into play that must be followed. The disruption test of *Tinker* (see CASE 4) is usually referred to in these disputes. The following cases discuss various issues related to religion and school, including school displays, religious clubs, and prayer in school or school-related ceremonies.

CAN A STATE REQUIRE SCHOOL CLASSROOMS TO POST THE TEN COMMANDMENTS?

Stone v. Graham (1980)

When Kentucky passed a law requiring public school classrooms to display a copy of the Ten

Commandments, a group of parents sued the state for violating the Establishment Clause of the First Amendment. The Supreme Court reviewed *Lemon* and found that the law failed the first part of the test. They ruled that the law was unconstitutional—that posting the Ten Commandments "had no secular legislative purpose and that it was plainly religious in nature." Although secular matters such as murder and stealing are part of the Commandments, others such as the worship of God and observing the Sabbath are obviously religious.

This case and others that are similar do not apply to private schools, since they don't receive federal funding and can therefore establish their own rules about religious symbols and instruction.

IS PRAYER ALLOWED AT PUBLIC SCHOOL CEREMONIES?

***Lee v. Weisman* (1992)**

Robert E. Lee was the principal of a middle school in Rhode Island. He invited a rabbi to speak and offer a prayer at the school's graduation ceremony. Deborah Weisman was fourteen and a member of the graduating class. She and her father opposed the practice of clergy praying at public school ceremonies.

In a 5–4 decision, the Supreme Court agreed with Weisman and found the practice unconstitutional. The Court held that the school's plan for the ceremony created "a state-sponsored and state-directed religious exercise." The practice was considered a subtle form of coercion since the students were required to stand respectfully and silently during the prayer. The policy forced students to act in ways that, the Court ruled, could be considered as the establishment of a state religion.

> ### IN OTHER WORDS
>
> **"The lessons of the First Amendment are as urgent in the modern world as in the 18th Century when it was written.... [A]ll creeds must be tolerated and none favored."**
> —Justice Anthony M. Kennedy, *Lee v. Weisman* (1992)

CAN RELIGIOUS CLUBS AND ORGANIZATIONS BE ESTABLISHED IN PUBLIC COLLEGES AND UNIVERSITIES?

Christian Legal Society v. Martinez (2010)

The Hastings College of Law in California refused to recognize the Christian Legal Society

(C.L.S.) as an official student organization. The C.L.S. required members to sign a statement specifying that they believed in the Christian God and the Holy Spirit, and that Jesus Christ "is Lord of my life." The college argued that the organization's membership conflicted with state law, which required all registered student organizations to allow "any student to participate, become a member, or seek leadership positions, regardless of their status or beliefs."

> ### Did You Know?
>
> In 2001, the Supreme Court ruled that excluding a Bible club from meeting after hours on public school property constituted **viewpoint discrimination** when other groups were allowed to meet on the property (*Good News Club v. Milford Central School*, 2001). In another case, the Court required equal treatment of Bible clubs in high schools (*Westside Community Board of Education v. Mergens*, 1990). In other words, if the school permits a chess or French club, it may not exclude a Bible club.

The Supreme Court upheld the school's decision to deny official recognition of the club. They found that the First Amendment does not require a public university to support or validate practices that discriminate.

CAN STUDENTS IN PUBLIC SCHOOLS BE REQUIRED TO RECITE MORNING PRAYERS?

Abington School District v. Schempp (1963)

A Pennsylvania law required all public school students to start the day with a reading of ten verses from the Bible. Following the Bible reading, the Abington School District required students to recite the Lord's Prayer. With a parent's written note, a student could be excused from the daily religious exercises.

Edward and Sidney Schempp had three children in Abington schools and opposed both the verses and the prayer. In an 8–1 decision, the Supreme Court agreed with the Schempps and struck down the readings and recitations as essentially religious ceremonies that were "intended by the State to be so." The Court went on to state that study of the Bible for its literary and historic qualities and study of religion, when presented objectively as part of a secular program of education, may pass First Amendment scrutiny.

> ## Talk, Think, and Take Action
> Consider the following decisions where freedom of religion has confronted a school

rule or state law. See if you agree with the outcomes of each case.

- In these cases, the federal courts determined that the activity did *not* violate the First Amendment:

  * Yoga classes, which are viewed by some as a spiritual practice and others as a secular experience, offered as part of a high school physical education program
  * A student sharing "Jesus" pencils at lunch or after school
  * A display at school showing one symbol for each religion
  * The words "under God" in the Pledge of Allegiance recited in schools
  * Observance of religious holidays, such as Christmas, in public schools, since these traditions can be seen as cultural or secular
  * A moment of silence at the start of the school day to reflect, meditate, pray, or simply do nothing, since non-religious students are not forced to endorse any religion.

- In these cases, the federal courts determined that the activity *did* violate the First Amendment:

  * Student-initiated and student-led prayers before high school football games
  * Students performing "Ave Maria" and proselytizing during speeches at their graduation ceremonies

* A high school coach "taking a knee" during a pregame prayer led by students
  * Student-created banners with religious messages displayed in classrooms
  * A teacher's criticism of a particular religion during class

• What do you think about *McCreary County v. American Civil Liberties Union*? If you walked into a public building and saw the Ten Commandments on the wall, would it bother you? Why or why not? Do you think the display of a menorah or copy of the Koran would generate similar feelings? Why or why not? What would you do in such a situation?

• Does your school have a Bible club or other religion-oriented organization? If not, are you interested in starting one—or starting a group for atheists, agnostics, or people of other beliefs? If you and a few friends are thinking about founding this type of group, talk with the principal or other administrator about the rules for clubs on campus.

• What do you think about high school sports teams reciting prayers together before a game? What if the players were to run through a banner with a Bible verse on it before the start of the game? Do you think either of these should be allowed at public schools? Why or why not?

• What do you think the solution is if a student's religious clothing or symbols violate a public school's dress code? If a Native American boy has long hair as part of his heritage and spirituality, for example, should a school's policy requiring short hair apply to him, or would his First Amendment rights protect him?

• In 2015, seven high school students successfully challenged school administrators regarding the protection of students' First Amendment rights at school. Some students at one school convinced the faculty to allow the students to hang a "Black Lives Matter" poster. Other students succeeded in getting faculty to approve a new morning announcement informing students of their right not to say the Pledge of Allegiance. In the words of one of the students, "Questioning authority is not always a bad thing, especially if you want to create change in your community or school."

Consider your views on this issue and the many scenarios the First Amendment might affect. For example, what if a school has a policy for everyone to remove hats during the Pledge of Allegiance? In this case, what do you think this should mean for female Muslim students who wear head coverings? What kind of exceptions, if any, do you think are appropriate to the general rule? If reciting the Pledge of Allegiance is important to you—or if the right *not* to recite it is important to you—talk to your school administrators and other students about the issue, and try to gain support for policies in line with your views.

Did You Know?

The Court has sometimes described the religion clauses as erecting a "wall" between church and state (*Lynch v. Donnelly*, 1984).

Did You Know?

- Under the Equal Access Act of 1984, public school students are guaranteed the right to form extracurricular groups with a religious, political, or philosophical purpose. If some groups are permitted, a school cannot exclude others based on their specific positions or viewpoints.
- As of 2015, the constitutions of seven states prohibit individuals who don't believe in God from holding any public office: Arkansas, Maryland, Mississippi, North Carolina, South Carolina, Tennessee, and Texas. Although still on the books in these states, these laws cannot be enforced. The Supreme Court ruled in 1961 that requiring a person to declare a belief in God as a test for public office invaded a person's freedom of belief and religion. Not to mention that the U.S. Constitution, Article

VI, states that "No religious test shall ever be required as a qualification to any office or public trust under the United States."

Closing Comments

As this chapter revealed, cases involving religious freedoms brought before our courts demonstrate the blurred line between church and state. Courts have approved and disapproved government action whose purpose was presumably religious. As the Supreme Court stated in *McCreary*, the Establishment Clause is left "with edges still to be determined." In other words, since "establishment" has not been clearly defined by the Constitution, what constitutes the "establishment of religion" depends on the facts of each case. Actions that will pass constitutional review can only be determined on a case-by-case basis. This explains the diverse decisions from state and federal courts.

IN OTHER WORDS

"It is difficult to discern a serious threat to religious liberty from a room of silent, thoughtful schoolchildren.... A moment of silence is not inherently religious."

—Justice Sandra Day O'Connor, *Wallace v. Jaffree* (1985)

Further Reading and Resources

Primary Case: *McCreary County v. American Civil Liberties Union*, 125 S.Ct. 2722 (2005).

"Inconsistent Guideposts: *Van Orden, McCreary County*, and the Continuing Need for a Single and Predictable Establishment Clause Test" by Frank. J. Ducoat, 8 *Rutgers Journal of Law and Religion* 14 (Spring 2007).

"Public Displays of Affection ... for God: Religious Monuments After *McCreary* and *Van Orden*" by Edith Brown Clement, 32 *Harvard Journal of Law and Public Policy* 231 (Winter 2009).

CASE 6

Board of Education v. Lindsay Earls (2002)

Key Issue: Drug Testing at School
Can a public school randomly drug test students who participate in extracurricular activities?

Are you familiar with the Fourth Amendment and how it protects us against "unreasonable searches and seizures" by the government? Should kids and teens be given this same protection in school settings, and who decides what is reasonable and what isn't? Do you have less of a right to protection or privacy if you participate in a school sport or club than if you are a student at the school who is not involved in extracurricular activities?

The following case and related cases explore what school officials can do without invading your constitutional right to privacy. We'll also look at how you can protect your rights when confronted with a search and possible seizure of yourself or your property while at school. The Supreme Court's 5–4 decision in the *Earls* case affected the power of public schools to regulate student behavior.

Facts of the Case

Lindsay Earls was a sixteen-year-old junior at Tecumseh High School in Oklahoma in 1999. She was a member of the choir, marching band, academic team, and National Honor Society. Her school district adopted a drug testing policy that required all middle and high school students to undergo drug testing before participating in any extracurricular activity. The policy outlined the procedures for the drug screening: Urine samples were examined for controlled substances only. The results were not reported to police, and students who tested positive did not face disciplinary action by the school. Test results were confidential and kept separate from the student's educational record. The only consequence of a failed drug test was a limit on participation in extracurricular activities. Counseling was offered to those who failed, and a student could be reinstated to the activity after a clean drug test.

In order to continue with her activities, Earls complied with the drug testing, and passed. However, she took the matter to court, claiming that the policy amounted to an unreasonable search and so violated the Fourth Amendment.

The Court's Ruling and Reasoning

A 1967 ruling (*Camara v. Municipal Court of San Francisco*) established that the Fourth Amendment's purpose is to "safeguard the privacy and security of individuals against arbitrary invasions by government officials." When the police want to conduct a search, they must either obtain permission from the person to be searched or get a search warrant from a judge that is based on probable cause. "Probable cause" exists when the facts and circumstances that an officer is aware of are sufficient to cause a reasonable person to believe that a crime has been or is being committed.

The probable cause standard does not apply to school officials since they are not law enforcement personnel or prosecutors. Instead, a lesser standard called "reasonable suspicion" (see *T.L.O.,*) is used in school situations. This means that school officials need to have only a reasonable suspicion that a school rule or a law has been broken in order to search a student's locker, cell phone, or other property, including a car parked on campus. If reasonable suspicion exists, the school does not need a search warrant.

IN OTHER WORDS

"The right of the people to be secure in their persons, houses, papers, and effects, against unreasonable searches and seizures, shall not be violated, and no warrants shall issue, but upon probable cause, supported by oath or affirmation, and particularly describing the place to be searched, and the persons or things to be seized."

—The Fourth Amendment to the U.S. Constitution

The Court Speaks

"While schoolchildren do not shed their constitutional rights when they enter the schoolhouse, Fourth Amendment rights are different in public schools than elsewhere."

In this case, the Court noted the differences between criminal activity that occurs in a school setting versus outside of the school. Fourth Amendment rights call for probable cause to justify a search of an individual suspected of breaking the law. However, a school's relationship with students is unique. It is both custodial and educational. Justice Clarence Thomas wrote for the majority that sometimes compelling governmental interests exist for random, suspicionless drug testing of certain students.

This raises a question about privacy at school. While you do have a right to privacy, that right is limited depending on the circumstances. A student's expectation of privacy is balanced against a school's duty to maintain a safe and secure environment.

Did You Know?

Riley Stratton was thirteen in 2012 when school officials in her Minnesota town, trying to combat cyberbullying, demanded she tell them her Facebook password. She did and, after reading her messages, they gave her detention for criticizing a hallway monitor and

> talking to a boy about things of a "sexual nature." Stratton and her parents sued for invasion of privacy and an unreasonable search. A cash settlement was reached in 2014 and the school agreed to change its policies and limit its searches of students' email or social media accounts to times when it has a "reasonable suspicion" that school rules have been violated.

Since the Fourth Amendment protects you from unreasonable searches, the Court in *Earls* reviewed the school district's policy for reasonableness. They determined that the prevention, deterrence, and detection of drug use by students were compelling governmental interests that justified a minimal intrusion of a student's privacy. The Court had already decided (see *Vernonia*) that students who voluntarily participate in school athletics agree to legal intrusions on certain rights and privileges, including privacy. In *Earls*, they extended that rationale to students who joined any extracurricular activity, and ruled in the school's favor.

> ### Did You Know?
> In 2014, the Supreme Court ruled unanimously on a case involving privacy rights in the digital age. In this criminal case, they

> decided that police and other government officials generally do not have the right to search devices that contain data, such as cell phones, without a search warrant. The reasoning of this Court case may be applied to students and their cell phones and other digital devices. For more information, see *Riley v. California*.

"Without first establishing discipline and maintaining order, teachers cannot begin to educate their students," the Court wrote in *T.L.O. v. New Jersey* in support of the policy. The Court in *Earls* noted that students who are under the influence of alcohol or drugs at school can present a danger to themselves and everyone around them. It stated, "The school has the obligation to protect pupils from mistreatment by other children, and also to protect teachers themselves from violence by the few students whose conduct in recent years has prompted national concern."

Four justices disagreed with the majority decision. They thought the drug testing policy was unreasonable and unjustly invaded the privacy of students.

What If...?

As a result of *Earls*, public schools may implement a suspicionless drug testing policy for students in clubs or other school organizations. However, the decision does not require schools to create a testing policy—it is up to individual school districts to determine whether or not to use drug testing for students in extracurricular activities. One more vote against the policy would have hampered schools' efforts to combat drug abuse.

> ### Did You Know?
> According to the National Institute on Drug Abuse, in 2014, 6.5 percent of eighth graders, 16.6 percent of tenth graders, and 21.2 percent of twelfth graders reported using marijuana in the previous month.

If schools weren't able to perform random drug tests for these students, students and teachers could be exposed to unnecessary risks at school and school events. Identifying students who are using drugs or who are under the influence of drugs or alcohol on campus fits within the school's *in loco parentis* obligation toward all students—that is, the school's responsibility to take on the role of a parent during the school day. In the specific case of Lindsay Earls's school, the respectful method they used to collect samples, the confidentiality of the test results, and the lack of prosecution or school discipline for a positive test added up to a reasonable approach to a legitimate problem. The Court recognized that "a nationwide drug epidemic makes the war against drugs a pressing concern in every state," and that Earls's school was faced with a drug problem.

Related Cases

Schools are continuously working to create drug-free environments. Most public and private schools have zero-tolerance policies against drugs on campus and at school events. Consequences for violating the rules include suspension or expulsion. Although public schools may legally require athletes and students involved with extracurricular activities to submit to testing, most schools don't have these programs because of the expense involved. The responsibility lies with the family and community to keep young people away from drugs and alcohol. The following cases addressed different issues related to drug searches, including canine searches at school, testing school athletes, and random drug tests at work.

CAN STUDENT ATHLETES BE REQUIRED TO TAKE RANDOM DRUG TESTS?

Vernonia School District v. James Acton (1995)

A few years before *Earls* was decided, the Court considered another challenge to drug testing in public schools. James Acton was a twelve-year-old seventh grader in Vernonia, Oregon. The school district required all student athletes to comply with a student athlete drug policy that included drug testing before the sports season and random urine tests throughout the season.

Acton wanted to try out for the football team but he and his parents objected to the drug policy since there was no reason to suspect he was using drugs or alcohol. Acton's parents refused to sign the consent form that would allow him to be tested. The school, following its policy, suspended Acton from sports, and he and his family challenged the school's action in court.

The Supreme Court found that the school's concern with the safety of students was more important than the privacy of student athletes, especially since the drug testing required only a limited invasion of their privacy. According to the Court, providing a urine sample was just another type of privacy that student athletes must give up, much like they lose a bit of privacy by sharing a locker room and changing and showering in a common area.

In its decision, the Court noted that "The effects of a drug-infested school are visited not just upon the users, but upon the entire student body and faculty, as the educational process is disrupted."

CAN OFFICERS SEARCH A CAR WITHOUT A WARRANT BASED ON A CANINE ALERT?

Florida v. Harris (2013)

Clayton Harris was stopped for an expired registration on his car. The officer who stopped Harris had a drug detection dog that alerted him to the presence of drugs. A warrantless search of the car followed, and it uncovered over two hundred pills and other supplies for making methamphetamines. Harris was charged and convicted of possession of controlled substances.

He appealed, claiming that an alert by a dog does not give an officer probable cause to conduct a search and so the evidence found in his car could not be used in court.

The Supreme Court concluded unanimously that an alert from a trained canine may constitute probable cause to carry out a warrantless search. Justice Elena Kagan wrote that "A sniff is up to snuff ... if, when viewed through the lens of common sense, it would make a reasonably prudent person think that a search would reveal contraband or evidence of a crime." This applies whether it's your car or a friend's that you're driving. The driver is assumed to be in control of the vehicle and may be held responsible for its contents.

Although the facts of this case involved an adult, it could have just as easily been a teen driver. Once you get your driver's permit or license, all traffic laws apply to you.

CAN EMPLOYERS RANDOMLY DRUG TEST THEIR EMPLOYEES?

Treasury Employees v. Von Raab **and** *Skinner v. Railway Labor Executives' Association* **(1989)**

Adults as well as minors are required to undergo suspicionless drug testing in some instances, depending on the person's occupation and inherent risks in the job. Those with safety-sensitive jobs may be randomly tested. Consider the following situations.

In 1989, the Supreme Court decided two cases regarding employee drug testing. In *Treasury Employees v. Von Raab,* random testing of customs officials was approved because their work intercepting smuggled drugs creates special safety and national security risks. In *Skinner v. Railway Labor Executives' Association,* the Court ruled that testing railway employees was constitutional "to avoid enormous risks to the lives and limbs of others ... even a momentary lapse of attention can have disastrous consequences."

Other occupations where privacy rights have given way to the safety of others include airline pilots, school bus drivers, and nuclear power plant employees.

Talk, Think, and Take Action

• Have there been instances when you thought school officials invaded or violated your privacy? If so, what did you do? Different schools have different policies to protect students and some require students to give up more privacy rights than others. In some schools, students have to walk through metal detectors, face random searches for weapons, or have their lockers, backpacks, or cars subject to drug-sniffing canines on occasion. How do you think schools can best strike a balance between protecting the privacy rights of students and ensuring the safety of other students and adults on campus? Talk with friends and classmates about your ideas for accomplishing this.

• Consider the following issues that involve Fourth Amendment rights. Do you think these searches should be allowed or banned? These situations came up at schools across the country.

* Calling students out of class for questioning about a school-related matter (a rumored fight after school, for example)

* Searching a student who leaves campus but then returns on the same day

* Conducting a schoolwide search for weapons even when no individual student is suspected of misconduct

* Searching a student who is off-campus by a school security guard

* Searching a student's backpack for weapons without having a reason to suspect the student is violating school policy

* Using drug detection dogs to conduct random "sniffs" of student lockers and vehicles in the school parking lot

• What is your school's policy about carrying or using digital devices on campus? Student handbooks often spell out rules for using cell phones, tablets, MP3 players, and other technologies in school. You may already know from personal experience the consequences for breaking these rules. As technology becomes more and more a part of our everyday lives, do you think your school's policy needs to be updated? If so, what could you do to help change your school policy or to at least voice your opinion?

• What do you think about schools monitoring students' social media accounts? In your view, would it be okay for a school to monitor a student's Twitter profile? Why or why not? What about requiring students to provide their social media passwords? Or do you believe that what a student does away from campus should not be subject to review by school officials and possible disciplinary action?

In 2013, the Lodi Unified School District in California adopted a new social media contract and wanted all student athletes and those involved with extracurricular activities to sign it. The contract specified that students would be suspended for inappropriate posts on social media. After hundreds of students protested and drew attention to the issue, the school district decided to drop this new policy. If you are interested in changing your school's policy, consider collecting signatures from students, parents, and school officials to petition the school board to revise the policy.

Closing Comments

Random drug testing of students in activities is not the only type of search that has passed the reasonableness test of the Fourth Amendment. Indeed, most students can expect their backpacks, desks, lockers, and cars on campus to be subject to a search by school officials. Courts have considered challenges to canine searches in high schools, as well as strip searches for contraband, and "reasonable suspicion" has been the test supporting or rejecting such searches. Advances in digital technology are keeping the courts and legislatures busy interpreting and applying the Fourth Amendment in the twenty-first century. For instance, a proposed Student Digital Privacy Act has been considered by Congress and by some states (Delaware, Georgia, Kentucky, Louisiana, and New York) to protect the privacy of students' digital personal information, including user names and passwords. In addition, the collection of student data by education companies and others must now comply with existing federal laws, such as the Family Educational Rights and Privacy Act of 1974 (FERPA), aimed at ensuring the privacy of student records. In 2015, President Barack Obama commented that "data collected on students in the classroom should only be used for educational purposes—to teach our children, not to market to our children."

Further Reading and Resources

Primary Case: *Board of Education v. Lindsay Earls*, 536 U.S. 822 (2002).

"The Disappearing Schoolhouse Gate: Applying *Tinker* in the Internet Age" by John T. Ceglia, 39 *Pepperdine Law Review* 939 (April 2012).

The Earls Case and the Student Drug Testing Debate: Debating Supreme Court Decisions by Kathiann M. Kowalski (New York: Enslow Publishers, 2006).

"Shedding Rights at the College Gate: How Suspicionless Mandatory Drug Testing of College Students Violates the Fourth Amendment" by Jeremy L. Kahn, 67 *University of Miami Law Review* 217 (Fall 2012).

CASE 7

Boy Scouts of America v. James Dale (2000)

Key Issue: Freedom of Association
Does the Boy Scouts' ban on gay leaders violate the First Amendment right to freedom of association?

The First Amendment is well known for giving us freedom of speech, but it also guarantees that we can participate in and pursue a wide variety of political, social, economic, educational, religious, and cultural goals. The clause of the amendment that covers this is often called the right of expressive association, and it gives us the right to freely associate with like-minded people. This right helps prevent a majority group from forcing its views on smaller groups that have other, perhaps unpopular, ideas.

However, this right is not absolute. Like anything else, it has limits. This means that, in some cases, it may be unconstitutional for the government to interfere with how an organization is set up or what it does. On the other hand, a person may—as in this case—be excluded from joining a club or organization if joining would interfere with the organization's main message. There is a delicate balance between an organization's right to free expression and an individual's right to association.

For example, forcing a group to accept certain members may limit that group from fully expressing its views. Having freedom of association means we also have a freedom *not* to associate. Think about that idea as you read this chapter. The issues involved are definitely complex, which helps explain why they divided the Supreme Court in this case.

Facts of the Case

When he was eight years old, James Dale became a Cub Scout and over the years progressed through the scouting ranks until, ten years later, he achieved the rank of Eagle Scout. He went on to apply for adult membership in the Scouts, and at age nineteen Dale became an assistant scoutmaster.

In college, Dale came out as gay and became active in the student lesbian/gay alliance. He was even featured in a news story about the need for role models for gay teenagers.

> ### Did You Know?
> Public accommodations laws were originally intended to prevent discrimination in traditional places where the public is invited, such as hotels, trains, restaurants, and bars. The scope of these laws has been expanded to include public organizations and associations.

Shortly thereafter, Dale received a letter from the Boy Scouts revoking his membership because the Scouts "specifically forbid membership to homosexuals." Dale sued the Scouts for violating New Jersey's public accommodations law, which prohibits discrimination based on sexual orientation in public places. Before reaching the Supreme Court, different lower courts ruled in favor of both Dale and the Boy Scouts. These courts were divided over the way they interpreted the state law and the First Amendment's right of expressive association. In

2000, the Supreme Court agreed to hear the case and resolve this conflict.

The Court's Ruling and Reasoning

The First Amendment states: "Congress shall make no law ... abridging ... the right of the people peaceably to assemble." In this case, the Court was called on to determine if forcing the Boy Scouts to include Dale would affect their ability to promote the values embodied in the Scout Oath and Scout Law, and if it would infringe on the Scouts' First Amendment rights. Remember, the Boy Scouts are a private, not-for-profit organization that works to instill a system of values in young people. They state that homosexual conduct is inconsistent with those values, and they argued that allowing James Dale to be an assistant scoutmaster would interfere with the Scouts' choice not to promote a point of view contrary to their beliefs.

The Court ruled in favor of the Boy Scouts and agreed that being forced to accept Dale, a gay-rights activist, would impair the Boy Scouts' view that homosexual conduct was an unacceptable form of behavior. It said, "The Boy Scouts has a First Amendment right to choose to send one message but not the other." Allowing Dale to remain an assistant scoutmaster would significantly burden the organization's right to "oppose or disfavor homosexual conduct."

The majority opinion, written by Chief Justice William Rehnquist, also concluded that "the presence of an avowed homosexual and gay rights activist in an assistant scoutmaster's uniform sends a ... message" and the Boy Scouts of America, as a private organization, is entitled to exclude that message. "The forced inclusion of an unwanted person in a group infringes on the group's freedom of expressive association if the presence of that person affects in a significant way the group's ability to advocate public or private viewpoints."

The four justices who dissented felt that New Jersey's public accommodations law did not prevent the Boy Scouts from communicating its message. They argued that keeping Dale in his position as an assistant scoutmaster would not contradict the Scouts' basic goals and values. The mere inclusion of gays in the Scouts membership and leadership would not force them to proclaim a message it does not want to send.

In 2013, the Boy Scouts of America voted to lift the ban on openly gay youth members. However, the ban on gay leadership remained. Upon hearing the news, Dale commented, "I don't know how they can create guidelines that tell [members] a young kid is acceptable and once they turn eighteen, they're not. It's half discrimination." (See "Did You Know?" in section entitled "DOES A PRIVATE ORGANIZATION HAVE THE RIGHT TO EXCLUDE GAY AND LESBIAN GROUPS FROM A PUBLIC PARADE?" for an update.)

The Court Speaks

"The First Amendment protects expression, be it of the popular variety or not."

In the majority opinion, Chief Justice William Rehnquist wrote that although homosexuality has gained greater acceptance in society, this alone is not a sufficient argument to deny First Amendment protection to those who don't accept these views. In fact, he pointed out that the more an idea is embraced and advocated by increasing numbers of people, the more reason there is to protect the First Amendment rights of those who wish to voice a different view.

What If...?

If the Supreme Court had voted that the Boy Scouts' policy was discriminatory and unconstitutional, the Scouts' membership and leadership might look different today. Some would argue that it would more accurately represent the current face of America, since the more inclusive an organization is, the more diverse its membership is likely to be. Similarly, a different conclusion by the Court would have forced groups like the Scouts to accept members with contrary viewpoints. Churches might have to include members with views that conflicted with the beliefs and practices of the church. Veterans groups would be forced to accept non-veterans who held different views on the military and service in the armed forces. The Court held that limiting freedom of expression and association by requiring an all-inclusive policy was not consistent with the principles of the founding documents of the United States.

Related Cases

Have you ever been surprised by news of events or organizations that are very controversial—from neo-Nazis or skinheads marching in a parade to the formation of an atheist club at school to teens who express support for jihad or ISIS? Are these activities protected speech or expression? Do you see the difference between expressing a belief or idea and taking action in pursuit of the belief?

The following cases may help you better understand the concepts of "inciting" behavior and "actual threats." When speech crosses the line, it becomes criminal and, consequently, subject to prosecution. These cases about association and expression apply to both teens and adults. They involve controversial speech involved in a demonstration, hate speech, and the right of a private organization to exclude a group with speech that conflicted with their own beliefs.

IS MARCHING WITH A SWASTIKA AND OTHER SYMBOLIC SPEECH LEGAL?

National Socialist Party v. Skokie (1977) and Village of Skokie v. National Socialist Party of America (1978)

In 1977, the National Socialist (Nazi) Party of America informed the police department in Skokie, Illinois, that they planned to demonstrate in a march on May 1 of that year to protest the town's fee for park permits. The population of Skokie was approximately 70,000 people, and more than half of them were Jewish. The leader of the organization told the police chief that up to fifty members of the Party would walk in single file in front of the Skokie Village Hall in full dress, including Nazi uniforms and swastika armbands. They did not intend to make derogatory statements or disregard police instructions.

After holding a hearing on the matter, the district court released an order stopping the group from marching, walking, parading, or otherwise displaying the swastika on the scheduled day. The case made its way to the Supreme Court, who voted 5–4 to send it back to the state court for reconsideration. The Illinois Supreme Court eventually ruled that the use of the swastika is a symbolic form of free speech entitled to First Amendment protection. Displaying such a symbol in a public demonstration did not constitute a "fighting words" exception to free speech, and expecting a hostile audience did not justify prior restraint.

IS HATE SPEECH LEGALLY PROTECTED?

Brandenburg v. Ohio (1969)

A state law in Ohio prohibited speech that advocated crime, sabotage, violence, or terrorism. It also outlawed getting together with others to preach or discuss these behaviors, which the law called "criminal syndicalism." The law's intent was to keep people from advocating social change through violence, sabotage, or other methods of terrorism.

Clarence Brandenburg was a leader of the Ku Klux Klan in Ohio. He organized a rally at a farm where he said, among other statements, "if our President, our Congress, our Supreme Court, continues to suppress the white, Caucasian race, it's possible that there might have to be some revengeance taken." Members gathered around a wooden cross and burned it. In a state court, Brandenburg was charged and convicted of violating the criminal syndicalism statute. He was sentenced to one to ten years in prison and a $1,000 fine.

On appeal, the Supreme Court voted unanimously that the law and the ruling of the lower court violated Brandenburg's right to free speech. They ruled that speech can be prohibited if it is directed at inciting or producing imminent lawless action and if it is likely to provoke such action. The key word here is *imminent*, which means ready to take place or hanging threateningly over one's head. There was no evidence that this was the situation here.

DOES A PRIVATE ORGANIZATION HAVE THE RIGHT TO EXCLUDE

GAY AND LESBIAN GROUPS FROM A PUBLIC PARADE?

Hurley v. Irish-American Gay, Lesbian and Bisexual Group of Boston, Inc. (1995)

A private group called the South Boston Allied War Veterans Council received approval by the City of Boston to organize a St. Patrick's Day Parade. The council consisted of individuals elected from South Boston veterans groups. Historically, they didn't promote any particular message and weren't choosy about who was given permission to march in the parade. However, the Council refused a place in the event for the Irish-American Gay, Lesbian, and Bisexual Group of Boston (GLIB). GLIB intended to express their members' pride in their Irish heritage as openly gay individuals. The council argued that being forced to include GLIB members in their privately organized parade violated their free speech.

Did You Know?

A 2013 Gallup poll showed that 70 percent of eighteen- to twenty-nine-year-olds supported same-sex marriage. A 2014 *New York Times*/CBS news poll found that 56 percent of Americans favored legalizing same-sex marriage. And a February 2015 poll from Greenberg

Quinlan Rosner Research found that 60 percent of people likely to vote in 2016 were in favor of same-sex marriage.

In 2015, the president of the Boy Scouts of America, Robert M. Gates, called for a change in the ban on gay adult leaders. He said a change of policy would allow local Scout organizations the freedom to decide whether to accept gay volunteers and paid staff. He also noted that some state laws ban discrimination based on sexual orientation, and commented on the impending decision by the Supreme Court on gay marriage—both signs that the national consensus on the issue was changing. He said, "We must deal with the world as it is, not as we might wish it to be." In July of that year, the Scouts voted to end the national ban on gay adult leaders, effective immediately (although local faith-based groups will still be able to set their own hiring policies). In a statement on the decision, Gates said, "For far too long this issue has divided and distracted us. Now it's time to unite behind our shared belief in the extraordinary power of Scouting to be a force for good in a community and in the lives of its youth members."

Similar to the ruling in *Boy Scouts of America v. Dale*, the Supreme Court ruled unanimously in this case that "the government may not compel anyone to proclaim a belief with which he or she disagrees." Requiring private citizens to include a group in a parade with a message different from their own violates their First Amendment right to choose their message and, conversely, what not to say.

In 2014, the South Boston Allied War Veterans Council announced that gay groups would no longer be banned from marching in the annual parade. In 2015, gays marched in the parade under rainbow banners for the first time in its 114-year history.

Talk, Think, and Take Action

- In *Boy Scouts of America v. Dale,* do you agree with the Court's majority ruling or with the dissent? Why or why not? What do you think about the change in policy the Boy Scouts made in 2015?

- Does your school have organizations for students interested in politics, such as a Young Republicans, Young Democrats, or Green Party club? If not, who could you talk to about starting one? How else could you begin getting involved in politics in your area?

- Think about the various political parties. Do you know each one's platform and position on issues that are important to you? What could you do to challenge a party position that you don't agree with?

- How do you feel about the idea of voting the "party line"? Do you feel that it's more important to always vote with the same party, or to vote according to your conscience on certain issues? Why?

• Your right to freedom of association means that you have the opportunity to join a wide variety of clubs and organizations in high school and beyond. Look into those that interest you, even if their purpose may be controversial. For example, No Más Muertes (No More Deaths) is a humanitarian organization whose mission is to end death and suffering of migrants in areas along the U.S.-Mexico border. Also consider the difference that one student can make. For example, Zana Alattar, a junior at Arizona State University, founded Students Organize for Syria (SOS), a student-led movement to educate, bring awareness to the Syrian revolution, and provide humanitarian relief to the Syrian people.

• Does your school have a Gay-Straight Alliance (GSA) club? If not, and if you're interested in fighting homophobia and transphobia in your school, consider starting a GSA. Thousands of these alliances exist in schools throughout the country, started by students who wanted to create a safe school environment for all and empower other students. For more information, visit GSAnetwork.org.

Closing Comments

The Supreme Court has often wrestled with freedom of speech, freedom of expression, and the right of association. Because these rights overlap and create especially complex questions, the Court's ruling on individual challenges to the First Amendment often comes down to one vote. In addition, the Court can rule one way and years later reverse themselves when the same or similar issue comes before them again. It is not uncommon for the Court to consider the national consensus on a certain topic along with scientific developments to arrive at a final decision. We've seen this with issues including the juvenile death penalty (*Roper v. Simmons*, 2005), life without parole for crimes committed as a minor (*Miller v. Alabama*, 2012), and issues related to same-sex relationships (*Lawrence v. Texas*, 2003). It only takes one vote by the nine justices to create a major change in society.

Further Reading and Resources

Primary Case: *Boy Scouts of America v. James Dale*, 530 U.S. 640 (2000).

"Freedom of Expressive Association and Discrimination on the Basis of Sexual Orientation" by Grace Cretcher and Kellyn Goler, 12

Georgetown Journal of Gender and the Law 385 (2011).

The Gay-Straight Alliance Network
www.gsanetwork.org

The Gay-Straight Alliance Network works to empower and train youth activists in schools to fight homophobia and transphobia.

Judging the Boy Scouts of America: Gay Rights, Freedom of Association, and the Dale Case by Richard J. Ellis (Lawrence: University Press of Kansas, 2014).

"Scouts' (Dis)Honor: The Supreme Court Allows the Boy Scouts of America to Discriminate Against Homosexuals in *Boy Scouts of America v. Dale*" by Scott Kelly, 39 *Houston Law Review* 243 (2002).

The Trevor Project
www.thetrevorproject.org

This organization provides crisis intervention and suicide prevention services to lesbian, gay, bisexual, and transgender young people ages thirteen to twenty-four.

CASE 8

Texas v. Gregory Lee Johnson (1989)

Key Issue: Symbolic Speech
Can expressions of ideas without talking be subject to government restrictions or control?

In this criminal case the Supreme Court considered the issue of flag burning. Does an individual have the right to burn this symbol of democracy and unity? This case deals with the right to freedom of expression through nonverbal actions rather than the spoken word.

Facts of the Case

The 1984 Republican National Convention was held in Dallas, Texas. Party members gathered to formally nominate President Ronald Reagan for reelection. Twenty-eight-year-old Gregory Lee Johnson took part in a political demonstration protesting policies of the Reagan administration. Approximately 100 protesters gathered in front of the Dallas City Hall where Johnson unfurled an American flag, doused it with kerosene, and set it on fire. While the flag burned, the protesters chanted "America, the red, white, and blue, we spit on you." Although no one was physically injured or threatened with injury by the flag burning, several witnesses testified that they were offended by the act.

Johnson was charged with violating a state law that prohibited the desecration of a state or national flag. He was convicted by a jury, sentenced to one year in prison, and fined $2,000. Johnson appealed his case through the state and federal courts.

The Court's Ruling and Reasoning

In a 5–4 decision, the Supreme Court stated in this case that although "the First Amendment literally forbids the abridgement only of speech, we have long recognized that its protection does not end at the spoken or written word." In other words, symbolic speech that is intended to express an idea without words may fall within the scope of the First Amendment. Since Johnson's flag burning was expressive conduct, he could claim protection under the First Amendment.

IN OTHER WORDS

A principal "function of free speech under our system of government is to invite dispute. It may indeed best serve its high purpose when it induces a condition of unrest, creates dissatisfaction with conditions as they are, or even stirs people to anger."
—Justice William O. Douglas, *Terminiello v. City of Chicago* (1949)

The Supreme Court held that even if society at large finds an idea offensive, it does not justify restricting or punishing someone for expressing that idea. Similarly, when considering public safety, the government cannot assume that every time a provocative idea is expressed it will lead to a riot. Instead, authorities must look to the actual circumstances surrounding the expression.

One exception to this principle is the "fighting words" concept regarding free speech. Speech that agitates a listener and has a tendency to provoke retaliation may not be protected by the First Amendment. The "N" word, for example, or a display of the Confederate flag (see section entitled "IS THE DISPLAY OF THE CONFEDERATE FLAG AT SCHOOL PROHIBITED?") in certain environments may constitute fighting words.

The Court did not find Johnson's act of burning the flag to be a breach of the peace, or what's referred to in criminal cases as "disorderly conduct." A person can upset the peace of others by causing a disturbance without inciting a riot or criminal activity. The state's interest in preserving the flag as a symbol of national unity did not justify Johnson's conviction for political expression. The Court ruled in Johnson's favor. The judgment and sentence in his case were thrown out.

IN OTHER WORDS

> "[F]reedom to differ is not limited to things that do not matter much. That would be a mere shadow of freedom. The test of its substance is the right to differ as to things that touch the heart of the existing order."
> —Justice Robert H. Jackson, *West Virginia Board of Education v. Barnette* (1943)

The four justices who disagreed with the Court's majority opinion wrote that Johnson's act dishonored all those who had carried the flag into battle. They felt that the majority opinion disregarded 200 years of the flag's "unique position as the symbol of our Nation" and that Johnson had other ways to express his disagreement with the government's policies.

The Court Speaks

"If there is a bedrock principle underlying the First Amendment, it is that the government may not prohibit the expression of an idea simply because society finds the idea itself offensive and disagreeable."

Writing for the majority, Justice William Brennan stated that in a case twenty years earlier, it was determined that states could not punish someone for verbally criticizing the flag. Americans have the right to be intellectually diverse or even contrary. Opinions that seem defiant or disrespectful are protected expressions under the First Amendment. On the other hand, the government may not force people to respect the flag, and public schools may not require a student to stand or recite the Pledge of Allegiance or salute the flag.

Brennan wrote, "We do not consecrate the flag by punishing its desecration, for in doing so we dilute the freedom that this cherished emblem represents."

What If...?

If the Court had upheld Johnson's conviction for desecrating the flag, it would have opened the door to across-the-board restrictions on other forms of expression—especially expression that is political or controversial. Consider vehicle license plates displaying the Confederate flag, or message T-shirts worn during incidents of civil unrest such as "I can't breathe" in New York. Although some people disagree with these expressions, are these examples of speech so disruptive to the community as to merit censorship?

> ## IN OTHER WORDS
>
> "It is poignant but fundamental that the flag protects those who hold it in contempt."
>
> —Justice Anthony M. Kennedy, *Texas v. Johnson* (1989)

All speech is subject to the scrutiny of the First Amendment. That includes "pure speech" (the spoken word), as in the *Fraser* case, as well as symbolic speech, as in the *Johnson* case. Recent examples of symbolic speech include antigay signs at military funerals, T-shirts that are for or against gun control, and pro-life and prochoice messages regarding abortion.

> ## Did You Know?
>
> Teens in North Korea are prohibited from expressing themselves through their hairstyles. The government enforces a list of eighteen approved haircuts for girls and ten for boys.

Additional incidents of nonverbal acts that have met with government action include students wearing black armbands to school to make an antiwar statement, or participating in a sit-in to protest segregation or other social injustices. Courts have found these instances to be protected expression under the First Amendment.

By and large, the First Amendment protects offensive or disagreeable speech.

Related Cases

You may find some of the behavior in the following cases disturbing. It is important to remember that the founding fathers of the United States included the right of free speech to protect the minority. Even people who hold what seem to be the most outrageous opinions have a right to express their beliefs. As Justice Anthony M. Kennedy concurred in *Johnson,* "The hard fact is that sometimes we must make decisions we do not like. We make them because they are right, right in the sense that the law and the Constitution, as we see them, compel the result." That is because our democracy and judicial system recognize the value in expression and free speech for all. The related cases deal with symbols that may be considered racist, anti-American, or simply disrespectful.

IS THE DISPLAY OF THE CONFEDERATE FLAG AT SCHOOL PROHIBITED?

Barr v. Lafon (2008)

Derek Barr attended William Blount High School in Tennessee. During his time as a student there, graffiti on school buildings included a depiction of a Confederate flag and a noose. Interracial fights and hit lists of students' names written on walls were also a concern to school officials. Due in part to the atmosphere on campus, the dress code prohibited any clothing or apparel that would disrupt the school environment.

> ### Did You Know?
> In 2015, the Supreme Court voted 5–4 that states can refuse to add the Confederate flag to vehicle license plates. They ruled that, because the flag is a racially charged symbol of oppression, excluding it from appearing on state property does not violate free speech. (*Walker v. Sons of Confederate Veterans*, 2015)

Barr wore a shirt to school that depicted the Confederate flag, two dogs, and the words "Guarding our Southern Heritage." The principal told Barr his shirt violated the dress code and asked him to change it. Barr complied but, together with his parents, sued the school for violating his right to free speech. Because of a history of racial tension at the school, the federal court upheld the dress code in the interest of maintaining a safe environment for all students. In 2009, the Supreme Court declined without comment to review this case.

> ## IN OTHER WORDS
>
> **In a 2011 case challenging the sale and rental of violent video games to minors, Justice Samuel Alito commented, "Our cases hold that minors are entitled to a significant degree of First Amendment protection. Government has no free-floating power to restrict the ideas to which they may be exposed"** (*Brown v. Entertainment Merchants Association*). **The Court voted 7–2 against the ban.**

Some courts have viewed Confederate symbols as "fighting words," thereby justifying banning them on campus. The right to free speech is not absolute—there are exceptions to its protection.

IS DISPLAYING AN UPSIDE-DOWN AMERICAN FLAG PROTECTED SPEECH?

Spence v. Washington (1974)

Harold Spence was a college student in Seattle, Washington, when he attached a peace symbol to both sides of the American flag and hung it upside down from his apartment window. The three-by-five-foot flag was clearly visible to people on the street but it didn't cause any sort of disruption or fight. When the police saw it, Spence was arrested and charged with improper use of the flag. A jury found him guilty and he was sentenced to ten days in jail and a small fine.

Spence testified that he was protesting the U.S. invasion of Cambodia and the recent killings at Kent State University. "I wanted people to know that I thought America stood for peace," he said. The Supreme Court overturned the conviction, finding his speech protected as political expression under the First Amendment.

IS WEARING THE U.S. FLAG AS CLOTHING OR ACCESSORIES

CONSIDERED EXPRESSIVE CONDUCT?

Smith v. Goguen (1974)

The police in Massachusetts saw Valarie Goguen on a street corner talking with friends. They noticed he had an American flag on his back pocket. The four-by-six-inch flag was sewn on to his blue jeans. He was arrested for treating the flag "contemptuously." State law prohibited such conduct but failed to define what acts would be viewed as contemptuous. A jury found Goguen guilty and sentenced him to six months in jail. He served part of the sentence before being released pending his appeal.

The Supreme Court reversed the conviction holding that the law was "void for vagueness." This means that if a law is unclear or ambiguous, it is not valid. The law provided insufficient notice of what exactly constituted a violation. The Court wrote, "What is contemptuous to one man may be a work of art to another."

Talk, Think, and Take Action

• Do you think the *Johnson* decision went too far in protecting flag burning? If yes, where would you draw the line on freedom of expression? Does protecting this behavior confirm our nation's belief in freedom, inclusiveness, and tolerance of criticism? Imagine a world where the government restricted what message we could wear on buttons or T-shirts or what political slogans or stickers we could display. (Note: School dress codes are permitted for all messages on clothing if consistently enforced.) What do you think might be negative or positive about this scenario?

• Whether you're interested in politics at the local or national level, or other social causes such as climate change or the environment, there are many ways to participate. You don't have to wait until you're eighteen to get involved in the world around you. Consider attending rallies or joining a peaceful demonstration. You can also support a candidate or ballot proposition by volunteering to collect signatures or hand out literature or bumper stickers. Many national organizations have local chapters that you may find interesting.

• The Arizona Supreme Court has ruled that tattoos involve "constitutionally protected speech." That means if you live in Arizona, you have the right to tattoo potentially offensive or obscene messages on your body. Do you agree that this right should be protected by the First Amendment? Why or why not? In what ways could such tattoos create challenges in your life, either now or in the future? In what ways could they benefit your life?

• Members of the Westboro Baptist Church of Topeka, Kansas, believe that the death of U.S. troops is punishment for the nation's immorality, particularly its tolerance of homosexuality and abortion. Some of its church members travel the country protesting at military funerals. Their protests sometimes include trampling on the American flag and wearing and displaying it upside down. Do you think this type of activity is (or should be) protected speech? Why or why not? (To learn what the Supreme Court said about the Westboro's practices, read about the 2011 case *Snyder v. Phelps*.)

• Each year, on the Day of Silence, students in thousands of schools across the country vow to carry out a form of silence for the day to bring attention to the silencing effect that anti-LGBTQ bullying has on schools. This has caused controversy at some schools over students' rights to participate, and instead of not speaking, some students wear buttons, stickers, and T-shirts in support of the day. If you'd like to learn more about this event, your right to participate, and how to organize an event at your school, visit DayofSilence.org.

Closing Comments

You're not limited to talking or writing as a way to express yourself. Communication may be protected by the First Amendment regardless of its method.

> ### IN OTHER WORDS
>
> **"I've learned that life is a lot more interesting if you stand up for what you believe in and don't do what's considered popular."**
>
> —Mary Beth Tinker, student-plaintiff in the 1969 case about black armbands at school in protest of the Vietnam War

This chapter illustrates the strength of the First Amendment and the will of the Supreme Court to uphold its values even in cases involving unpopular ideas. At first glance, permitting the American flag to be burned or flown upside down may seem unpatriotic and it may be. But from a Constitutional perspective, the greater injustice would be limiting an individual's freedom of expression regardless of the message.

Further Reading and Resources

Primary Case: *Texas v. Johnson*, 491 U.S. 397 (1989).

Burning the Flag: The Great 1989–1990 American Flag Desecration Controversy by Robert Justin Goldstein (Kent: OH: Kent State University Press, 2013).

"Constitutionality of Restricting Public Speech in Street, Sidewalk, Park, or Other Public Forum" by William M. Howard, 70 *American Law Reports*, 6th 513 (2011).

Flag Burning and Free Speech: The Case of Texas v. Johnson by Robert Justin Goldstein (Lawrence, KS: University Press of Kansas, 2000).

CASE 9

Island Trees School District v. Steven Pico (1982)

Key Issue: Censorship at School
Can a public school ban books due to their language or content?

The Supreme Court tries to stay out of issues involving the U.S. public education system. They have left those decisions about what's best for children and teens to local governing boards and parents. However, they agreed to review this case because it involved a very specific question about censorship in public schools.

This 5–4 decision illustrates how different people, including Supreme Court justices, consider different aspects of an issue to be most important when they cast a vote. Some justices consider themselves as strict "constructionists" or "originalists" when it comes to interpreting the Constitution and the Bill of Rights. As they see it, if the Founding Fathers didn't include a certain right, such as privacy, in either document, then it's not the justices' job to create one in the twenty-first century. On the other extreme, some justices view the Constitution as a "living" document open to interpretation with societal changes. In this case, you'll see how these different views can affect the outcome of a case.

Facts of the Case

In 1976, the school board of the Island Trees School District in New York ordered that certain books be removed from the district's junior high and high school curriculum and that the same books be removed from school libraries in the district. They explained their action by describing the books as "anti-American, anti-Christian, anti-Semitic, and just plain filthy." The books had been included on a list published by a politically conservative parental organization. The board stated, "It is our duty, our moral obligation, to protect the children in our schools from this moral danger as surely as from physical and medical dangers."

> **IN OTHER WORDS**
>
> **"I burned to learn to read novels and I tortured my mother into telling me of every strange word I saw, not because the word itself had any value, but because it was the gateway to a forbidden and enchanting land."**
> —Richard Wright, *Black Boy*

The banned books included:
- *The Best Short Stories by Negro Writers* edited by Langston Hughes
- *Black Boy* by Richard Wright
- *Down These Mean Streets* by Piri Thomas
- *Go Ask Alice* by an anonymous author
- *A Hero Ain't Nuthin' But a Sandwich* by Alice Childress
- *Laughing Boy* by Oliver La Farge
- *The Naked Ape* by Desmond Morris
- *Slaughterhouse Five* by Kurt Vonnegut
- *Soul on Ice* by Eldridge Cleaver

The challenged books were not required reading for students, but were only in the library for optional reading and study. After the ban, these books were removed from the libraries and could not be assigned to students. However, teachers were not prohibited from discussing them or the ideas expressed in them. A group of students, including high school student Steven Pico and his mother, filed a lawsuit against the school district. They claimed that the board censored the books because they found that certain passages offended their political, social, and moral tastes, not because the books lacked educational value.

The Court's Ruling and Reasoning

In the opinion written by Justice William J. Brennan Jr., the Supreme Court acknowledged that a school's role is to educate young people for citizenship. It follows, then, that there is reason to carefully protect a student's constitutional freedoms. School boards must use their "important, delicate, and highly discretionary functions" within the limits and constraints of the First Amendment. This idea was articulated in the Court's 1968 decision of *Tinker* (see CASE 4).

In a 5–4 vote, the Court ruled in favor of Pico and his mother. It said that a public school may not remove books from school library shelves simply because administrators dislike the political ideas or social perspectives contained in the books. Doing so does not teach children to respect the diversity of ideas that is core to American values. "This Court has repeatedly stated that First Amendment concerns encompass the receipt of information and ideas as well as the right of free expression.... State operated schools may not be enclaves of totalitarianism," wrote Justice Harry Blackmun in a concurring opinion.

> ## IN OTHER WORDS
> **"A student's rights, therefore, do not embrace merely the classroom hours.... When he is in the cafeteria, or on the playing field, or on the campus during the authorized hours, he may express his opinions, even on controversial subjects."**
> —Justice Abe Fortas, *Tinker v. Des Moines Independent Community School District* (1969)

In this case, the Supreme Court recognized school libraries as unique places where students are "free to inquire, to study and to evaluate, to gain new maturity and understanding. Students learn that a library is a place to test or expand upon ideas presented to him or her, in or out of the classroom."

The four justices who dissented felt that the issue was not subject to federal court review. Otherwise, the Supreme Court would become a "super censor" of school board decisions. They believed that parents, teachers, and local school boards—not judges—should determine how standards of morality and vulgarity are handled in the school setting.

The dissenters wrote that the majority in this case created a new "right to receive ideas" and information not found in the Constitution or the Bill of Rights. In addition, they pointed out that, although excluded from the school library, the nine books were still available from public libraries or other sources.

IN OTHER WORDS

"The vigilant protection of constitutional freedoms is nowhere more vital than in the community of American schools."

—Justice Potter Stewart, *Shelton v. Tucker* (1960)

The Court Speaks

Quoting *Tinker*, the Court wrote in its majority opinion, "'In our system, students may not be regarded as closed-circuit recipients of only that which the State chooses to communicate.'"

Expressed in Justice Harry Blackmun's concurring opinion is the importance of public schools in preparing students for participation as informed citizens. Educators are charged with promoting civic virtues and cultural values. Schools may not be run in such a manner as to "prescribe what shall be orthodox in politics, nationalism, religion, or other matters of opinion."

What If...?

Had the Court agreed that the school board had a constitutional right to remove these books, your school library might be a lot smaller today. A single complaint by any parent or student about the appropriateness of a book might result in its removal. If they wanted to, you could probably find a word, phrase, or idea in *any* published book that someone would find offensive. So whose standards should apply in determining what reading material is acceptable and what is not? In some schools, certain books are available for parents to check out for their children, but students themselves are not allowed to check out the books. And some books may be banned as required class reading but still be available in the school library.

> ## IN OTHER WORDS
>
> **"Let us pick up our books and pens. They are the most powerful weapons."**
> —Malala Yousafzai, teen Association publishes a list of banned and activist for education and

Each year, the Office for Intellectual Freedom of the American Library challenged books in schools and public Nobel Peace Prize recipient libraries. Complaints from individuals and groups about the language, violence, and sexual content of a book may lead to its ban. You may be surprised at the books on the list each year, which have included *To Kill a Mockingbird*, *The Hunger Games*, and *Twilight*. You can see the list at www.ala.org.

Related Cases

Imagine living where the government controlled all media—where government propaganda was the only thing shown on television, or where the Internet was unavailable or restricted to government-approved websites. Are we speaking of centuries ago or past events? No. Just search for information on freedom of speech in such countries as China, North Korea, Saudi Arabia, or Iran. Censorship is rampant in these and other countries.

To a limited degree, censorship has also been practiced in American schools. The Supreme Court has addressed the issue and acknowledged the need for schools to exercise some control over student expression in newspapers, yearbooks, and artistic productions. On the other hand, a few states have passed laws giving students greater free speech rights than what was allowed under *Hazelwood*. These Student Free Expression laws protect journalism students and teachers or advisors from censorship as long as the material is not obscene, libelous, or encourages lawlessness or disruption at school.

(See *Lange v. Diercks*, 2011, for a discussion of censorship of student productions.)

> ### Did You Know?
>
> In 2014, a school board in Idaho banned Sherman Alexie's coming-of-age novel *The Absolutely True Diary of a Part-Time Indian* from its tenth-grade curriculum. The book tells the semi-autobiographical story of a fourteen-year-old Native American boy in an all-white school. Parents complained about profanity and references to masturbation.
>
> Seventeen-year-old Brady Kissel, a junior at Mountain View High School in Idaho, was one student who had opposed the ban. She had circulated a petition against the ban, and gathered 350 signatures in support. After the ban went through, she took another step and organized a giveaway of *The Absolutely True Diary of a Part-Time Indian* on World Book Night in 2014. Kissel worked with a local bookstore to raise funds to buy copies of the book, and also collected donated copies. When Alexie's publisher heard of Kissel's efforts, they also donated copies. On April 23, 2014, Kissel and several of the bookstore employees started handing out the books to teens in a local park. A parent complained about the giveaway without parental consent. The police arrived, spoke with Kissel, and determined that no laws were broken and the event continued. Alexie

> praised the students for their love of books and support for this event.

In the following cases, other types of communication at school are considered, along with speech that is sexually suggestive, and a teacher's right to challenge censorship regarding the curriculum.

CAN A SCHOOL CENSOR A STUDENT NEWSPAPER?

Hazelwood v. Kuhlmeier (1988)

In May 1983, Cathy Kuhlmeier was the layout editor of the *Spectrum,* the student newspaper at Hazelwood High School in Missouri. She and two classmates worked on the final issue of the year, which included articles about the impact of divorce on students and one about teen pregnancy. Both of these articles quoted and either named other students or gave enough details that the students could be identified. Before the paper was printed, the principal pulled the articles as inappropriate, highly personal, and too sensitive for younger high school students.

The three students, with their parents' help, challenged the principal's authority to censor the paper. They sued the school district claiming a violation of their First Amendment right to freedom of expression. The Supreme Court ruled against the student journalists, stating that schools are allowed to control the newspaper's content within reason, along with certain other forms of student expression on campus or at a school event.

> ### IN OTHER WORDS
>
> *"Hazelwood has bleached far too many schools of any discussion of issues that might be sensitive or controversial. It's impossible to have truly effective, participatory civics education so long as Hazelwood remains on the books."*
>
> —Frank LoMonte, director, Student Press Law Center (April 2014)

The Court said that schools must be able to set high standards for student speech made under their supervision. As Justice Byron White wrote for the majority, "Educators do not offend the First Amendment by exercising editorial control over the style and content of student speech in school-sponsored expressive activities so long as their actions are reasonably related to [valid educational] concerns."

CAN A SCHOOL DISCIPLINE STUDENTS FOR SPEECH MADE IN AN UNDERGROUND NEWSPAPER?

Boucher v. School Board of Greenfield (1998)

Justin Boucher was a seventeen-year-old junior when he wrote *The Last,* an underground newspaper written and printed off-campus but distributed at his high school in Greenfield, Wisconsin. In a June 1997 issue, he provided a blueprint for hacking into the school district's computer system. The newspaper was banned from the school and Boucher was expelled for endangering school property. Boucher challenged the school's action, but the federal court upheld the expulsion. Based on the reasonable forecast rule, which judges the likelihood of disruption based on recent events, substantial disruption of a school activity was possible.

CAN A SCHOOL REMOVE SEXUAL CONTENT FROM A STUDENT NEWSPAPER?

R.O. v. Ithaca City School District (2011)

The Tattler was the student newspaper at Ithaca High School in New York. Approximately

3,000 copies were printed each month and distributed on campus and in the local community. In 2005, the faculty advisor reviewed an upcoming issue that included an article written by a graduate of the school that was titled "Alumni Advice: Sex is fun." Attached to the article was a cartoon with eight drawings of stick figures in various sexual positions. Both were removed from the paper before it went to press. A later issue included a revised article but excluded the cartoon.

Robert Ochshorn (R.O.) and his parents sued the school district, challenging censorship of the cartoon. The federal court agreed with the school's decision to prohibit publication of the cartoon, in line with *Hazelwood* and other decisions addressing student expression. The Court decided that censorship was appropriate due to the sexual content of the cartoon, its intended audience (which included some young students), and potential disruption of the educational environment.

WHAT HAPPENS WHEN TEACHERS CHALLENGE CENSORSHIP LAWS AFFECTING SCHOOL CURRICULUM?

Censorship has also been the subject of lawsuits by teachers regarding specific subjects and methods of teaching. Although these cases were decided decades ago, they continue to impact education in the United States.

In one case, *Epperson v. Arkansas* (1968), a tenth-grade biology teacher in Arkansas challenged a law that banned the teaching of human evolution (Darwin's theory) in public schools. A lower court ruled against the law because it "tends to hinder the quest for knowledge, restricts the freedom to learn, and restrains the freedom to teach." In 1968, the Supreme Court agreed and struck down the law as vague and a violation of the First Amendment.

In another case, *Meyer v. Nebraska* (1923), a 1919 Nebraska law prohibited teaching any foreign language in public schools until a student started high school. English was the only language allowed to be spoken. Violation could result in a fine or a jail sentence. Robert T. Meyer taught a reading class in German at an elementary school in Nebraska. He was charged with breaking the law, found guilty, and sentenced to pay a $25 fine. Meyer appealed his conviction and in 1923, the Supreme Court ruled in his favor. It found that teaching a foreign language is "not injurious to the health, morals, or understanding of the ordinary child." They went on to say that "The American people have always regarded education and acquisition of knowledge as matters of supreme importance. Imparting knowledge in a foreign language is not inherently immoral or inimical to the public welfare."

Talk, Think, and Take Action

• The books at the heart of *Pico* were removed because the school board determined they were "irrelevant, vulgar, immoral, and in bad taste." Have you read any of the books that were banned in this case? If so, did you learn anything from them? Were you shocked or entertained? Do you agree that these books should be banned from your school library? Why or why not?

• In *Tinker*, the Supreme Court stated that classrooms are a "marketplace of ideas" and depend on a robust exchange of thoughts and viewpoints. What do you think about this? Do you believe that *all* ideas should be fair game for students to weigh and discuss in school? Why or why not?

• What amount of say do you have in matters of speech and censorship at your school? If you were a class officer, how could you contribute to the school's discussion about censorship? Does your school board include a student representative? If not, how could you go about expressing your views to the leadership of your school or to your school or public library? In order to challenge an incident of censorship at your school, you could start a petition and collect classmates' signatures, create a Facebook page, or use other social media to spread awareness about the issue and to gain support.

- If you're interested in censorship issues in the school system, consider participating in Banned Books Week, sponsored by the American Library Association. Banned Books Week events take place across the country every September. Find out more by visiting BannedBooksWeek.org. Also, think about volunteering at your school or local public library to gain an insider's view of how books become banned in the library.

- Student actors at a high school in Connecticut fought for the right to put on the show *Rent* after the principal pulled the plug on it because it dealt with "challenging issues." After students circulated a petition, held public meetings, and started a Facebook page to track media coverage of the story, the principal relented and the show was allowed to go on. If you are passionate about a book, play, musical piece, or another artistic expression that has been censored at your school, mobilizing support for your cause and gaining media attention may be helpful tools.

Closing Comments

The First Amendment contains just forty-five words, but it affects your daily life in many ways.

Questions of censorship are an important aspect of applying the First Amendment. Censorship is a four-letter word to many people in the United States. Throughout history great works of fiction and nonfiction have included profanity, sexual content, and rebellious ideas, but are those reason enough to ban those materials? For instance, do you think *Tom Sawyer* or *Huckleberry Finn*, written in the language of their time, should be off limits to students because they include the "N" word? Do you think the surge in reading fantasy novels (sparked in part by the Harry Potter and the Twilight series) has negatively influenced teens or given them dangerous ideas? Are all ideas equally valuable, or do you think some are more harmful than helpful? These are just some of the issues related to the cases in this section.

IN OTHER WORDS

"The Nation's future depends upon leaders trained through wide exposure to that robust exchange of ideas which discovers truth out of a multitude of tongues."

—Justice Lewis F. Powell, *Regents of the University of California v. Bakke* (1978)

Further Reading and Resources

Primary Case: *Island Trees School District v. Pico,* 457 U.S. 853 (1982).

The American Library Association
www.ala.org
The American Library Association works to improve library and information services. The ALA's Office for Intellectual Freedom promotes the free expression of ideas and the right to read all viewpoints, even those that may be considered unorthodox. It compiles and circulates a list of banned and challenged books each year in an effort to promote freedom of speech and choice.

Book Banning in 21st-Century America by Emily J.M. Knox (Lanham, MD: Rowan and Littlefield Publishers, 2015).

"[Censored]: Book Banning in the U.S. Education System" by Michael Brenyo, 40 *Journal of Law and Education* 541 (July 2011).

The First Amendment Center
www.firstamendmentcenter.org
The First Amendment Center provides a forum for the study and exploration of First Amendment issues, including freedom of expression and freedom of speech. Its website provides information, news, and commentary on First Amendment issues.

The Student Press Law Center

www.splc.org
The Student Press Law Center advocates for First Amendment rights and also provides information, training, and legal assistance to student journalists and educators.

CASE 10

Plyler v. Doe (1982)

Key Issue: Public Education for All
What does the Equal Protection Clause of the Fourteenth Amendment guarantee? Does it apply to children who are in the United States illegally?

The United States has been called the land of freedom and opportunity. Jobs, education, and freedom of religion are listed among the many reasons that people want to immigrate here. Also, in a democracy such as the United States, a person's background or class is not supposed to matter—we all are said to possess the same rights to pursue our dreams. The Equal Protection Clause of the Fourteenth Amendment is intended to ensure that laws are applied equally to all; this includes laws that restrict what we do as well as laws that offer us opportunities. The clause helps protect our civil rights.

The question put to the justices of the Supreme Court in this case was whether this protection applies to illegal immigrants, particularly children who are not citizens of the United States. The Court needed to decide whether living in a state was enough to warrant receiving a free basic education. Could a state rightly exclude undocumented children because it had limited resources and wanted to use them for lawful residents? Or would doing so amount to discrimination and therefore violate the Fourteenth Amendment? The nine justices of the Court were faced with a decision that would affect not only the amount of money states had to spend on educating students but the day-to-day lives of millions of children and their futures.

Did You Know?

> The Equal Protection Clause of the Fourteenth Amendment to the U.S. Constitution states in part:
> "...nor shall any State deprive any person of life, liberty, or property, without due process of law; nor deny to any person within its jurisdiction the equal protection of the laws."

Facts of the Case

The Texas legislature passed a law in 1975 that provided free public education for all children between the ages of five and twenty-one who were either citizens of the United States or legally admitted immigrants. With this law, the state withheld money to school districts for educating students who were in the country illegally, and it authorized schools to deny a whole group of children the right to attend school.

As a result of this law, some schools began refusing to enroll students who could not verify their legal status or citizenship. The school district in Tyler, Texas, required undocumented children to pay a full tuition fee in order to enroll, $1,000 per school year. A lawsuit was brought on behalf of all undocumented Latino children in the school district who were denied free access to public school. At the heart of the challenge was the purpose and meaning of the Equal Protection clause.

The Court's Ruling and Reasoning

More than 100 years ago, in *Wong Wing v. U.S.* (1896), the Supreme Court wrote, "A resident, alien born, is entitled to the same protection under the laws that a citizen is entitled to. He owes obedience to the laws of the country in which he is domiciled, and, as a consequence, he is entitled to the equal protection of those laws."

The *Plyler* Court, in an opinion written by Justice William Brennan, ruled against the school district. It said that anyone who lives within a state's jurisdiction "is subject to the full range of obligations imposed by the State's civil or criminal laws. And until he leaves the jurisdiction, either voluntarily or involuntarily in accordance with the Constitution and laws of the United States, he is entitled to the equal protection of the laws that a State may choose to establish." *Plyler* held that the Equal Protection Clause directs that all persons in a similar situation shall be treated alike (for example, two school-age children, one of whom is a citizen and one of whom is an undocumented immigrant). *All* school-age children are eligible for the same educational opportunities.

If a state provides the opportunity of an education for its residents, that opportunity is a right that must be made available to everyone on equal terms. The Court rejected the argument that undocumented immigrants, because of their immigration status, are not persons within the jurisdiction of the State of Texas and therefore had no right to equal protection of Texas law. The Court stated that an illegal immigrant is a "person" under the Fourteenth Amendment and, as such, the principles of due process and equal protection "extend to anyone, citizen or stranger, who is within its jurisdiction" and subject to the laws of the state.

IN OTHER WORDS

"**Illiteracy is an enduring disability. The inability to read and write will handicap the individual deprived of a basic education each and every day of his life.**"

—Justice William Brennan, *Plyler v. Doe* (1982)

The Court recognized the existence of a "shadow population" made up of illegal residents. Some of these residents remain in the United States as a source of cheap labor "whose presence is tolerated. Defenseless against any abuse, exploitation or callous neglect, the existence of such an underclass presents most difficult problems for a Nation that prides itself on adherence to principles of equality under law." The majority opinion said that "charging tuition to undocumented children constitutes a ludicrously ineffectual attempt to stem the tide of illegal immigration." Furthermore, the Court rejected the argument that educating undocumented children was an unbearable financial burden to the state.

The majority decided that a state may withhold public benefits such as food stamps and public housing to adults who are illegal immigrants. But, the Court ruled, punishing children for their parents' misconduct goes against basic concepts of justice. "Obviously, no child is responsible for his birth and penalizing the child is an ineffectual as well as unjust way of deterring the parent."

IN OTHER WORDS

"The children involved in this litigation should not be left on the streets uneducated."

—Justice Harry Blackmun, concurring opinion, *Plyler v. Doe* (1982)

The four dissenting justices argued that the Court did not have the authority to make policy or even become involved with the matters that other branches of government were responsible for. They said it was the job of Congress to enforce immigration laws, not the Court's job to solve problems that should be handled by the states and Congress.

The Court Speaks

"Each person is to be judged individually and is entitled to equal justice under the law."

This statement is from Chief Justice Warren Burger, who was one of the four dissenters in this case. Burger prefaced his comment by stating that denying a free education to illegal alien children is not a choice he would make as a legislator. However, he noted that policy arguments against the Texas law do not necessarily make the law unconstitutional. Burger argued that, except in cases of clear constitutional violations, state legislatures are an independent branch of government with the power to create laws for their citizens.

IN OTHER WORDS

"Visiting condemnation on the head of an infant for the misdeeds of the parents is illogical, unjust, and contrary to the basic concept of our system that legal burdens should bear some relationship to individual responsibility or wrongdoing."

> —Justice William Powell, concurring opinion, *Plyler,* citing a 1972 case: *Weber v. Aetna Casualty & Surety Co.*

What If...?

If the Court in the *Plyler* case had determined that the Texas law was constitutional, it could have resulted in a growing number of illiterate adults. In *Brown v. Board of Education* (1954), the Supreme Court wrote, "Education is the very foundation of good citizenship.... It is perhaps the most important function of state and local governments." Expanding on that belief, the *Plyler* decision said that "By denying these children a basic education, we deny them the ability to live within the structure of our civic institutions, and foreclose any realistic possibility that they will contribute in even the smallest way to the progress of our Nation."

Did You Know?

- At the time of the *Plyler* decision in 1982, the number of undocumented residents

> in the United States was estimated at three to six million. Today, the number is approximately eleven million.
>
> • In 2015, Arizona became the first state to require students to pass a civics test in order to graduate. The administration of the American Civics Test begins in the 2016–2017 school year.

In contrast, millions of children who received a public education due to the Court's decision are now taxpayers. Whether or not they have become citizens, they can be contributing members of their communities and no longer have to live in the shadows, where they may be subject to the abuse, exploitation, and neglect which the Court spoke about in *Plyler*.

Related Cases

Did you know that education is not a fundamental right granted by the U.S. Constitution? Nor is education mentioned in the Bill of Rights. However, because Americans consider education to be so important, both the courts and society in general have come to assume that education is a protected right. And since the Fourteenth Amendment calls for equal protection of all people who live within a state's jurisdiction, state laws must not discriminate among its residents. This means that if a state law, like the one in Texas, provides public education for its children, it cannot discriminate against on school funding and the source of such funding, as well as the impact that property taxes have on the quality of education in different school districts.

> ### IN OTHER WORDS
> "Upon the subject of education, I can only say that I view it as the most important subject which we as a people may be engaged in."
> —President Abraham Lincoln

DOES FUNDING SCHOOL DISTRICTS THROUGH PROPERTY TAXES VIOLATE EQUAL PROTECTION?

San Antonio School District v. Rodriguez (1973)

State and federal courts have studied our education system in a number of cases through the lens of discrimination. For example, the practice of funding public schools through local property taxes was challenged in Texas (in a separate case from *Plyler*). A school district with a high percentage of families living in poverty sued the state for discrimination on the basis of wealth. In other words, school districts in areas with a lower tax base—because they have less expensive homes and/or fewer industries or businesses to pay taxes—received less money for their schools than districts with a higher tax base. The Supreme Court ruled 5–4 against the school district, holding that there was no evidence that the system failed to provide an adequate education for all children.

IS THERE A RIGHT TO A CERTAIN QUALITY OF EDUCATION?

Bonner v. Daniels (2009)

A similar challenge as in *San Antonio School District v. Rodriguez* was made three decades later in Indiana. A group of nine public school students and their parents sued the governor and state education officials claiming that the state's school finance system denied them a quality education, as guaranteed under the Indiana constitution. The state supreme court looked to the exact language of the state's constitution. It said nothing about the quality of education or achievement, only that the state legislature was required to provide a system of schools equally open to all and without charge. What constitutes the best school system is up to the legislature, not the judicial system. The lawsuit was dismissed.

Talk, Think, and Take Action

- DREAMers are a growing group of people who were brought to the United States as undocumented immigrants when they were babies or young children, and who want to remain in the United States. The name DREAMers comes from the Development, Relief, and Education for Alien Minors (DREAM) Act, which is pending in Congress. DREAMers would like to continue their education and path to citizenship. In 2012, President Obama granted temporary relief to these young immigrants, lessening the threat of deportation. Certain immigrant students can apply for "deferred action" that grants them legal status in the United States for a period of two years.

In the meantime, Congress continues to debate the issue and is trying to resolve this aspect of the immigration dilemma. It is estimated that approximately 1.4 million DREAMers are in the country. Do you support or oppose the DREAMers' pursuit of citizenship? If you have a friend, family member, or classmate who is a DREAMer, how does their status affect your thoughts on this subject? Consider writing to your representatives in Congress or joining a grassroots organization to communicate your views.

• Another immigration issue involves men and women, age eighteen and older, who serve in the military. Some noncitizens who have completed a tour in Iraq or Afghanistan come home and end up being deported for even minor incidents with the law. This is true even though U.S. military veterans are guaranteed medical care and education benefits. How do you think the government should respond in these instances? Do you think they should deport vets? Why or why not?

• What do you think about minors who are locked up in detention or are serving time with the Department of Juvenile Corrections? Do you believe that the right to an education should continue to apply to them? Currently, the required daily hours in school and the quality of education varies from state to state.

• The right to public education extends to all, including students with disabilities, LGBTQ students, HIV-positive students, and those who become pregnant. A student cannot be kicked out of school for any of these reasons. Additionally, federal law guarantees students with disabilities an education that is appropriate for them. If you are interested in the right to equal education for all and want your voice to be heard, consider attending school meetings, joining student government, and talking with your friends and other students about these issues.

• The Sparkle Effect is a national organization that brings together students with and without disabilities to participate on cheerleading and dance squads. It's a great way to make cheer and dance equally available and inclusive for all students. The president of the organization explains that the teams "are not about perfection, they are about connection." If you are involved with your school's cheer or dance program, consider starting a Sparkle Effect team at your school. For more information, visit www.thesparkleeffect.org.

Closing Comments

The *Plyler* Court held that "Education has a fundamental role in maintaining the fabric of our society." The Court also distinguished education from other government benefits based on its importance in America, regardless of students' immigration status. U.S. citizens have access to social programs such as food stamps, aid to the blind and disabled, Medicare, Medicaid, and social security income. These programs are not available to undocumented residents. However, a free public education is considered a right available to everyone under the Equal Protection Clause of the Fourteenth Amendment that prohibits discrimination by states in all matters among its citizens, including education. America's future depends on a well-informed, educated population.

Further Reading and Resources

Primary Case: *Plyler v. Doe*, 457 U.S. 202 (1982).

"From the Border to the Schoolhouse Gate: Alternative Arguments for Extending Primary Education to Undocumented Alien Children" by Maria Pabon Lopez and Diomedes J. Tsitouras, 36 *Hofstra Law Review* 1243 (Summer 2008).

No Undocumented Child Left Behind: Plyler v. Doe *and the Education of Undocumented Schoolchildren* by Michael A. Olivas (New York: New York University Press, 2012).

"Protecting *Plyler:* New Challenges to the Right of Immigrant Children to Access a Public School Education" by Udi Ofer, 1 *Columbia Journal of Race and Law* 187 (2012).

"Searching for Equality: Equal Protection Clause Challenges to Bans on the Admission of Undocumented Immigrant Students to Public Universities" by Danielle Holley-Walker, *2011 Michigan State Law Review* 357 (2011).

CASE 11
Regents of the University of California v. Allan Bakke (1978)

Key Issue: Affirmative Action
Does it violate your equal protection rights if a college creates an admissions quota system that is based on race?

Are you accepted into college based solely on your achievements and educational merits, or do other factors matter? If you are a minority or a female student, should that help or hinder your chances of getting into a school or program, or make no difference at all?

Some schools and employers have an affirmative action policy—a plan designed to overcome past wrongs and discrimination by breaking down barriers and providing equal opportunity. In a message to Congress in 1963, President Kennedy proposed legislation that became the Civil Rights Act of 1964. He said, "Simple justice requires that public funds, to which all taxpayers of all races contribute, not be spent in any fashion which encourages, subsidizes or results in racial discrimination." He instructed federal contractors to take "affirmative action" to hire minorities.

The Civil Rights Act of 1964 states, "No person in the United States shall, on the ground of race, color, or national origin be excluded from participation in, be denied the benefits of, or be subjected to discrimination under any program or activity receiving Federal financial assistance." In the *Bakke* case, Justice John Paul Stevens said that when Congress passed that law, it was focused on the "glaring ... discrimination against Negroes which exists throughout our Nation." One of the law's original goals was to prevent federal funding of segregated facilities. At the same time, the law prohibits discrimination against *any* person, regardless of race. Bakke's case was referred to as "reverse discrimination" since he claimed that, as a white applicant, he was discriminated against in the admission's process.

Is it right to give one group an advantage if it will help level the playing field for all? Or does creating an artificial advantage for some people discriminate against others? The issue before the Supreme Court in the *Bakke* case concerned the use of race as a factor in achieving diverse student bodies at public universities or colleges.

Facts of the Case

Allan Bakke was a white resident of California when he applied for admission to the medical school at the University of California at Davis in 1973. He applied again in 1974. The school admitted 100 students each year, using two admission tracks—one general admissions program for white students and a special admissions program for students of certain ethnic groups. Sixteen of the 100 spots in the medical school were reserved for students who were African American, Mexican American, American Indian, or Asian American.

IN OTHER WORDS

"The assertion of human equality is closely associated with the proposition

> that differences in color or creed, birth or status, are neither significant nor relevant to the way in which persons should be treated."
> —Justice William Powell, *Regents of the University of California v. Allan Bakke* (1978)

Bakke had earned a high grade point average in college and scored well on the medical college admission test. He was interviewed twice for admission and found to be "a very desirable applicant to the medical school." However, he was denied each year, even though he was more qualified (according to his GPA and test scores) than the minority students who were admitted through the special admissions program during those two years.

Bakke filed a lawsuit in federal court claiming discrimination based on race. He argued that the university's special admissions program violated the Civil Rights Act of 1964 and the Equal Protection Clause of the Fourteenth Amendment. The question in *Bakke* was whether an educational institution that received federal funds could engage in racial discrimination in its admission policies in an effort to increase minority enrollment. The University responded that its affirmative action program was intended to help integrate the medical profession and increase the number of doctors willing to serve minority patients.

The Court's Ruling and Reasoning

The Court found that minority applicants to the special admissions program were evaluated only against each other and not with applicants to the general program. Additionally, those applying through the general admissions process needed a college GPA of 2.5 or better to be considered for admission but those applying through the special admissions program had no minimum GPA to meet. White applicants could not compete for the sixteen places reserved for the special admissions slots. The Court was reviewing the constitutionality of what amounted to a quota system.

IN OTHER WORDS

"It is not merely the history of slavery alone but also that a whole people were marked as inferior by the law. And that mark has endured. The dream of America as the great melting pot has not been realized for the Negro: because of his skin color he never even made it into the pot."

> —Justice Thurgood Marshall commenting on the *Bakke* case

The Court concluded that the goal of achieving a diverse student body justifies considering a student's race in admission decisions under some circumstances. However, the Court ruled that the university's special admissions program, which focused *solely* on ethnic diversity, was unconstitutional—that is, quota systems are not allowed. The Court stated that race may be a consideration *along* with other factors in evaluating an applicant, such as a personal interview, recommendations, the applicant's goals, and the needs of the profession and of society at large. An applicant's work or service experience, leadership potential, maturity, and demonstrated compassion could also be factored in.

The Court also noted that the university's program told applicants who were not black, Asian, Latino, or American Indian that they were excluded from sixteen places in an entering class. In the majority opinion, Powell wrote, "No matter how strong their qualifications, quantitative and extracurricular, including their own potential for contribution to educational diversity, they are never afforded the chance to compete with applicants from the preferred groups for the special admissions seats."

> ## IN OTHER WORDS
>
> **"Discrimination on the basis of race is illegal, immoral, unconstitutional, inherently wrong, and destructive of democratic society."**
> —Alexander M. Bickel, *The Morality of Consent*

The protections of the Fourteenth Amendment extend to all persons: "No state shall ... deny to any person within its jurisdiction the equal protection of the laws." These are personal rights guaranteed to each individual. *Bakke* concluded with the idea that "'The nation's future depends upon leaders trained through wide exposure' to the ideas and mores of students as diverse as this Nation of many peoples."

Five of the justices agreed that any racial quota system supported by the government violated the Civil Rights Act of 1964 and the Equal Protection Clause. Bakke had been discriminated against and, consequently, the university was ordered to admit him. The four dissenting justices thought that considering a person's race when making college admission decisions was constitutionally permissible and that the university's policy was an acceptable way to achieve diversity.

The Court Speaks

"The guarantee of equal protection cannot mean one thing when applied to one individual and something else when applied to a person of another color."

In writing for the majority, Justice Lewis Powell Jr. asserted that the guarantees of the Fourteenth Amendment are personal rights that extend to all people. Legal restrictions in a school's admissions policy are immediately suspect. That is not to say that all such restrictions are unconstitutional, but they must be carefully scrutinized. In this case, the quota system used to achieve diversity was unacceptable.

> ## IN OTHER WORDS
>
> "Distinctions between citizens solely because of their ancestry are, by their very nature, odious to a free people whose institutions are founded upon the doctrine of equality."
> —Chief Justice Harlan Stone, *Hirabayashi v. U.S.* (1943)

What If...?

If one more vote had been against Bakke, a quota system would be considered an acceptable way to obtain diversity in a study body and would have likely altered many college admissions policies. If quotas were allowed and a university had a goal of reaching a 50 percent student population composed of ethnic minorities, it could reach their goal quicker. At the same time, these schools might be denying more qualified applicants in some instances.

Related Cases

Affirmative action is a program that has been in practice for more than fifty years. Since the *Bakke* decision in 1978, hundreds of affirmative action cases have been filed in federal courts. In this section, you'll read about a few that reached the Supreme Court. Critics of the policy argue that affirmative action is no longer needed, while supporters urge the courts to maintain the policy, or at least allow states to decide individually whether to ban it or not. Also presented is a recent case involving discrimination in the workplace, which some argue is a valid reason to keep affirmative action policies.

CAN RACE BE CONSIDERED AS A FACTOR FOR LAW SCHOOL ADMISSION?

Grutter v. Bollinger (2003)

In 1997, Barbara Grutter applied to the University of Michigan Law School. Barbara was a white student with a 3.8 college GPA and a high law school admission test score. After being denied admission and learning that the school considers race in its review of applicants, she sued the university for violating her equal protection rights under the Fourteenth Amendment. (Lee Bollinger was the president of the University of Michigan at that time, which is why the case name is *Grutter v. Bollinger.*)

IN OTHER WORDS

"Effective participation by members of all racial and ethnic groups in the civil life of our Nation is essential if the

> **dream of one Nation, indivisible, is to be realized."**
> —Justice Sandra Day O'Connor, *Grutter v. Bollinger* (2003)

In a 5–4 vote, the Court ruled in favor of the school. Justice Sandra Day O'Connor wrote for the majority that the university did not harm nonminority students with its race-conscious admissions program. Its limited use of race helped the school achieve its valid goal of having a diverse student body. With similar reasoning as in the *Bakke* case, Justice O'Connor wrote that race was *a* factor only, not *the* determining one. Again, racial *quotas* cannot be used, but race, as one of many factors, can be taken into account.

CAN COLLEGES USE AFFIRMATIVE ACTION PLANS AS A LAST RESORT TO DIVERSIFY STUDENT POPULATION?

Fisher v. University of Texas (2013)

Abigail Fisher was a white high school senior who applied to the University of Texas at Austin in 2008. She was not in the top 10 percent of her high school graduating class. Otherwise she would have been automatically admitted due to the state's Top Ten race-neutral law. She had to compete with all other applicants not in the top 10 percent, and she was denied admission. The university explained that it considered race in admission to help build a diverse student body.

In deciding the case in 2013, the Supreme Court did not throw out affirmative action but ruled that using racial preferences was allowed as a last resort in creating a diverse student population. Diversity in all its forms, according to the Court, is an important goal in higher education and an essential part of a complete education. The challenge becomes how to achieve that diversity. The Court agreed that affirmative action plans are allowed if the school can prove that "no workable race-neutral alternatives would produce the benefits of educational diversity."

In this instance, the Court ordered the university to reconsider its admission process. It ruled that the method of selecting students must be narrowly tailored to "ensure that each applicant is evaluated as an individual and not in a way that makes an applicant's race or ethnicity the defining feature of his or her application." (Justices Antonin Scalia and Clarence Thomas also inferred that they would prefer to banish affirmative action altogether.) In 2014, a lower federal court approved the university's admissions policy, and in June 2015, the Supreme Court agreed to hear the case again in its 2015–2016 term.

CAN STATE LAWS BAN AFFIRMATIVE ACTION?

Schuette v. Coalition to Defend Affirmative Action (2014)

Some states have passed laws that ban any use of racial preferences in admissions to public universities. Voters in Michigan approved such a ban in 2006 and groups that supported affirmative action sued. In 2014, the Supreme Court ruled in *Schuette* that states have the right to ban racial preferences in university admissions.

CAN A COMPANY REFUSE TO HIRE AN APPLICANT BECAUSE SHE WEARS A HEADSCARF?

Equal Employment Opportunity Commission (EEOC) v. Abercrombie & Fitch (2015)

Although this is not a school case, it does involve discrimination based on the religious beliefs of a minor. Samantha Elauf was seventeen years old when she applied for a job at the clothing store Abercrombie & Fitch. The company had a no-headwear policy that they claimed Elauf didn't meet. She is a practicing Muslim and wore a black hijab during her interview. She did not mention that her religious beliefs required her to wear a headscarf. When Elauf was not hired, she claimed that the store had discriminated against her based on her religion. The Court ruled 8–1 in Samantha's favor. They said that employers cannot consider a person's religion or religious practices when deciding whether or not to hire them.

Talk, Think, and Take Action

- If you plan to go to college, have you started the application process yet? If you're a junior or senior in high school, you may be thinking about schools you want to attend. Do you know which, if any, have affirmative action policies regarding admissions? Regardless of your ethnicity, an affirmative action admissions policy could affect your chances of being accepted to certain schools. As of 2014, eight states have banned the use of affirmative action in college admissions. If this is an issue you're concerned about when you apply to a college, check the school's website or contact the admissions office for information.
- What are your thoughts on the idea behind affirmative action—to help bridge the gap in diversity where historically there has been a lack of equal opportunity? Do you think this policy has a place in some parts of society? If so, do you think it should be used on a temporary or permanent basis?

- In addition to creating diversity in school, affirmative action has been used for the workplace and for government contracts. What are your thoughts on this practice? If you think it's appropriate, what are some geographic areas or some industries where equal opportunities may be lacking? Talk to friends and classmates to see if you agree on this issue. Also consider talking to some adults you know about this issue to learn about their perspectives.
- What do you think about minimum wage laws? Minimum wage was originally created out of the Fair Labor Standards Act in 1938, designed to protect employees against exploitation (especially women, children, and other vulnerable groups) and to help guarantee workers a living wage. The federal minimum wage is currently $7.25 per hour. However, many states and cities have passed laws raising the minimum wage in that state or city. In 2015, for example, the mayor of Los Angeles, California, signed into law a measure to increase the minimum wage over the course of several years until it reaches $15 per hour. What is the minimum wage in your state? Your city? Do you or any of your friends have a part-time job? Could you imagine living off of your earnings, even if you were working full time? What if you had children? If you feel strongly about this issue, consider writing to

your mayor or state representatives and expressing your views.

Did You Know?

"Why is it taken for granted that women must earn less than men? No! They have the same rights. The discrepancy is pure scandal."—Pope Francis, April 2015

In the United States, women earn 78 cents for every dollar a man makes in a similar job. This gap has narrowed significantly since 1960, when women earned 61 cents on the dollar compared to men, but it still is far from equal pay. What can you do to help close the gap? Contact your representatives in Congress with your views. You can also visit the U.S. Department of Labor's website at www.dol.gov/equalpay to express yourself on the subject. In addition, if you go on to attend college, you can look into the American Association of University Women. This group advocates for equal pay and gender equality in the workplace. For more, see www.aauw.org.

Closing Comments

In the *Grutter* case, Justice Sandra Day O'Connor wrote, "We expect that 25 years from now, the use of racial preferences will no longer be necessary to further the interest approved today." Ten years later, in the 2013 *Fisher* case, the nation seemed to be closer to realizing her expectation. Yet more progress was still needed.

Bakke spoke of America's professed goal of a society that is not race conscious. Until then, race-conscious admission programs remain constitutional. Justice Harry A. Blackmun wrote in *Bakke*, "I yield to no one in my earnest hope that the time will come when an 'affirmative action' program is unnecessary and is, in truth, only a relic of the past.... At some time the United States must and will reach a stage of maturity where persons will be regarded as persons, and discrimination of the type we address today will be an ugly feature of history that is instructive but that is behind us."

Further Reading and Resources

Primary Case: *Regents of the University of California v. Bakke*, 438 U.S. 265 (1978).

For Discrimination: Race, Affirmative Action and the Law by Randall Kennedy (New York: Pantheon, 2013).

"*Grutter* and *Fisher*: A Reassessment and a Preview" by James F. Blumstein, 65 *Vanderbilt Law Review En Banc* 57 (July 23, 2012).

The Morality of Consent by Alexander M. Bickel (New Haven, CT: Yale University Press, 1977).

"Percent Plans: A 'Workable, Race-Neutral Alternative' to Affirmative Action?" by Marvin Lim, 39 *Journal of College and University Law* 127 (2013).

"Requiem for Affirmative Action in Higher Education: Case Analysis Leading to a *Fisher v. University of Texas at Austin*" by Philip T.K. Daniel and Scott Greytak, 279 *Education Law Reporter* 539 (July 7, 2012).

For more information about segregation in America, see Case 14: *Palmer v. Thompson*.

CASE 12

Ingraham v. Wright (1977)

Key Issue: Corporal Punishment
Does the Eighth Amendment right to be free from cruel and unusual punishment apply to public school students?

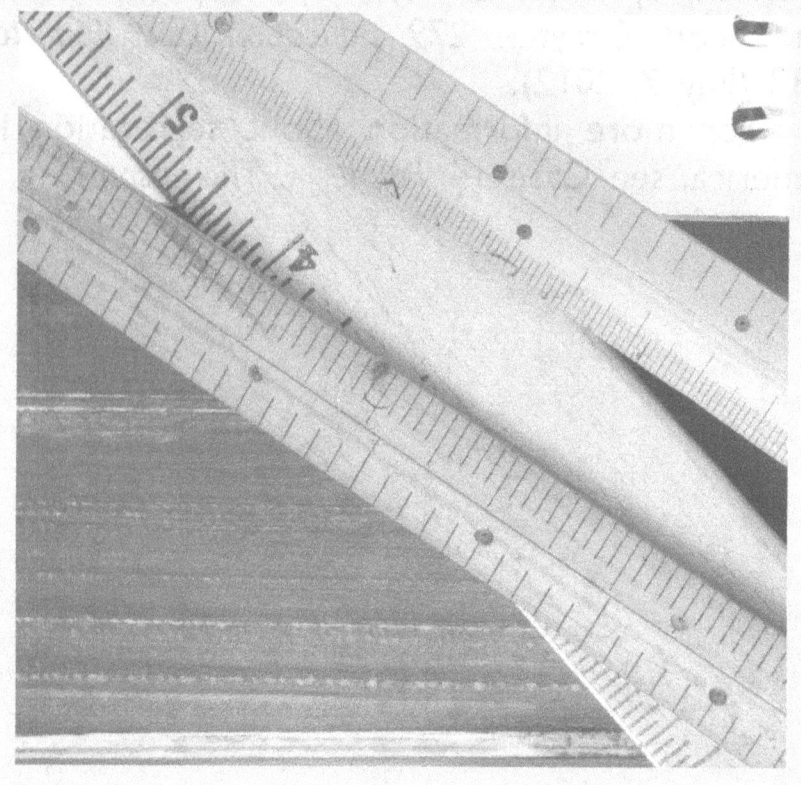

The Eighth Amendment to the U.S. Constitution states in full: *"Excessive bail shall not*

be required; nor excessive fines imposed, nor cruel and unusual punishments inflicted."

> ### IN OTHER WORDS
> **"The paddling of recalcitrant children has long been an accepted method of promoting good behavior and instilling notions of responsibility and decorum into the mischievous heads of schoolchildren."**
> —Justice William Powell, *Ingraham v. Wright* (1977)

In this case from the 1970s, the issue before the Supreme Court was whether the prohibition against "cruel and unusual punishments" applied to the ways students were disciplined at school. Was it acceptable for a teacher or principal to use physical punishment (such as a swat with a paddle, yardstick, cane, or strap) on a student who had broken a school rule?

Once again, the votes made by the justices in this case would have a significant impact on the lives of many. In this case, their ruling would affect how students are treated in schools today.

Facts of the Case

Florida law authorized public schools to use **corporal punishment** to discipline students. Corporal punishment has been defined by the United Nations Committee on the Rights of the

Child as "any punishment in which physical force is used and intended to cause some degree of pain or discomfort, however light." The punishment was not to be "degrading or unduly severe." Teachers were allowed to paddle students on the buttocks with a wooden paddle no longer than two feet or thicker than a half inch. Punishment was limited to five swats and a second adult had to be present.

Roosevelt Andrews attended a junior high school in Florida. (This case is named after Andrews's fellow plaintiff, James Ingraham.) He had been paddled numerous times during the school year for being late for his physical education class, for not changing clothes for gym, and for not having his tennis shoes. He explained that they were stolen and his mother couldn't afford to replace them. On one occasion, he was struck on his wrist, which swelled and resulted in Andrews having only limited use of his arm for a week.

James Ingraham was in the eighth grade and went to the same school as Andrews. He was paddled for walking too slowly when told by a teacher to leave an area. Both boys and their parents joined in a lawsuit against the school for the use of corporal punishment, claiming a violation of their Eighth Amendment rights as well as a violation of their Fourteenth Amendment rights to due process—that is, the right to be heard and to have a hearing before the paddling.

The Court's Ruling and Reasoning

As a part of considering this case, the Supreme Court reviewed the history of the Eighth Amendment and found that bail, fines, and punishment were all traditionally associated with the criminal process. Accordingly, the Court ruled that the Eighth Amendment was designed to protect criminals from excessive punishment and that it does not apply to disciplining schoolchildren. The Court said, "The prisoner and the schoolchild stand in wholly different circumstances, separated by the harsh facts of criminal conviction and incarceration." Andrews and Ingraham lost the case.

The five justices in the majority reasoned that extending Eighth Amendment protection to public school students was unnecessary, because teachers and administrators were already subject to the oversight of parents and the community. In addition, every state has civil and criminal laws against excessive or unreasonable corporal punishment, and educators face legal consequences for breaking those laws. This was another reason, according to the Court, that students did not need the additional protection offered by the Eighth Amendment. In its opinion, written by Justice William Powell, the Court said that the established rule in this country allows a teacher or an administrator to use the amount of force that he or she "reasonably believes to be necessary for (the child's) proper control, training, or education."

> ### Did You Know?
>
> Fewer states authorize corporal punishment in schools now than allowed it in 1977 when Ingraham v. Wright was decided. As of June 2015, thirty-one states have outlawed corporal punishment in public schools, as have the District of Columbia and Puerto Rico. In New Jersey and Iowa, the ban extends to private school students. Canada and most European countries also prohibit corporal punishment in public and private schools.

However, the Court's ruling does not mean there are no limits on physically disciplining students. In states that allow corporal punishment in schools, teachers may use reasonable but not excessive force to discipline a student. They must be cautious and use restraint. The Court suggested a test to determine if physical discipline is called for. The school should consider the seriousness of the offense, the student's attitude and past behavior, the nature and severity of the punishment, the age and strength of the child, and the availability of less severe but equally effective forms of discipline.

The Court Speaks

"The use of corporal punishment in this country as a means of disciplining schoolchildren dates back to colonial times."

In writing for the majority, Justice Lewis Powell Jr. noted that, under English law, a teacher could inflict "moderate correction" on a student. This was when the teacher believed such action was necessary for the child's control or education. The common law test of reasonableness was recognized as well as the practice of parental notice and infliction by the principal in the presence of an adult witness.

Did You Know?

Corporal punishment is still being debated in the United States (as well as in other countries). Across the United States, some organizations are campaigning for laws that would prohibit all forms of corporal punishment in homes and in schools. However, it is unlikely that Congress will act, since states have full authority to legislate on this issue.

The four dissenting justices in Andrews's case argued that the Eighth Amendment should be read to prohibit all "barbaric punishments" regardless of the offense. They held that spanking was punishment and that due process requires a discussion between student and teacher before the student is paddled, so the student has a chance to explain his or her side of the story.

What If...?

If the Court in *Ingraham v. Wright* had decided that the Eighth Amendment did apply to students, a strong argument could be made in future cases that the Eighth Amendment also applies to physical discipline by parents. This would have resulted in parent-child and family relationships being challenged in federal rather than state court. As it is, the question of whether corporal punishment at school or in the home is excessive depends on the laws of a specific state. Civil and criminal statutes set the boundaries for school officials and parents. If the line is crossed, consequences may include fines, incarceration, and additional financial loss if a civil lawsuit against the parents or school is successful. In the eyes of the Court, these are effective ways to deal with alleged abuse by a teacher, principal, or parent.

As the Court stated in its opinion: "We think it a misuse of our judicial power to determine, for example, whether a teacher has acted arbitrarily in paddling a particular child for certain behavior or whether in a particular instance of misconduct five licks would have been a more appropriate punishment than ten licks."

Related Cases

The practice of corporal punishment for misbehaving children dates back several hundred years in America. The following cases concern physical discipline at home and at school. Every state allows parents to spank their children with "reasonable force." However, what is considered reasonable is based on community norms and the degree of injury inflicted. The same physical discipline used on a child may be viewed as abuse according to the laws in one state but may be considered acceptable in another.

While most states have outlawed corporal punishment in schools, some states still allow it, though it is used less and less in recent years. In 2015, a bill was introduced into the U.S. House of Representatives that would withhold federal funds from schools that allow corporal punishment. The Ending Corporal Punishment in Schools Act of 2015 (H.R. 2268) was referred to the House Committee on Education and the Workforce, and is still pending.

DO PARENTS HAVE THE RIGHT TO PHYSICALLY DISCIPLINE THEIR CHILDREN?

State of Iowa v. Rollins (2013)

Otis Rollins returned home after a night out to find his children—ages nine, eight, and six—still awake and playing in their room. He confronted them while allegedly holding a knife and made them stand in the corner. Later that night, he hit the nine-year-old with a belt, leaving bruises. Rollins was convicted of child endangerment and sentenced to five years in prison.

On appeal, the state court upheld Rollins's conviction, stating, "The control and proper discipline of a child by the parent may justify acts which would otherwise constitute assault and battery, but the right of parental discipline clearly has its limits. And if the limits are exceeded, the parent may be criminally liable for assault or other offenses." The conviction and sentence were affirmed.

> ### Did You Know?
>
> There are no federal laws on parental discipline—it is a matter left to each state. The states assume this responsibility under their child welfare laws and the Supreme Court defers to the states to enforce their laws designed to protect children.
>
> But while most states have a child welfare agency that is responsible for investigating reports of abuse and neglect, and removing children from dangerous situations, simply having child protective services does not guarantee that children will be safe when left with or returned to their parents. Under the civil and criminal laws of each state, excessive discipline of a child or teen at home or at school may result in prosecution. Child abuse, child endangerment, and assault are crimes in every state that may lead to incarceration.

MUST PARENTS LIMIT THEMSELVES TO "REASONABLE FORCE" WHEN USING PHYSICAL DISCIPLINE?

***Simons v. State of North Dakota* (2011)**

Ben Simons and his wife, Traci Simons, had eight children in their home. Two of them were foster children, and one was under a guardianship. (A guardian is created by court order.) As guardians of the child, the Simons had legal responsibility for his care and welfare.

The Simons couple required all of their children to respond to them with "yes, sir" or "yes, ma'am." At church one Sunday, their two-year-old refused to respond to a question as the parents required, so he was given two swats on the bottom. Later that day, the boy again refused to answer his father as required and was swatted three times on the bottom with a wooden backscratcher. He was wearing a diaper and pants at the time. This pattern of three swats and a talk with his father continued for the next two hours. The boy refused to say "yes, sir." He received a total of twenty-four swats. Upon changing the boy's diaper, the parents discovered two purple bruises, each the size of a fifty-cent piece, on his buttocks.

After receiving a tip, social services investigated the incident and determined that the child had been abused and that the family needed counseling and support services. The parents appealed the decision, arguing that the child had not been abused and that there was not enough evidence to prove the spankings caused him physical pain. The court upheld the ruling of the agency, stating that the father failed to use reasonable force in disciplining his son.

WHAT CONSTITUTES EXCESSIVE CORPORAL PUNISHMENT BY SCHOOL OFFICIALS?

Teresa Garcia v. Miera (1987)

Teresa was a nine-year-old student in the third grade at Penasco Elementary School in New Mexico. A boy at school kicked her and she hit him back. Teresa was called to the principal's office where she was told to bend over to be paddled. She refused and a teacher was called in to assist with the punishment. The principal gave Teresa five swats while the teacher held her upside down by her ankles. The swats were inflicted on the front of Teresa's legs between her knees and waist. Blood was seen coming through her pants, and upon inspection her teacher saw a welt on her leg that left a permanent scar.

A year later, Teresa was paddled five times for saying she saw a teacher kiss another student's father during a field trip. The paddling left severe bruises on her buttocks and caused pain for three weeks.

Teresa and her parents sued the school district over the two incidents, alleging that the school violated Teresa's due process right to a hearing before being paddled.

> ### Did You Know?
>
> Most cases regarding violations of any of the twenty-seven amendments to the Constitution are filed in federal court. Some are filed in state court claiming violations of a state constitution in addition to violating the federal laws, but these cases are usually dismissed in state court and bumped up to the federal system. This avoids duplicate lawsuits and is more efficient.

The court in Teresa's case stated that "punishments that are so grossly excessive as to be shocking to the conscience" violate a student's rights. School officials in this case were not entitled to immunity, and the trial was allowed to proceed. However, in the meantime, the federal court dismissed the lawsuit on the basis that such matters should be left to school officials and state law. The Supreme Court declined without comment to hear the case.

> ### Talk, Think, and Take Action
>
> • What does the Eighth Amendment mean to you? Do you interpret it to include physical discipline at home or school? Why or why not? By stating that bail and fines are not to be excessive and punishment is not to be cruel and unusual, do you think the authors of the Eighth Amendment meant to reach into schools

and homes in this regard, even if they didn't say so specifically? Or do you think it's more likely they were intending to set restrictions on the criminal justice system only?

- What is your state law regarding corporal punishment in public or private schools? If it is allowed, do you think it should be banned? If you do, consider working with your friends to start an online petition or write a resolution calling for an end to this policy in schools and distribute it to anyone you think could help make a difference. Your list could include the governor, the legislature (especially members of education committees), the state director of education, school district superintendents, and school board members. You could also contact the media and the editorial page of local newspapers requesting their support. For more information on this issue, take a look at www.stophitting.com and www.findlaw.com.
- Minors who are locked up in juvenile detention centers or state corrections facilities are sometimes placed in solitary confinement as punishment for their behavior. What do you think about this? Do you think solitary confinement is "cruel and unusual" punishment as meant under the Eighth Amendment? In 2015, New York City officials and officials at Rikers Island—the nation's second-largest jail system—reached an agreement banning solitary

confinement for inmates under age twenty-one. Do you agree with this decision? Why or why not? What do you think it would be like to be in solitary confinement? What would be most difficult about it?

- In an unrelated case to this chapter, Justice Clarence Thomas commented, "The historical evidence shows that the founding generation believed parents had absolute authority over their minor children and expected parents to use that authority to direct the proper development of their children" (*Brown v. Entertainment Merchants Association*, 2011). After considering this comment, how do you think Justice Thomas would rule if faced with a case involving corporal punishment at school or home? Do you think he would vote in favor of or against corporal punishment? What about *you*? How would you rule if you were on the court, and why?

IN OTHER WORDS

"Parental autonomy ... is not absolute. The state is the guardian of society's basic values.... [T]he state has a right, indeed, a duty, to protect children. State officials may interfere in family matters to safeguard the child's

> **health, educational development, and emotional well-being."**
> —Judge P.J. Caldecott, *In re Phillip B.* (1979)

Closing Comments

The Supreme Court has held that it respects the fundamental right of parents to raise their children, and the right of schools to manage themselves without interference from the courts. Accordingly, as this case revealed, young people are not protected by the Eighth Amendment. Still, those who teach and care for children and teens are held responsible if they mistreat or abuse them, and society has a number of safeguards in place to help protect children. In addition, the judicial system does pay attention to and review cases involving serious violations of young people's basic rights by educators and parents.

Further Reading and Resources

Primary Case: *Ingraham v. Wright*, 430 U.S. 651 (1977).

Beating the Devil Out of Them: Corporal Punishment in American Families and Its Effect on Children by Murray A. Strauss (Piscataway, NJ: Transaction Publishers, 2001).

"Can They Do That to Me?! Does the Eighth Amendment Protect Children's Best Interests?" by Maryam Ahranjani, 63 *South Carolina Law Review* 403 (Winter 2011).

"Corporal Punishment in K–12 Public School Settings: Reconsideration of its Constitutional Dimensions Thirty Years After *Ingraham v. Wright*" by Lewis M. Wasserman, 26 *Touro Law Review* 1029 (2011).

Corporal Punishment in Public Schools: Legal Precedents, Current Practices, and Future Policy by Elizabeth Gershoff, Kelly M. Purtell, and Igor Holas (New York: Springer, 2015).

CASE 13

Goss v. Dwight Lopez (1975)

Key Issue: Prison Suspension Terms for or Expulsion Young People from School

Can Do students a juvenile have be a sent right to to prison for "due life process" without the before possibility being of earning suspended release or expelled on parole? from school?

Every state has laws about children and teens attending school. Called compulsory attendance laws, these vary from state to state but generally they require children between certain ages (six to sixteen, for example) to be in school during the school year. However, schools also have the right to suspend or expel students who break the school rules or laws. In this case, the Supreme Court considered whether students had the right to "due process" before being disciplined in this way. Due process of law is defined as the right to know what you are accused of and a chance to respond to the accusation.

> ### IN OTHER WORDS
>
> **"The touchstone of due process is protection of the individual against arbitrary action of government."**
> —Justice David Souter, *County of Sacramento v. Lewis* (1998) quoting *Wolff v. McDonnell* (1974)

Facts of the Case

In 1971, the state of Ohio had a law that allowed public school principals to suspend a student for misconduct for up to ten days, or to expel the student for more serious behavior. The principal was required to notify the student's parents of the discipline within twenty-four hours and explain the reasons for the action. The law did not require giving notice to the student or allowing them an opportunity for a hearing before or after the suspension or expulsion.

Nineteen-year-old Dwight Lopez attended Central High School in Columbus, Ohio. The school had experienced racially motivated tension regarding Black History Month, including demonstrations and property damage. One day, Lopez was in the lunchroom when a few students started overturning tables. He and his friends left, taking no part in the disturbance. However, Lopez was suspended, along with other students at his school. No specific reasons were given for his suspension, and no hearing was scheduled. There was also some confusion about the length of his suspension, and he stayed out of school a week longer than he was supposed to. A month later, the school transferred him to another school in the district. In addition to claiming that he was not treated fairly, Lopez said he had been an innocent bystander. In a **class action** lawsuit, Lopez and eight other students who had been suspended from various schools in the Columbus school district challenged the suspension, arguing that they were suspended without any notice or hearing.

The Court's Ruling and Reasoning

The Supreme Court noted that Ohio law provides a free public education to all residents between the ages of five and twenty-one. The law requires students to attend school for at least thirty-two weeks each year and states that schools may suspend students for up to ten days for certain offenses. Since the law offers the right to education, the Court ruled that this right cannot be withdrawn without first investigating what happened and verifying that the misconduct actually occurred. The Court noted that misconduct charges could seriously damage a student's reputation as well as interfere with the young person's chances of getting into college or finding a job. They voted in favor of Lopez. Actions by school officials against a student must comply with certain safeguards. In the majority decision, written by Justice Byron R. White, the Court noted, "A 10-day suspension from school is not *de minimus* [of little concern] in our view and may not be imposed in complete disregard of the Due Process Clause."

IN OTHER WORDS

> **The Court has long recognized the importance of education and graduation. As Justice Anthony M. Kennedy said in the 1992 case *Lee v. Weisman*, "Everyone knows that, in our society and in our culture, high school graduation is one of life's most significant occasions."**

Due process requires that a student be told or given written notice of the charges against him or her. In addition, if the student denies those charges, the school must explain the evidence and give the student a chance to present his or her side of the story. Depending on the circumstances, the notice and hearing should follow as soon as possible. As the Court said in its majority opinion, "Students facing suspension must be given some kind of notice and offered some kind of hearing.... The student's interest is to avoid unfair or mistaken exclusion from the educational process, with all of its unfortunate consequences."

Most school suspensions are for less than ten days. Usually, a teacher will talk to the student about what happened within minutes of the incident, an informal conversation which generally meets the requirements of due process. If something more serious happens and greater discipline is possible, the Court said students could be immediately removed from the school if their presence posed a danger or would likely disrupt the classroom. It also said, "Longer suspensions or expulsions for the remainder of the school term, or permanently, may require more formal procedures." The Court commented that, "The classroom is the laboratory in which this lesson in life [about consequences for one's actions] is best learned." However, the Court did not require a formal hearing for minor incidents.

It is clear from *Goss v. Lopez* that the Supreme Court acknowledges the importance of educators concentrating on their primary mission without involvment from the judicial system. However, this doesn't grant teachers and administrators free rein over students in all situations. Discipline for misbehavior must meet minimum due process protections, which includes informing students of what the consequences will be and giving them a chance to explain the situation. The Court did not require a full hearing or trial, since this would make it difficult for schools to discipline students in any situation, and often immediate action is called for.

Four of the justices disagreed with the decision. They felt that granting a new constitutional right (due process) specifically for students would require courts to continually intervene in public school operations. The dissenters remarked that there was value in disciplining students. Justice William Powell wrote, "School discipline, like parental discipline, is an integral and important part of training our children to be good citizens—to be better citizens.... One who does not comprehend the meaning and necessity of discipline is handicapped not merely in his education but throughout his subsequent life."

The Court Speaks

"Due process of law has little reality or worth unless one is informed that the matter is pending and can choose for himself whether to contest."

Justice White, in his majority opinion, summarized the matter of due process at school quite simply: anyone whose rights will be affected is entitled to be heard and must first be notified. The risk of an undeserved suspension is not trivial, and it is in students' interest to avoid unfair or mistaken exclusion from school. White also clarified, however, that the due process clause is *not* a way for students to evade justified and properly imposed suspensions.

What If...?

If due process did not apply at all to cases of school discipline, school officials would be free to punish students at will. Every unruly, disrespectful, or disruptive act that teachers and principals became suspicious of could lead to suspension without challenge. As a result, schools could seriously impact a student's future and psychological state. The majority of the Court saw this as an unacceptable result.

Related Cases

The concept of due process applies to all students in a variety of situations at school. The related cases that follow all deal with decisions made by educators that involved students' due process rights. They include cases concerning students with special needs, students given in-school suspension or time-outs, and students who are placed in alternative programs separate from mainstream educational programs.

WHAT DUE PROCESS RIGHTS DO SPECIAL NEEDS STUDENTS HAVE?

Couture v. Board of Education of Albuquerque Public School (2008)

M. Couture (M.C.) was six years old when his school district determined that he was emotionally disturbed and therefore eligible for special education services. M.C. was defiant, uncooperative, argumentative, and aggressive toward other students and his teachers. The school developed an individualized education plan for M.C. that included supervised time-outs when he became disruptive.

In first grade M.C. was placed in time-out twenty-one times for a total of twelve hours. His mother claimed that this amounted to a deprivation of his right to an education. She sued the school district and various school officials, claiming they discriminated against him on the basis of his disability. Although she had signed off on the plan, she later challenged it as inappropriate and said that the use of the time-outs deprived him of due process.

The federal court ruled that "Time-outs are intended to settle down a child while keeping him within close proximity to the classroom." Given M.C.'s severe emotional and behavioral difficulties, teaching him self-control was among the most important components of his education program. The court denied the mother's claims, and no further appeal was taken.

DOES IN-SCHOOL SUSPENSION DEPRIVE STUDENTS OF EDUCATIONAL OPPORTUNITIES?

Laney v. Farley **(2007)**

Victoria Laney was in the eighth grade at West Wilson Middle School in Tennessee. At the beginning of the school year her cell phone started ringing during class. Her teacher took the phone and sent it with a discipline sheet to the principal. Because possessing a phone during school hours violated the school's code of conduct, Victoria was given a one-day in-school suspension and her phone was confiscated for thirty days. Victoria and her father sued, alleging her due process rights were violated since she did not receive a hearing before this discipline was implemented.

The court ruled against her, saying that in-school suspension did not deprive Victoria of any educational opportunities since, although she wasn't in her regular classroom, she was "required to complete academic requirements." The court found that the suspension was not detrimental to her future and the lawsuit against the principal was dismissed.

CAN JUVENILE DELINQUENTS BE FORCED TO ATTEND AN ALTERNATIVE SCHOOL?

D.C. v. School District of Philadelphia (2005)

D.C. was a sixteen-year-old high schooler who was found **delinquent** in juvenile court for joyriding. He was sent to a residential facility for juvenile delinquents for a few months. Pennsylvania law barred juveniles released from placement or on probation from returning to a regular classroom. Instead, they were to attend alternative education programs.

When D.C. was released, he was sent to an alternative school for disruptive students rather than his old high school. He challenged this decision, alleging that the program did not offer the same educational opportunities or intra-scholastic sports as his regular high school. The court found that "the absence of any opportunity for returning students to challenge their transfer to an alternative educational setting violates due process." D.C. was entitled to a hearing by the school administration to determine if he could return to his regular high school.

Talk, Think, and Take Action

- Have you ever had a teacher who seemed to have it out for you? Have you ever been disciplined for your behavior, dress, or attitude at school? Were you suspended or expelled or given time in detention? If any of these have happened to you, how did you feel? How did you respond? Have you ever experienced, or heard about another student at your school experiencing, a form of discipline without being given a chance to explain your side of the story? If so, what happened?
- Schools have disciplined students for many years. In 1906, two sisters in Wisconsin were suspended and fined forty cents for writing a poem making fun of their school. The state's highest court upheld the discipline, stating that "school authorities have the power to suspend a pupil for an offense committed outside of school hours" if disruptive to the educational environment.

Today, students can get in trouble for expressing themselves online, whether or not they write their comments while at school. Although a student would never be fined forty cents for something said online, students do continue to face suspension and even expulsion for all types of speech—just as they did 100 years ago. However, unlike speech a century ago, online speech is traceable. Students may face discipline for behavior that occurred outside of school hours and off campus.

• What can you do if you think your First Amendment freedom of speech and expression is threatened at school? If you were facing a suspension or expulsion from school, do you know how you could challenge it? Discuss the situation with your parents and take a look at your student handbook or the school district's policy manual to learn about the appeals process. Even if you're not in this situation, learning about the process and its consequences may allow you to help yourself or a friend in the future.

• Do you feel that suspensions and expulsions occur too frequently at your school, or do you think they are given out when needed—or are not given out enough? Do you think they are handled arbitrarily, or appropriately? How do you think students are affected when they are suspended or expelled? In what ways could this affect them academically and emotionally? Think about action you could take if you disagree with the disciplinary process at your school. First, you could review the rules and policies listed in your student handbook and the school district's policy manual to learn about the appeals process. Then you could begin the discussion by talking with your friends, classmates, and school officials about strategies to make positive changes in the disciplinary policies at your school. What else could you do?

• Read the following cases of students who were disciplined for expressing themselves online. In each case, consider whether you think the punishment fit the crime. Why or why not?

* Michelle E., a high school senior, was unhappy with a grade she received on an essay. She wrote on a friend's Facebook wall, "I say we shoot our English teacher in the face." She was suspended for ninety days.

* Brothers Steven and Sean W. created a website containing racist and sexually explicit comments about female classmates. Their speech disrupted the school environment and therefore was not protected under the First Amendment. A six-month suspension was upheld by a judge.

* Taylor B. wrote and posted a rap song on YouTube criticizing two coaches at school. Using vulgar language and threatening lyrics, he accused them of improper conduct with female students. Taylor's speech was not protected, and he was suspended for seven days and required to transfer to an alternative school.

* D.J.M. sent a friend an instant message from a home computer. He talked about taking a gun to school and killing certain students. He was suspended for the remainder of the school year—approximately six months.

* Have you ever heard of the "school-to-prison pipeline"? This phrase used by civil rights organizations and academic scholars describes the policies and practices of school systems that are said to be pushing students out of school and into the juvenile justice system. They argue that zero-tolerance policies and other disciplinary policies adopted by school districts are contributing factors to this pipeline. In addition, they say that students of color and those with special needs are disproportionately affected.

If you believe this is happening at your school, take action. Consider circulating a petition to change your school's policies on discipline. For instance, some schools have police officers present at all times and students may be arrested for minor offenses. If you oppose this practice, you might work to encourage school officials to reconsider their policies and, rather than arresting students, discipline them through the school or even refer them to a teen court. If a school doesn't have a teen court, it can start one—and you can advocate for this change, too.

Closing Comments

Many teachers and administrators are stretched to the limit. If they had to worry about being sued every time a student was suspended or expelled, it would make their jobs even more difficult. Most situations involving disputes about how a student is disciplined never reach the courts and are instead resolved at the school level—between the teacher, student, and parents. The few that result in a lawsuit are usually settled before trial. Only rarely are cases fully litigated.

The Supreme Court has emphasized that public school officials need to create rules and expectations for student behavior and then enforce those rules in daily school life. The court system should play only a limited supervisory role in public schools. In 1968, the Supreme Court held in *Epperson v. Arkansas* that "By and large, public education in our Nation is committed to the control of state and local authorities. Courts do not and cannot intervene in the resolution of conflicts which arise in the daily operation of school systems and which do not directly and sharply implicate basic constitutional values." In the Court's view, in-school or off-campus suspensions for less than ten days do not violate basic constitutional principles. Anything longer than ten days calls for following due process procedures. Even then, most situations can be resolved without involving lawyers and the court system.

Further Reading and Resources

Primary Case: *Goss v. Lopez*, 419 U.S. 565 (1975).

Middle School, The Worst Years of My Life by James Patterson and Chris Tebbetts (New York: Little, Brown and Co., 2012).

Prelude to Prison: Student Perspectives on School Suspension by Marsha Weissman (Syracuse, NY: Syracuse University Press, 2015).

"Upholding Students' Due Process Rights: Why Students Are in Need of Better Representation at, and Alternatives to, School Suspension Hearings" by Simone Marie Freeman, 45 *Family Court Review* 638 (October 2007).

"Youth with Learning Disabilities: Seven Things Juvenile Courts Should Know" by Christopher A. Mallett, 63 *Juvenile and Family Court Journal* 55 (Summer 2012).

CASE 14

Hazel Palmer v. Thompson (1971)

Key Issue: Segregation
Did a city close its public swimming pools because they could no longer be segregated? If so, was this an unconstitutional act?

This case may be more than forty-five years old, but the subject of race relations and discrimination in the United States is still relevant today. Even as minorities have risen to the highest offices in government and business, the struggle for equality and justice continues. You only have to consider such incidents as the death of Freddie Gray in Baltimore, Maryland (and the protests that followed), Samantha Elauf's workplace discrimination lawsuit (see section entitled "CAN A COMPANY REFUSE TO HIRE AN APPLICANT BECAUSE SHE WEARS A HEADSCARF?"), and renewed attempts to create obstacles to voting to see that the issues of this case remain important in the twenty-first century.

Facts of the Case

In 1962, the city of Jackson, Mississippi, maintained five public parks, along with golf courses, tennis courts, and swimming pools that were all racially segregated. Four of the pools were used by white residents only, and one was for use by black residents only. After the city lost a lawsuit finding that this segregation violated the constitutional rights of black citizens, it responded by desegregating its public parks, auditoriums, zoo, and golf courses. However, citing economic concerns as well as worries about violence among Jackson's citizens due to racial tensions, the city decided to close all of the pools.

An elementary school janitor named Hazel Palmer and eleven other citizens sued the city to force it to reopen the pools and make them available to all, regardless of race. The trial court found that the city's decision to close the pools was justified to preserve peace and order, and because it would be financially difficult to operate the pools if they were integrated. Since the trial court did not find any discrimination in the city's actions, Palmer appealed the decision to the Supreme Court. The Supreme Court was faced with deciding whether the city had acted to avoid desegregation and, in doing so, denied black residents equal protection of the law.

The Court's Ruling and Reasoning

The Supreme Court reviewed the history of the Fourteenth Amendment, stating that it was designed, in part, to safeguard African Americans from laws that discriminated against them. The justices also noted that the Equal Protection Clause of the Fourteenth Amendment did not apply only to white people, but to all citizens of the United States. The Fourteenth Amendment prohibits any government action that treats one group differently from another.

The Court recognized that the issue before it was not one where whites were permitted to use public facilities while blacks were denied access. Nor was the city offering different facilities for blacks and whites, forcing the races to remain separate in recreational activities. Instead, the city had closed *all* of the pools, thereby denying access to all citizens of Jackson, regardless of color. Justice Harry Blackmun summed it up by stating, "I cannot read into closing of the pools an official expression of inferiority toward black citizens."

Palmer argued that the city's action did violate the Equal Protection Clause because, she said, the city closed the pools to avoid integrating the races. The Court rejected this argument since it "is difficult or impossible for any court to determine the sole or dominant motivation behind the choices of a group of legislators." It was not willing to speculate about motivation in this case. It further commented that "the issue here is whether black citizens in Jackson *are* being denied their constitutional rights when the city has closed the public pools to black and white alike. Nothing in the history or language of the Fourteenth Amendment nor in any of our prior cases persuades us that the closing of the Jackson swimming pools to all its citizens constitutes a denial of the equal protection of the laws." The Court could not find a denial of equal protection of the law and so voted in favor of the city.

Four of the justices disagreed with the majority opinion. They felt that a government should not discontinue any of its services to the public because it found life in a multiracial community difficult or unpleasant. Doing so would constitute a pronouncement that African Americans were unfit to swim with whites and support a view that they were inferior. Justice William O. Douglas expressed his dissent, writing, "The closing of the City's pools has done more than deprive a few thousand Negroes of the pleasures of swimming ... Negroes will now think twice before protesting segregated public parks, segregated public libraries, or other facilities. They must first decide whether they wish to risk living without the facility altogether, and at the same time engendering further animosity from a white community which has lost its public facilities also through the Negroes' attempts to desegregate these facilities."

The Court Speaks

"Officially segregated public facilities were not equal."

In a dissenting opinion, Justice Byron White reviewed the cases decided by the Court since the 1954 decision in *Brown v. Board of Education*. *Brown* held that separate educational facilities were by nature unequal and no longer permissible under the Fourteenth Amendment. Over the following decade, the principles of *Brown* were applied in cases involving public recreational facilities including beaches, city parks, fishing lakes, golf courses, and buses. Justice White concluded that the pools in this case would have remained open had there not been a court order to open them to all citizens without regard to race.

> ### Did You Know?
> Recent reports in a few southern states show efforts to resegregate public schools. Referred to as clustered classrooms and clustered schools, the rezoning of school districts and new transfer policies has created predominantly white or black schools. Such incidents are under review and being watched by the courts and **interest groups** focused on or affected by separate but equal policies, including school districts in North Carolina and Texas.

What If...?

If the Court had decided that discrimination was the main reason the city closed all of its pools, they could have weakened the standing and reputation of the Court, since its job is to decide cases based on sound evidence, not assumptions. Such a decision could therefore have opened the door for cases based on speculation, not facts. For example, claims of racial profiling in traffic stops, detentions, and arrests could be "proven" based *solely* on a person's allegations against a police officer. (Although such claims should be investigated, the number of actual cases that enter the court system is small.) Or a claim of wage discrimination might be pursued even without supporting facts and figures. Similarly, some lawmakers have tried to pass legislation allowing businesses to discriminate against the LGBTQ community, on the basis of the right to religious freedom. Such proposed legislation has stated that if a business owner "sincerely held" a religious belief, he or she could refuse service to a customer. The question, however, is how to legally assess someone's "sincerely held" religious beliefs to determine if the refusal to serve a customer is legitimate.

At the same time, such cases are in the unique and nearly impossible position of requiring proof of a police officer's intent or motivation. As in the *Palmer* case, how do you prove intent behind discriminatory conduct without an admission of some sort?

Related Cases

The following cases present a timeline of Supreme Court decisions over seventy years on the issue of racial segregation. The section begins with a case from 1857, Scott v. Sandford, and a ruling that has been called the Court's worst decision in its history. The Scott decision led, in part, to the Fourteenth Amendment of 1868, which granted full freedom to former slaves and other African Americans. In the years that followed, decisions by the Court addressed the policy of "separate but equal," segregation of public facilities and schools, and interracial marriage.

CAN A BLACK MAN SUE FOR HIS FREEDOM?

Scott v. Sandford (1857)

Dred Scott was born into slavery in 1795. He was later purchased in 1831 and became the slave of U.S. Army surgeon John Emerson. When Emerson died, Scott tried unsuccessfully to buy his freedom from the doctor's widow. Scott decided to take the matter to court and sue for his freedom. Over the next eleven years, the case worked its way through state and federal courts, ending up before the Supreme Court. The Court ruled in a 7–2 decision that a black man, whether enslaved or not, could not be an American citizen and, therefore, had no standing to sue in federal court. Chief Justice Roger B. Taney wrote that slaves and their descendants had "no rights which the white man was bound to respect."

Scott returned to his owner's residence. Three months later, she returned Scott to his original owners who granted Scott and his family their freedom. He became a porter in St. Louis and died the next year of tuberculosis.

IS "SEPARATE BUT EQUAL" PUBLIC TRANSPORTATION CONSTITUTIONAL?

Plessy v. Ferguson (1896)

Homer Adolph Plessy was seven-eighths white and one-eighth "of African blood," but under Louisiana law he was considered black. In 1892, Plessy boarded a train in Louisiana and took a seat in the white car. He was told to move to the car for black passengers. When he refused, he was forcibly ejected, arrested, and taken to jail. Plessy was convicted of violating the state's segregation law and fined $25. He appealed, arguing that the law violated the Equal Protection Clause of the Fourteenth Amendment.

Did You Know?

> Just as one vote can make a monumental difference in matters large and small, one action can as well. When Rosa Parks refused to move from the front of a bus in 1955, her action sparked a bus boycott that lasted a year and inspired the civil rights movement. A decade later the Civil Rights Act and Voting Rights Act were passed by Congress. And more than half a century later, in 2013, President Barack Obama commented that Parks's "singular act of disobedience launched a movement" that lasts to this day. He said, "Rosa Parks tells us there's always something we can do. She tells us that we all have responsibilities, to ourselves and to one another."

On appeal, the Supreme Court voted 7–1 that "separate but equal" is constitutional "so long as white men are distinguished from the other race by color." The Court's opinion further stated that "The object of the Fourteenth Amendment was undoubtedly to enforce the absolute equality of the two races before the law, but in the nature of things it could not have been intended to abolish distinctions based upon color ... or to enforce a commingling of the two races."

Homer Plessy lost and "separate but equal" became the court-sanctioned rule for over fifty years, not ending until 1954 when *Brown v. Board of Education* was decided. The lone dissenter in

Plessy, Justice John Marshall Harlan, commented, "Our Constitution is color-blind, and neither knows nor tolerates classes among citizens. In respect of civil rights, all citizens are equal before the law."

ARE "SEPARATE BUT EQUAL" SCHOOLS CONSTITUTIONAL?

Brown v. Board of Education (1954)

The landmark case of *Brown v. Board of Education* reversed the *Plessy* decision, ruling that "separate but equal" was unconstitutional. Chief Justice Earl Warren wrote for the unanimous Court that "Segregation of white and colored children in public schools has a detrimental effect upon the colored children.... A sense of inferiority affects the motivation of a child to learn.... Separate educational facilities are inherently unequal." Schools throughout the United States began desegregating.

Did You Know?

An African-American woman named Ruby Bridges was born in 1954, the year the Supreme Court ordered that public schools be integrated, and that attendance would no longer be based on a student's race. Integration did not happen immediately though. It wasn't until

1960 that a federal court order forced schools in New Orleans, Louisiana, to desegregate. Ruby was one of six black children selected to start the school year in all-white schools in New Orleans, and the only one to attend William Franz Public School. She was six years old when federal marshals first escorted her and her mother to the school. As they entered the school, they faced angry, violent crowds of white parents who were protesting. While it was a frightening time, the situation gradually improved. Ruby completed elementary school and moved on to other integrated schools. She eventually became a travel agent, married, and had four sons. After three decades, she reunited with her first white teacher, Barbara Henry. Together, they have traveled the country speaking to groups and students about education and racism.

CAN PUBLIC LIBRARIES LEGALLY DISCRIMINATE?

Brown v. Louisiana (1966)

In 1964, Henry Brown and four friends entered the Audubon Public Library in Louisiana. As members of a civil rights organization (CORE, or Congress of Racial Equality), they claimed that blacks had been locked out of public libraries in three Louisiana parishes. The men sat quietly without disturbing anyone. However, since they were black they were asked to leave. When they refused, they were arrested and convicted of disturbing the peace. The Supreme Court ruled 5–4 that the arresting police officer had violated their constitutional rights since maintaining separate libraries for blacks and whites was discriminatory. (Note that this happened ten years after the Court outlawed segregation of the races in *Brown v. Board of Education*. Desegregation had not yet been fully implemented.)

The dissent in this case argued that, in their interpretation of the evidence, the library did not deny Brown service or intend to discriminate against him. Furthermore, they said that the state of Louisiana had the right to make it unlawful to stage "sit-ins" in their public libraries. Brown, they claimed, had no right to use the library to express his "dissident ideas" (meaning, in this case, his disagreement with established rules or policies).

ARE LAWS AGAINST INTERRACIAL MARRIAGES CONSTITUTIONAL?

***Loving v. Virginia* (1967)**

In 1958, eighteen-year-old Mildred Jeter, who was black, married Richard Loving, a twenty-four-year-old white man, in Washington, D.C. The state of Virginia, where they lived, outlawed interracial marriages. The Lovings were indicted (charged) by a grand jury and pled guilty. They were sentenced to one year in jail, but the sentence was suspended on the condition that they leave Virginia for twenty-five years. They moved out of Virginia while their case was on appeal. In 1967, the Supreme Court ruled unanimously in their favor and declared Virginia's law against interracial marriage unconstitutional.

Did You Know?

After *Loving v. Virginia*, the Supreme Court did not consider another marriage case for almost fifty years. In 2015, they ruled 5–4 that marriage for same-sex couples was a constitutional right, making it legal nationwide. (*Obergefell v. Hodges*, 2015)

Are Supreme Court Decisions Effective Immediately?

You may be wondering why some of the cases presented in this chapter were still being brought to court decades after the *Brown v. Board of Education* case. *Brown* was decided in 1954 and the Court declared "separate but equal" an unconstitutional practice. Shouldn't that have been the end of the discussion? Why did segregation continue following *Brown*, and even after the Civil Rights Act of 1964?

The fact is that the wheels of justice move slowly. In addition, because individual rights are highly valued by the U.S. Constitution, laws and court decisions can be continuously challenged. One could argue that a ruling from the Supreme Court is not necessarily final. Over a period of time, and with a change of justices and national consensus on particular issues, the Court can reverse itself—and has.

For example, the Court went from a nearly unanimous decision (7–1) in *Plessy*, ruling that blacks and whites could legally be segregated in public, to reversing that decision and ruling unanimously (9–0) in *Brown* that segregation was clearly unconstitutional and violated the Equal Protection Clause. This happened over a fifty-year period, due in part to an entirely new Court and nine justices appointed by presidents who took office after the *Plessy* decision.

Also, consider life without parole for minors or the juvenile death penalty (see CASE 1). What was once the law of the land became history through subsequent Supreme Court decisions. Current issues that the Court may one day revisit include campaign finance (especially regarding super PACS—political action committees that are allowed to raise and spend unlimited funds to support or oppose political candidates) and the national healthcare program (often called Obamacare).

Talk, Think, and Take Action

• Do you think the city of Jackson, Mississippi, would have closed all of the pools if keeping them open on a segregated basis had not been challenged? In your opinion, was the Supreme Court right in not finding discrimination since all of the pools were closed? Why or why not?

• What connections do you see, if any, between the desegregation of public libraries, schools, and other facilities with the closure of public swimming pools? Does it make sense to you that a city would integrate all of its public services and amenities except one? Why or why not? The Court considered the proposition that once a city provides a service, it cannot eliminate it without being charged with discrimination. Even if an underlying desire to keep the races from swimming together existed, should this trump a valid financial decision to end a program that costs too much?

• LGBTQ rights and equality are sometimes referred to as the civil rights movement of the twenty-first century. What are your thoughts on this and on these issues? Should a person who is lesbian or gay be discriminated against when applying for a job? If asked about your sexual orientation in a job interview, what would you say? Do you have to answer the question at all?

• Some schools have come under criticism in recent years for denying students the right to dress in nonconforming ways at prom and other school dances. Several students have fought for their right to bring same-sex dates and to wear what they want, including male students wanting to wear prom dresses and female students wanting to wear tuxedos. If your school prevents LGBTQ students from participating at school dances as they would like to, consider writing a letter to the principal, starting a petition, or speaking up at the next school meeting. If you need additional help with this issue at your school, contact your local ACLU office. Many schools across the country have embraced the changing society we live in, allowing male students to run for homecoming queen and female students to run for king—and in some schools, those students have won!

• Do you think a student who is transgender—for instance, someone who is born biologically male but identifies as female—should have to use the boy's bathroom and locker room at school? Do you think equal protection of the law requires schools to allow transgender students to use the facilities of the gender they identify with? What about transgender students playing on sports teams for the gender they identify with? What type of challenges might occur in these situations, and how do you think these could be addressed?

- Although the Supreme Court approved interracial marriage in 1967, a Louisiana judge refused to marry a mixed-race couple in 2009. He explained that he wasn't racist, but he didn't "believe in mixing the races that way." Write a letter to the judge explaining your thoughts about his decision to deny this couple their recognized right to marry. What legal principles would you use in your letter? Ethical principles?

- Since same-sex marriage is an issue that individuals, couples, and families are discussing throughout the country, how can you take a stand on this, whether you're for or against it? Does your school have a club that advocates for social issues? How can you exercise your right to free speech and express yourself peaceably on this or any other issues discussed in this book?

Did You Know?

In 2009, a private swim club in Pennsylvania agreed to allow children from a local childcare center to use the pool once a week during the summer. After sixty-five mainly black and Hispanic children showed up for their first swim day, the club canceled their membership. The Huntington Valley Swim Club—which was predominantly white—explained that there were concerns over the number of children, their safety, and noise levels.

The Department of Justice investigated and found racial hostility as the reason for canceling the contract with the club. A settlement was reached in 2012, dividing $1.1 million among the children and their families.

In response to this incident, actor Tyler Perry stepped up and paid for the children to fly to Florida to spend a few days at Disney World. He wanted them to see that although some people may be misguided, others care about them.

Closing Comments

The Supreme Court ruled in 1954 that the practice of "separate but equal" was unconstitutional in a school setting. They later considered similar situations in other parts of daily life in the United States, including segregated seats on public transportation and restaurants, and the use of public bathrooms. Each time, they ruled against segregation of the races. *Palmer*, however, presented a twist on segregation, and one vote made all the difference in whether a city's action was found to violate equal protection.

As you can see from the discussion in this case, as well as cases 10, 11, and 13 *(Plyler, Bakke,* and *Goss)*, the concepts of equal protection and due process are fluid. They depend on the specific circumstances of a case and the overall effect of the challenged action. The strength of the Constitution and the Bill of Rights relies on U.S. courts acting according to the underlying principles of those documents, even 200 years after they were written.

Further Reading and Resources

Primary Case: *Palmer v. Thompson*, 403 U.S. 217 (1971).

Gordon Parks: Segregation Story by Gordon Parks (photographer) (Göttingen, Germany: Steidl, 2015).

Miles to Go for Freedom: Segregation and Civil Rights in the Jim Crow Years by Linda Barnett Osborne (New York: Abrams, 2012).

"Race, Rights, and the Thirteenth Amendment: Defining the Badges and Incidents of Slavery" by William M. Carter Jr., 40 *University of California Davis Law Review* 1311 (April 2007).

"Segregation: A Modern Problem for Public Schools in the South," Grace Chen, www.publicschoolreview.com (blog), (2010).

CASE 15

Ernesto Miranda v. Arizona (1966)

Key Issue: Criminal Rights
What are your rights when taken into custody or deprived of your freedom in any significant way by the police?

Many Supreme Court cases are about finding the proper balance between the rights of different people or groups. In the *Miranda* case, the Court was tasked with weighing the constitutional rights of an individual taken into police custody with the rights of officers and other authorities to do their job most effectively. Are people in custody protected by the Fifth Amendment from incriminating themselves?

> **The Fifth Amendment states in part:** *"Nor shall any person be compelled in any criminal case to be a witness against himself."*

In this case, the Court needed to distinguish legitimate and necessary forms of questioning suspects from practices that may impair a suspect's ability to make a rational choice. It also needed to determine how important it was to inform a suspect of his or her rights before the questioning process and if not doing so would invalidate any confessions made during the interview.

> ## IN OTHER WORDS
>
> "The quality of a nation's civilization can be largely measured by the methods it uses in the enforcement of its criminal law."

> —Chief Justice Earl Warren, *Miranda v. Arizona* (1966)

The case named *Miranda* actually consolidated four cases involving police pressure during the interrogations, but the decision was announced under one defendant's name: Ernesto Miranda.

Facts of the Case

In March 1963, an eighteen-year-old woman in Phoenix, Arizona, was walking home from the movie theater where she worked when a car pulled up and a man got out and grabbed her. He forced her into the backseat of the car where he tied her hands and feet, held a sharp object to her neck, and told her not to scream. He said that he would not hurt her. He drove to another location where he raped her.

When the woman got away, she ran home and told her family what happened. The police were called, and they arrested twenty-two-year-old Ernesto Miranda a week later. He was taken to the police station, where the victim identified him in a lineup. Then two police officers interrogated him for two hours in a windowless room. They did not tell him that he could have a lawyer present. He signed a written confession that was used at trial. Miranda was convicted of kidnapping and rape, and sentenced to twenty to thirty years in prison.

Miranda appealed the conviction, claiming his confession should not have been used against him at trial since he was not told that he had a right to a lawyer or the right to remain silent.

The Court's Ruling and Reasoning

Miranda is about "custodial interrogation," that is, questioning by the police after a person has been taken into custody (arrested) or otherwise deprived of his or her freedom in any significant way. In determining whether a statement was given to police voluntarily, the Court considered a number of factors: threats, food or sleep deprivation, extended interrogation, and contact with an attorney or loved one (such as a spouse or parent, for example).

The Court ruled 5–4 in favor of the individuals taken into police custody. The governing principles of *Miranda* are that suspects be warned before questioning that they have the right to remain silent, that any statement they make may be used as evidence against them, and that they have a right to a lawyer before questioning begins (today, this is commonly referred to as the *Miranda* warnings). If a person can't afford a lawyer, one will be appointed to represent him or her. A person can waive (give up) these rights, but it must be a clear, intelligent waiver. That is, it needs to be clear that the person understands the warnings given by the police. Generally, police end the reading of a suspect's rights by asking, "Do you understand your rights?"

These became new protections (guaranteed rights) for people in custody, and are now required in all states. Before *Miranda*, it had been up to individual states to apply all, some, or none of these precautions when interrogating suspects who were in custody.

The Fifth Amendment protects every person against self-incrimination. In other words, criminal justice demands that the government produce the evidence against a person by its own independent labors rather than solely from the mouth of the suspect. The privilege against self-incrimination is an essential element of America's judicial system. In order for a confession to be admissible against a defendant at trial, the suspect must have given it freely, knowing the potential consequences, and without being pressured by the police. Once in police custody, a suspect must be advised of his rights before being questioned.

The Court Speaks

"One of our Nation's most cherished principles is that an individual may not be compelled to incriminate himself."

The majority opinion expresses concern with the atmosphere of police interrogations. They were referred to as "menacing procedures" in an unfamiliar police station. Chief Justice Earl Warren wrote that the officers failed to set up appropriate safeguards at the beginning of the interrogation to ensure that the statements were "truly the product of free choice" and voluntarily given without physical coercion or psychological ploys.

> ## IN OTHER WORDS
>
> **"These precious rights were fixed in our Constitution only after centuries of persecution and struggle."**
> —Chief Justice Earl Warren, *Miranda v. Arizona* (1966)

Lawyers need to be present during interrogations to make sure that any statement the suspect gives is made freely—that is, it is not coerced or dragged out of the person. Suspects have a right to have a lawyer before questioning even if they can't afford to hire a lawyer. The right against self-incrimination applies to all individuals, regardless of income. If a person states that he or she wants an attorney, the interrogation must stop until an attorney is present.

In addition, at trial the prosecutor may not mention that a suspect remained silent or chose not to give a statement in order to avoid self-incrimination. In the Court's majority opinion in this case, Chief Justice Earl Warren wrote, "Any evidence that the accused was threatened, tricked, or cajoled into a waiver will, of course, show that the defendant did not voluntarily waive his privilege." The Supreme Court wrote in *Miranda* that "Crime is contagious. If the Government becomes a lawbreaker, it breeds contempt for law; it invites every man to become a law unto himself; it invites anarchy."

IN OTHER WORDS

"**If you use your fists, you are not so likely to use your wits.**"
—Chief Justice Earl Warren, *Miranda v. Arizona* (1966)

The four justices who dissented from the majority believed that voluntary confessions should be admissible in court even if suspects were not warned of their rights. In the dissenting opinion, Justice John M. Harlan wrote that the Fifth Amendment privilege against self-incrimination does not apply "to the police station—that police questioning may inherently entail some pressure on the suspect and may seek advantage in his ignorance or weaknesses." They pointed out that, historically, the privilege was designed to prevent a court or judicial officer from pressuring suspects, not the police investigating a crime. They felt there was not enough evidence that police brutality regularly occurred in interrogations, that it was not a universal practice, and that the decision of the majority "represents poor constitutional law with harmful consequences." The new rules announced under *Miranda*, they wrote, would frustrate law enforcement and "markedly decrease the number of confessions."

Miranda was later retried, convicted by a jury, and again sentenced to twenty to thirty years in prison.

What if...?

If Ernesto Miranda had lost his case and it was determined that the Fifth Amendment does not require any warnings or precautions before questioning a suspect, each state could decide how to conduct police interrogations. People placed under arrest could be subjected to lengthy (hours or days) of interrogation without food, water, sleep, or any contact with a lawyer or loved one.

Do you believe that false confessions or admissions of guilt by an innocent person would be a problem? Even though *Miranda* warnings are now required before custodial interrogations, false confessions continue to occur at concerning rates. For example, according to the Innocence Project (www.InnocenceProject.org), one out of four wrongful convictions where the person was eventually found not guilty through DNA evidence involved a false confession or statement.

Related Cases

As mentioned in Case I *(Miller v. Alabama)*, two criminal justice systems exist in the United States: one for adults and one for juveniles. What the Supreme Court decided in *Miranda* applied only to adults who were in police custody. One year after the *Miranda* decision, the Court revisited the issue of police interrogations but this time as applied to juveniles. In the *Gault* case that follows, the Court needed to decide whether to extend the *Miranda* warnings to juveniles in police custody. The other cases deal with the use of *Miranda* rights when a minor volunteers to be interviewed and what exceptions to these warnings are allowed.

DOES THE RIGHT AGAINST SELF-INCRIMINATION APPLY TO JUVENILES?

In re Gault (1967)

Gerald Francis Gault was fifteen years old when he was arrested in Globe, Arizona, after a neighbor complained about receiving obscene phone calls. Gault was on **probation** at the time for an earlier offense. His parents weren't called, nor was Gault informed of any rights, including his right against self-incrimination. Following two **delinquency hearings** before a juvenile court judge where he was unrepresented by an attorney and where the neighbor failed to appear, he was found guilty and sent to the state industrial (reform) school until age twenty-one. The Supreme Court reversed his conviction and sentence, ruling that his due process rights had been violated. He wasn't able to face his accuser in court, was not given legal assistance, and his parents weren't notified of the charges against him.

Gault applied the principles announced in *Miranda* to juveniles. The Court wrote, "The greatest care must be taken to assure that the admission [of a juvenile] is voluntary, in the sense not only that it has not been coerced or suggested, but also that it is not the product of ignorance of rights or of adolescent fantasy, fright, or despair."

WHAT HAPPENS TO MIRANDA RIGHTS WHEN A JUVENILE INITIATES CONTACT WITH THE POLICE?

People v. T.C. (1995)

The statements of an eleven-year-old boy who contacted the police about a murder were determined to be inadmissible at trial. When T.C. was interrogated a second time he wasn't given his *Miranda* warnings nor were his parents present during questioning. The court concluded that the circumstances of the interrogation would lead a reasonable person in T.C.'s situation to feel that "he had no choice but to stay and listen to the officer."

IS THERE A PUBLIC SAFETY EXCEPTION TO THE MIRANDA RULE?

New York v. Quarles (1984)

After a rape victim gave police a description of her attacker, Benjamin Quarles was stopped and frisked in a nearby supermarket. The officer discovered an empty shoulder holster. When asked where the gun was, Quarles stated "the gun is over there" nodding toward some empty cartons. The officer retrieved the gun, placed Quarles under arrest, and read him his *Miranda* rights.

Since Quarles was not informed of his *Miranda* rights at the outset, the trial court excluded his statements and the gun itself from being used as evidence at trial. The state appealed, citing a public safety exception to the *Miranda* rule. In a 5–4 decision, the Supreme Court found in favor of the state, holding that "This case presents a situation where concerns for public safety must be paramount."

Did You Know?

The debate about the suspension of the *Miranda* warnings in the interest of public safety and intelligence gathering continues. Dzhokhar Tsarnaev was the nineteen-year-old suspect in the Boston Marathon bombings in 2013. He was interrogated for sixteen hours before he was given his Miranda warnings, under a public safety exception that applies when investigating the possibility of additional attacks. Whether *Miranda* was violated and whether Tsarnaev's statements were legally admissible was, at first, a point of dispute in the government's case against him. However, at trial, the prosecution chose not to introduce the statements in question. In 2015, Tsarnaev was convicted of all counts and sentenced to death.

Talk, Think, and Take Action

- What do you think about the Miranda requirement that you be advised of your rights before being interrogated by the police if in their custody? In what ways does this seem like an important right? Or, conversely, not that important? Some people think that if you're not guilty of anything, then there's no reason to fear that you'll make a false confession. What do you think? Have you ever been questioned by your parents or a teacher and taken responsibility for something you didn't do in order to help out a sibling or friend? If so, what happened? What are some reasons you think false confessions might occur?

- Do you agree with the public safety exception the Court announced in the *Quarles* case? Consider situations where the police might be justified in questioning suspects before telling them about their *Miranda* rights. Talk about this with your friends or family.

- If you were being questioned at school by the principal or a school resource officer, would you feel free to get up and walk out? *Miranda* does not apply to school officials, but do you think it should apply to your school's resource officer? What difference does it make if you're in "custody" or not? What difference does it make if the resource officer is in uniform or not?
- If you are passionate about the law and how it affects your life, consider starting a local chapter of the National Youth Rights Association (NYRA) or beginning your own youth rights club at school or online. NYRA is a youth-led civil rights group that advocates for the rights and liberties of young people. To learn more, visit www.youthrights.org. Creating a teen rights group on Facebook or another social media platform could be another great way to build a following and share ideas about important youth rights issues, not just locally, but nationally.
- What if you and your friends are stopped by a police officer while hanging out at the park or walking down the street? Would you feel free to leave if the officer began to ask you basic questions about what you're doing, where you're going, and so on? You wouldn't be in "custody," so the officer would not be required to read you your rights. Know that if you're unsure about what is happening,

> you can always ask an officer in a polite way, "Officer, am I being detained?" That would help you know for sure whether you are free to leave or not. What if an officer asked to see some form of identification? Are you required to provide it? As a minor, you may not have an identification card, especially if you are not driving yet. To know and protect your rights, research the rules that apply to these situations and discuss them with your friends and classmates.

Closing Comments

Why should the Fifth Amendment be important to you? In short, it protects against abuse by law enforcement. Since police interrogations are by nature designed to persuade a person to confess, the Fifth Amendment requires warnings before questioning begins. Otherwise any statements given during an interrogation that occurs when a person is in custody cannot be used in court against him or her.

Since the *Gault* decision applying the *Miranda* warnings to juveniles, courts and state legislatures have recognized additional rights and responsibilities of minors. Laws have been passed addressing both criminal and civil actions involving those who are under eighteen. For example, juveniles who are found guilty of crimes may be ordered to pay restitution to victims, perform community service, undergo random drug testing, or attend counseling sessions. However, if locked up, juveniles retain certain rights, including the right to an education.

Additional rights allow minors, under certain circumstances, to get help for problems such as drug abuse, medical care, and abortions without their parents' knowledge or consent, but with the approval of a judge. Minors of a certain age also have a right to appear and speak at court hearings involving them, as well as agree to their adoption if they are over age twelve, for example. And emancipation laws exist in some states for minors who meet the strict requirements spelled out in the law.

State laws differ on these subjects. You can check what the laws are in your state by conducting an Internet search of the name of your state and the issue you're interested in.

Further Reading and Resources

Primary Case: *Miranda v. Arizona*, 384 U.S. 436 (1966).

"Empty Promises: *Miranda* Warnings in Noncustodial Interrogations" by Aurora Maoz, 110 *Michigan Law Review* 1309 (May 2012).

Miranda: The Story of America's Right to Remain Silent by Gary L. Stuart (Tucson: University of Arizona Press, 2008).

Miranda v. Arizona: *Rights of the Accused* by Gail Blasser Riley (New York: Enslow Publishers, 1994).

"The United States Supreme Court Adopts a Reasonable Juvenile Standard in *J.D.B. v. North Carolina* for Purposes of the *Miranda* Custody Analysis: Can a More Reasoned Justice System for Juveniles Be Far Behind?" by Marsha L. Levick and Elizabeth-Ann Tierney, 47 *Harvard Civil Rights—Civil Liberties Law Review* 501 (2012).

"You Have the Right to Remain Thirteen: Considering Age in Juvenile Interrogations in *J.D.B. v. North Carolina*" by Nicole J. Ettinger, 60 *Buffalo Law Review* 559 (April 2012).

Additional Supreme Court 5–4 Decisions

The cases we've explored so far are not the only important Supreme Court cases that were decided by one vote. Subjects ranging from DNA cheek swabs to adoption and same-sex marriage have been considered by the Court and have also been decided narrowly. In this section, you'll find some of these cases and learn how the justices ruled.

Digging Deeper

As you read about the cases that follow, consider their meaning and implications. Do any of them matter directly to you? Which of the issues discussed do you feel strongly about, and why? Imagine how you, your family, your friends, and others might have been affected if one vote had been cast the other way in each case, leading to a different decision.

These cases are presented chronologically, with the most recent first. For more information, you can read the Court's full opinion in each case by visiting the Supreme Court's website at www.supremecourt.gov/opinions/opinions.aspx.

DO YOU HAVE ANY PRIVACY RIGHTS AS A CUSTOMER (OR OWNER) OF A HOTEL OR MOTEL?

City of Los Angeles v. Patel (2015)

In Los Angeles, California, a city law allowed the police to inspect the hotel records of any customer without a search warrant, and made it a misdemeanor for a hotel owner to fail or refuse to cooperate. Under this law, information available to the police included the guest's name and address; the number of people in the guest's party; the make, model, and license plate number of any vehicle that belonged to the guest parked on hotel property; the guest's date and time of arrival and scheduled departure date; the room number assigned to the guest; the rate charged and amount collected for the room; and the method of payment.

The Supreme Court ruled that the inspection of hotel records without a warrant or without giving the hotel owner a chance to obtain a neutral decision maker's ruling first was inconsistent with the Fourth Amendment's privacy expectation. In other words, the justices said that if a hotel owner objected to releasing information to the police, he or she should be allowed to obtain a second opinion from a local court or judge before further action was taken.

DOES THE FOURTEENTH AMENDMENT REQUIRE A STATE TO ALLOW SAME-SEX MARRIAGES?

Obergefell v. Hodges (2015)

Sixteen cases from Michigan, Kentucky, Ohio, and Tennessee challenged their states' definition of marriage as a union between one man and one woman. The petitioners were fourteen samesex couples and two men whose same-sex partners are deceased. James Obergefell was the first petitioner, and the Court's decision is known as the *Obergefell* case. Obergefell's partner died before the decision was announced in June 2015.

In this split decision, the Supreme Court came down on the side of marriage equality. The majority ruled that all people should be treated equal, and that same-sex couples have a fundamental, constitutional right to get married. The ruling effectively threw out existing state laws banning same-sex marriage. Justice Anthony Kennedy wrote for the majority, "The nature of marriage is that, through its enduring bond, two persons together can find other freedoms, such as expression, intimacy, and spirituality. This is true for all persons, whatever their sexual orientation."

ARE PRIVATE COMPANIES' HEALTHCARE PLANS REQUIRED TO COVER EMPLOYEES' CONTRACEPTIVES?

Burwell v. Hobby Lobby Stores (2014)

No. The Court ruled that some for-profit businesses may refuse to provide healthcare coverage that includes certain drugs or devices used to prevent pregnancy. The Court recognized the right of companies to hold religious beliefs against contraception. Companies can apply for an exemption from the contraception provision of the Affordable Care Act.

HOW DOES IQ AFFECT THE USE OF THE DEATH PENALTY?

Hall v. Florida (2014)

Freddie Lee Hall had an IQ of 71 and was convicted of murder. Under Florida law, he was sentenced to death since his IQ was over 70, the state's cutoff for the death penalty. The Supreme Court ruled that such a dividing line is too rigid. Instead, the Court said that such decisions should be made on a case-by-case basis. Justice Anthony M. Kennedy wrote that "intellectual disability is a condition, not a number" and that Florida's law "contravenes our nation's commitment to dignity." Hall remains in prison pending further evaluation and hearings on his mental state.

In a similar case in 2015, the Supreme Court voted 5–4 to send the question back to the trial court to determine if a convicted murderer with an IQ of 75 was intellectually disabled and therefore ineligible to be put to death. (*Brumfield v. Cain*, 135 S.Ct. 2269)

IS PRAYER ALLOWED AT PUBLIC MEETINGS?

Town of Greece v. Galloway (2014)

The town of Greece, New York, opened its public meetings with a prayer. Mostly Christian prayers were said but prayers from other faiths were added once the town's policy was challenged. The Court affirmed the practice, recognizing that "prayer is part of the nation's fabric, not a violation of the First Amendment." It also said, "Our tradition assumes that adult citizens, firm in their own beliefs, can tolerate and perhaps appreciate a ceremonial prayer delivered by a person of a different faith." However, the Court was careful to specify, "Our Government is prohibited from prescribing prayers to be recited in our public institutions in order to promote a preferred system of belief or code of moral behavior."

IS A FEDERAL BAN ON SAME-SEX MARRIAGE CONSTITUTIONAL?

United States v. Edie Windsor (2013)

The Court determined that the federal Defense of Marriage Act (DOMA) passed in 1996 was unconstitutional. DOMA allowed states to refuse to recognize same-sex marriages performed in other states. This, in turn, deprived same-sex couples of social security survivor's benefits, joint tax returns, and other federal benefits.

When the Court struck down this law, it gave homosexual federal employees the right to receive the same benefits as heterosexual couples. This includes healthcare benefits, pension payments, and insurance and tax benefits.

SHOULD RESTRICTIONS PLACED ON CERTAIN VOTING DISTRICTS FORTY YEARS AGO TO REDUCE DISCRIMINATION REMAIN IN PLACE?

Shelby County, Alabama v. Holder (2013)

The Voting Rights Act of 1965 required certain state and county governments with a history of discrimination to get approval from the federal government before making any changes to their voting laws. Due to improvements in these states, the Court sent the case back to Congress to reassess whether the federal oversight was still needed, based on current statistics of voting discrimination. Congress has yet to act on this mandate.

CAN A WORKPLACE BE HELD ACCOUNTABLE WHEN DISCRIMINATION OCCURS BETWEEN COWORKERS?

Maetta Vance v. Ball State University (2013)

Maetta Vance was the only African-American employee in Ball State University's catering department. She filed a lawsuit against the university claiming racial harassment by a coworker. The Supreme Court limited workplace discrimination lawsuits to supervisors who had the authority to hire, fire, promote, transfer, or discipline employees. Since Vance's lawsuit was against a coworker who did not have the power to affect Vance's status as an employee, the lawsuit was dismissed.

IF A SUSPECT ANSWERS SOME QUESTIONS DURING A POLICE INTERROGATION, HAS HE OR SHE WAIVED THE RIGHT TO REMAIN SILENT?

Salinas v. Texas (2013)

If you are arrested for a crime, the Fifth Amendment allows you to remain silent when interrogated by the police and not become a witness against yourself.

Genovevo Salinas was being questioned by a police officer, though he was not in custody and was not advised of his *Miranda* rights. He voluntarily answered some of the police officer's questions about a murder, but stopped talking when asked if his shotgun would match the shell casings found at the crime scene. At his trial, the prosecutor wanted to use Salinas's failure to answer the question as evidence against him but his attorney argued that his silence was protected by his Fifth Amendment right against self-incrimination. The Court ruled the evidence was admissible since Salinas had in effect waived his right to remain silent by answering some of the questions and not claiming the Fifth Amendment. Remaining mute when questioned by the police does not automatically invoke the protection of the Fifth Amendment—the suspect must actually say he or she wants this protection.

CAN POLICE CONDUCT A SEARCH BY CHEEK SWAB WITHOUT A WARRANT?

Maryland v. King (2013)

Alonzo Jay King Jr. was arrested and charged with first and second degree assault. As a part of Maryland's arrest process for violent suspects, a sample of King's DNA was taken by swabbing the inside of his cheek. When his DNA was entered into the state database, it matched a sample from an unsolved rape case. With this evidence against him, King was charged and convicted of first degree rape and sentenced to life in prison. King appealed, arguing that collecting his DNA amounted to a warrantless search that invaded his privacy, in violation of the Fourth Amendment, and that it should not have been allowed as evidence.

The Supreme Court ruled in favor of the state, holding that swabbing someone's cheek at arrest does not violate the Fourth Amendment because doing so serves a legitimate state interest and is not so invasive as to require a search warrant. They compared it to taking a suspect's fingerprints.

> **Did You Know?**
>
> Since the first challenge on the use of fingerprinting suspects was made in 1932, courts have consistently allowed for the use of fingerprints as evidence in criminal cases. Indeed, they have become an accepted part of booking someone who has been arrested and have not been found to violate the Fourth Amendment. (*U.S. v. Kelly*, 1932)
>
> Then in 2013, the Supreme Court stated in a case concerning DNA samples, *Maryland v. King*, that fingerprinting is accepted as a "widely known and frequently practiced" method of identifying persons charged with a crime.

IS IT CONSTITUTIONAL TO REQUIRE PEOPLE TO HAVE HEALTH INSURANCE?

State of Florida v. U.S. Department of Health and Human Services (2012)

This case about what is commonly known as "Obamacare" stemmed from the Patient Protection and Affordable Care Act (referred to as the ACA) that went into effect in 2010. The Supreme Court ruled that the Act was constitutional, including its mandate that everyone have health insurance by 2014. Those not covered would be taxed.

The ACA included an "individual mandate" requiring everyone over eighteen to purchase healthcare. Opponents of the ACA argued that the mandate violated Congress's power under the Commerce Clause by forcing individuals to buy a commodity or service. The Supreme Court considered the mandate a "tax" on those who didn't have health insurance and determined it was therefore constitutional.

DOES A PERSON HAVE THE RIGHT TO SUE OVER AN ISSUE OR LAW THAT DOES NOT AFFECT HIM OR HER?

Arizona Christian School Tuition Organization v. Winn (2011)

There is a concept in law called "standing," which means the right to sue. You can file a lawsuit against someone if you have been wronged or suffered harm in some manner by their actions. However, simply disagreeing with a certain policy or law doesn't give you *standing* to file a lawsuit to change or abolish it. Before considering a case and its merits, the Supreme

Court must first determine if standing exists in the case.

In the *Winn* case, plaintiffs challenged the constitutionality of a state's tuition tax credit program. The Court dismissed their lawsuit because the four plaintiffs did not participate in the program and were, therefore, not affected by it. In other words, the plaintiffs did not have standing to move forward with the lawsuit.

In *Hollingsworth v. Perry*, a 5–4 decision in 2013, the Court dismissed the case since the plaintiffs weren't directly affected by the state's ban on same-sex marriages and therefore lacked standing.

DO CORPORATIONS HAVE THE RIGHT TO FREE SPEECH?

Citizens United v. Federal Election Commission (2010)

In this case the Court decided that the First Amendment right to political speech applies to corporations and labor unions. They are allowed to spend their own money to support or oppose candidates through TV ads or printed materials, for example. However, donations are limited to organizations or political action committees, not to individual candidates.

> **Did You Know?**
>
> During the 2014 midterm elections, an estimated $3 billion was spent on political TV ads.

DO PEOPLE CONVICTED OF A CRIME HAVE A RIGHT TO ACCESS DNA EVIDENCE WHEN NEW TESTING METHODS BECOME AVAILABLE?

District Attorney's Office v. Osborne (2009)

William Osborne was convicted of kidnapping and sexual assault. He was sentenced to prison for twenty-six years. After new DNA testing methods became available, he requested that the biological evidence from his case be analyzed using the latest testing technologies. The Supreme Court ruled 5–4 that there is no constitutional right to obtain access to the state's evidence for DNA testing after a conviction—particularly one that included a confession.

HOW DOES FREE SPEECH APPLY TO ON-AIR PROFANITY?

FCC v. Fox Television Stations (2009) and *FCC v. Fox Television Stations* (2012)

A "fleeting expletive" is a swear word dropped during conversation or speech. Certain expletives, especially when said on television, have been controversial for some time. But is swearing that is broadcast into homes protected by the First Amendment?

The Federal Communications Commission (FCC) has the power to regulate profane speech in broadcast television (but not on satellite or cable TV). Typically, the commission allowed occasional swearing and only banned the repeated use of profane and obscene language during family viewing time (morning through early evening hours). In addition, several words are never allowed on broadcast television and would likely draw a fine from the FCC. However, after several stars, including Cher, Nicole Ritchie, and Bono, swore during award shows in 2002 and 2003, the FCC said it would fine the networks involved for not bleeping these words out of the broadcast. Fox challenged the FCC's new policy in court, arguing that it was too vague and broad and that they had not been warned of the change. Further, Fox said the commission should not have the right to prohibit free speech.

This case actually made its way to the Supreme Court twice. In a 5–4 decision in 2009, the justices ruled that the FCC could lawfully fine broadcasters for occasional swearing even though they had not given notice to the TV stations of the policy change. The Court did not rule on the First Amendment issue, instead sending the case back to the Second Circuit Court of Appeals. The appeals court ruled in favor of Fox, stating that the new FCC policy was unconstitutional. The FCC, in turn, appealed to the Supreme Court. And, in 2012, the Court was unanimous in finding that the TV broadcasters should have received notice that the policy was changing before fines were imposed (due process) and that the FCC's rules were too vague to enforce. The Court did uphold the FCC's authority to set decency standards for broadcasters but again declined to rule on whether a specific policy was constitutional.

DURING WHAT TIME FRAME MUST CONFESSIONS BE MADE BY SUSPECTS IN ORDER TO BE ADMISSIBLE IN COURT?

Corley v. United States **(2009)**

By law, someone arrested for a federal crime must be taken before a judicial officer as soon as possible. If the person confesses to a crime after being in custody for at least six hours, the confession cannot be used in federal court even if voluntarily made. This prevents lengthy or secretive questioning by the police.

Johnnie Corley was held and questioned for twenty-nine hours, during which time he voluntarily confessed. Then he was taken before a magistrate. He was eventually convicted of armed bank robbery and conspiracy, but appealed because his confession was not made within the six-hour window. The Supreme Court ruled that even voluntary confessions needed to be made within the specified time limit. However, the Court did not have enough evidence to determine if the confession was made within the time limit or whether any delay had been reasonable and acceptable under the circumstances. Consequently, the Court sent the case back to the lower court.

DO RESTRICTIONS ON GUN USE VIOLATE THE SECOND AMENDMENT?

District of Columbia v. Heller (2008)

In 1976, the District of Columbia passed a law that banned certain guns—including sawed-off shotguns and machine guns—required people to get licenses for all pistols, and mandated that all legal firearms be kept unloaded and disassembled or trigger locked. A group of private gun owners sued the district, arguing that the law violated their right to bear arms, as guaranteed in the Second Amendment.

The issue was whether the Second Amendment applied only to militias, such as the National Guard, or to private citizens as well. Can someone who is not in a state or regulated militia keep handguns and other firearms for private use in their homes?

The Court ruled 5–4 that the Second Amendment protects the right of individuals in the District of Columbia to possess a firearm within one's home. Two years later, in *McDonald v. Chicago*, the Court extended the ruling to apply throughout the United States. These two decisions do not prohibit all reasonable gun control laws, however. State and federal restrictions on gun possession by felons, the mentally ill, and in schools and government buildings remain intact.

In 2015, the Supreme Court declined to review two lower court decisions that required gun owners to secure their weapons at home and banned assault weapons and large-capacity magazines (over ten bullets). Consequently, the laws remain in effect.

CAN A CONVICTED RAPIST BE SENTENCED TO DEATH?

Kennedy v. Louisiana (2008)

Patrick Kennedy was convicted of aggravated rape of his eight-year-old stepdaughter and sentenced to death. The Supreme Court found that Louisiana's law allowing the death penalty for raping a child under age twelve years violated the Eighth Amendment. The death penalty in the United States is restricted to cases of murder and treason.

DOES PROPERTY TAKEN BY EMINENT DOMAIN ALWAYS NEED TO BE USED FOR PUBLIC USE?

Kelo v. City of New London (2005)

The phrase "eminent domain" means the right of the government to take private property for public purpose, for example, a neighborhood of homes in order to build a hospital, library, or highway. The Supreme Court considered a challenge to eminent domain in this case where private property was taken by the city to turn over to another private party to develop. The

Court deferred to local officials to determine what constitutes public use.

In her dissent, Justice Sandra Day O'Connor wrote, "Under the banner of economic development, all private property is now vulnerable to being taken and transferred to another private owner, so long as it might be upgraded—i.e., given to an owner who will use it in a way that the legislature deems more beneficial to the public."

DID THE FLORIDA SUPREME COURT OVERSTEP ITS AUTHORITY BY MAKING NEW ELECTION LAW?

Bush v. Gore **(2000)**

In this case, the Florida Supreme Court ordered a recount of 9,000 votes in one county, and a recount of all ballots statewide that did not indicate a vote for president (called under-votes). In a 5–4 vote, the U.S. Supreme Court stopped the recount, finding that the state's method of recounting ballots was unconstitutional and that election laws are up to the legislature, not state courts.

IN OTHER WORDS

"The right to vote is fundamental, and one source of its fundamental nature

> **lies in the equal weight accorded to each vote and the equal dignity owed to each voter."**
> —from the Supreme Court ruling in *Bush v. Gore*

The Court's ruling regarding the 2000 presidential election continues to be debated, including the question of whether the Court should have been involved in the first place. In 2013, Justice Sandra Day O'Connor commented, "Maybe the Court should have said, 'We're not going to take it, goodbye.'" Justice John Paul Stevens wrote a powerful dissent in the case, which included this statement: "Although we may never know with complete certainty the identity of the winner of this year's Presidential election, the identity of the loser is perfectly clear. It is the Nation's confidence in the judge as an impartial guardian of the rule of law." (For more information on the election process, see section entitled "The Election Process".)

DO SAME-SEX COUPLES HAVE A FUNDAMENTAL RIGHT UNDER THE CONSTITUTION TO ENGAGE

IN CONSENSUAL SEXUAL INTERCOURSE?

Bowers v. Hardwick (1986) and Lawrence v. Texas (2003)

When considering this question in the *Bowers* case of 1986, the Court said no, and ruled 5–4 that states had the right to outlaw "homosexual sodomy." Seventeen years later, the Court reversed itself and overruled *Bowers*. In *Lawrence v. Texas* (2003), the Court, in a 6–3 vote, overturned the convictions of John Lawrence and Tyron Garner for "deviate sexual intercourse" under Texas law. Justice Anthony Kennedy wrote: "Same sex couples ... are entitled to respect for their private lives." He added, "The state cannot demean their existence or control their destiny by making their private sexual conduct a crime."

IS A MINIMUM WAGE CONSTITUTIONAL?

Adkins v. Children's Hospital (1923) and West Coast Hotel Company v. Parrish (1937)

In 1918, Congress passed a law that guaranteed a minimum wage in the District of Columbia for women and children workers. The law was intended to protect women and children from work conditions that may damage their health and morals. In a 5–4 vote, the Supreme Court found the law to be unconstitutional due to its vagueness and said that it extended the police power of the state. Fourteen years later, the Court reversed itself in another 5–4 decision. In *West Coast Hotel Company v. Parrish* (1937), the Court ruled that it was constitutional to establish minimum wages for women.

Did You Know?

The Fair Labor Standards Act of 1938 set a national minimum wage, guaranteed time-and-a-half for overtime in certain jobs, and banned hiring minors for dangerous jobs. The eight-hour day and forty-hour work week were established and children under sixteen were prohibited from work during school hours.

Talk, Think, and Take Action

• Consider what life might be like for you and your family if some of the cases in this section had been decided differently. That could have easily happened, since each case was decided by one vote. Had one of the nine justices voted differently and tipped the balance the other way, consider this:

* Prayer at public meetings would be prohibited.

* Contraceptives would be available from all employer health plans with no exceptions.

* DNA evidence would be lost if the collection of cheek swabs was limited.

* The federal government would be legally able to deny benefits to same-sex couples.

* National healthcare would not be available for the sixteen million individuals (as of June 2015) currently enrolled.

• Discuss these issues with your friends and parents. It's important to gather information, share your opinion, and listen to the ideas of others. The more informed you are, the better able you are to make sound decisions not just about how to vote, which candidates to support, and what political causes you might want to get involved with, but also how to deal with some of life's daily challenges.

Closing Comments

The cases in this section represent the variety of issues the Supreme Court faces each term. Some of the cases seem to present a clear question calling for a simple "yes" or "no" answer. However, that's rarely the reality. The issues must be studied with the Constitution and the Bill of Rights in mind. Since the late 1700s when the Constitution was written, of course, the United States has changed and continues to change. These two documents, however, remain the foundation of our democracy and judicial system. The work of the Supreme Court in applying established principles to twenty-first-century life in the United States goes on.

> ### IN OTHER WORDS
>
> "In an election, every voice is equally powerful—don't underestimate your vote. Voting is the great equalizer. Your vote is not only important. It is imperative."
> —Maya Angelou, American poet

A Final Word

The cases in this book exemplify the power of one person to act and thereby influence over 300 million Americans. The same can be said about participating in elections. Every vote matters if our nation is to remain a democracy with liberty and justice for all.

If you're still not convinced that *your* voice can make a significant difference, consider the following examples of individuals who changed the world:

- Nicholas Lowinger of Rhode Island started the Gotta Have Sole Foundation when he was fifteen. Since 2010, they have provided over 23,000 pairs of shoes to children living in homeless shelters in thirty-five states. Nicholas was recognized in 2013 as a Young Wonder by CNN Heroes.
- Malala Yousafzai began speaking out about education for girls in Pakistan when she was eleven. Three years later, she was shot in the head by the Taliban because of her advocacy. She survived the attack and continues her mission on behalf of girls everywhere. In 2014, she won the Nobel Peace Prize at the age of seventeen, making her the youngest Nobel laureate in history.

- Wael Ghonim, age twenty-nine, was working at Google when he created a Facebook page that stimulated the first protests in Egypt in 2011. Twitter and Facebook were used extensively throughout the civil uprisings and demonstrations in the Arab world calling for democratic reforms (referred to as the Arab Spring).
- Nujood Ali was a child when her father arranged for her to marry a man three times her age. His abuse led her to become the first child-bride in Yemen to obtain a divorce—at age ten, setting an example for other girls in her situation. She tells her story in the book *I Am Nujood, Age 10 and Divorced*.
- In 2014, Kyle Tucker attended a charter school in Arizona. The school sits on private property managed by a condominium association. The sixteen-year-old Boy Scout was working on his project to become an Eagle Scout. His project was simple: Raise enough money to place a flagpole on his school's property. The association, however, told him he would need to pay for a $650,000 insurance policy to protect the building's owners from potential damage. Through the power of social media, Kyle convinced the association to allow him to

install the flagpole. Supporters donated the materials and labor.
- Matt Petronis was away at college when Hurricane Sandy hit the East Coast in 2012. His neighborhood of Breezy Point, New York, was devastated. Matt went to work setting up an online fundraiser. He ran the website and organized volunteers. His foundation raised more than $1 million for Sandy victims and Matt's hometown.

One person with inspiration and perseverance can improve the world. Let that person be you. And remember that one way you can bring about change is to express yourself through the voting booth. All you have to do is register to vote and get to the polls on Election Day. This is a right and a privilege that should not be ignored or wasted.

You can participate in the community in many other ways besides voting. If you feel strongly about something, or just want to make a difference and contribute some of your time to a worthy cause, consider the following:
- Volunteer at a local rescue shelter for animals.
- Get involved with scouting or with youth activities at your place of worship.
- Join the teen club at the public library.
- Volunteer at a food bank or soup kitchen.

- Look into literacy programs and become a tutor or teen mentor for other teens in need of help.
- Volunteer for one of the numerous national programs that promote healthy living, such as Girls on the Run or Michelle Obama's Let's Move program to fight childhood obesity.

> ### IN OTHER WORDS
> "Those who stay away from the election think that one vote will do no good. 'Tis but one step more to think one vote will do no harm."
> —Ralph Waldo Emerson

Wherever your interests lie, there's an organization that can use your help. Or, like some of the teens mentioned in this book, you can start your own organization and put your ideas to work. Whatever you decide to do, you and others will reap the benefits in many ways.

Talk, Think, and Take Action

- The cases in this book feature people who decided to take a stand on an issue that impacted their lives. They pursued their cause to effect change over years of litigation. Think about how your life might be different if they had chosen to accept the status quo and not challenge the system. Consider, for example, if Gerald Gault had not challenged his conviction. Children and teenagers could still be treated more like property of their parents—they wouldn't have a right to an attorney to represent them or the right to remain silent and not incriminate themselves.

• Is there an issue that you feel strongly about? How could you take a stand? Consider looking into an Explorer Program if your high school or community has one. These programs connect you with lawyers, law enforcement, and other professionals who mentor students and introduce you to various aspects of their profession. If you're interested in law, for example, you will meet with lawyers, judges, and others in the court system. You'll also have the chance to observe a variety of court proceedings. For more information, visit exploring.learningforlife.org.

• Now that you have finished *Every Vote Matters*, it's time to think about even more ways that you can help improve your school, community, country, and beyond. As you have read, there are many ways you can make your voice heard. As a reminder, here are some ideas to think about:

* Create an online petition for your cause.
* Circulate petitions for student signatures.
* Write a letter to the principal, local leaders, the mayor, and so on.
* Alert the media about your concern.

* Attend city council meetings.
* Speak out at community events.
* Join organizations dedicated to causes you support.
* Participate in or organize a peaceful demonstration.

Once you start the process of talking about your ideas and why you feel the way you do about an issue, it will become more and more comfortable. Your voice and contribution are needed more than ever. Keep us posted on your efforts through www.AsktheJudge.info. We might even include some information about your project on our website. We wish you well in your pursuits!

How to Do Legal Research

By following the simple instructions offered here, you can enhance your next term paper or presentation by adding information on one of the cases or legal articles discussed or cited in this book. Public libraries, law libraries, and the Internet can assist in your research. If you get stuck, ask a reference librarian for help.

Court Opinions

The published opinions of all of the country's **appellate courts** are found in a series of books called reporters. The series is divided into regions. For example, California decisions are found in the *Pacific Reporter*, while Maine decisions are located in the *Atlantic Reporter*. Each state also maintains its own set of reporters. This means that each decision may be found in both a regional reporter and a state reporter. The decisions of the United States Supreme Court can be found in several federal reporters. All of the Supreme Court cases cited in this book are located in either the *U.S. Supreme Court Reports* or the *Supreme Court Reporter*.

Each published opinion is assigned a citation number. For example, if you want to read the full opinion of the Supreme Court in *Miller v. Alabama* from case 1, start with the case citation, which is 132 S.Ct. 2455 (2012). This means you can find the opinion in volume 132 of the *Supreme Court Reporter* on page 2455. 2012 refers to the year of the decision. Similarly, you can find *Roper v. Simmons* (2005) from case 1 at 543 U.S. 551, which is volume 543 of the *U.S. Supreme Court Reports,* page 551.

You can also find information about some of the cases on websites, including Justia News (www.news.justia.com), Findlaw (www.findlaw.com), the Cornell Legal Information Institute (www.law.cornell.edu), the Chicago-Kent College of Law (www.oyez.org), and the American Association of Law Libraries (www.aallnet.org). The information is public, which means you don't have to be a lawyer, judge, or law student to access the material.

Legal Articles

The legal articles cited in this book usually list the name of the journal publishing the article, the author, a volume number followed by the page number, and the date the article was published. You can locate the article in a law library or online. If you visit the publication's website, search for the article by volume and page number. You might also locate it through a search engine using the title or author's name.

Law libraries are located on college campuses or at local courthouses. If there isn't one in your area, write or call the nearest one and ask for assistance. With the citation of the article, they may be able to send you a copy for a photocopying fee.

Glossary of Terms

Acquit. To find a criminal defendant not guilty of the crime charged.

Adjudicate. To make an official or judicial decision about who is right in a dispute.

Admissible. Refers to evidence that is introduced in a trial by the plaintiff and defendant according to rules of evidence and procedure.

Affirm. To uphold or agree with a decision made by a lower court.

Affirmative action. A term from the 1960s that refers to the policy of hiring and awarding contracts with diversity in mind. It was meant to remedy the effects of societal discrimination and applies to educational opportunities as well.

Amicus briefs. Written arguments presenting a party's position on an issue before the court.

Appeal. The legal process used to ask a higher court to review a decision of a lower court.

Appellate court. A court that reviews what happened in the trial court; there are no witnesses or evidence presented in appellate courts, only written and oral legal arguments by the lawyers. The U.S. Supreme Court is the highest appellate court in the country.

Ballot stuffing. When a person votes more than once in an election when usually only one ballot per person is permitted.

Burden of proof. In a lawsuit, the side that has the responsibility to go forward and prove the alleged facts carries the "burden of proof."

Capacity to sue. The ability of a person to file a lawsuit in his or her own name. This right is usually limited to adults and emancipated minors.

Certiorari. A Latin term used in cases filed with the Supreme Court asking for "review" of a lower court decision. Thousands of petitions for certiorari are filed each year but only 1 percent are granted.

Class action. A lawsuit that allows a large number of people who share common issues and have been subjected to similar consequences to sue or be sued as a group.

Common law. The law developed by judges through court decisions as opposed to laws passed by state legislatures.

Commute. To change a prison sentence or penalty to a less severe one; usually an act of a state's governor or the president.

Concurring opinion. A separate opinion written by a judge of an appellate court that agrees with the majority decision.

Controlled substance. Includes illegal drugs and prescription medications that are regulated by the government.

Conviction. A decision by a judge or a verdict by a jury determining that a person charged with a criminal offense is guilty beyond a reasonable doubt.

Corporal punishment. Physical discipline, including paddling or slaps, inflicted on the body of a criminal offender (defined below) or a child by a parent or teacher.

Criminal mischief. Behavior that involves damaging, defacing, or destroying someone's property; also referred to as vandalism or criminal damage.

Criminal offender. A person charged and convicted of a criminal act.

Defendant. The person or party sued in a civil case or the accused in a criminal case.

Delinquency hearing. A part of the juvenile justice system that may include a trial of the charges, review of status, or detention proceeding.

Delinquent. A person under eighteen years old who is found guilty in juvenile court of a crime. Delinquent may also be used to describe an act or behavior.

Discovery. The pretrial process by which one party becomes aware of the evidence gathered by the other party.

Discretion. The freedom to choose from available options: for example, when a judge decides an appropriate penalty or a prosecutor decides what charges to file or whether or not to file.

Disenfranchise. To prevent a person from exercising the right to vote.

Dissenting opinion. An opinion written by a judge of a court of appeals that explains why he or she disagrees with the majority decision.

Double jeopardy. Being tried twice for the same offense, which is prohibited by the Fifth Amendment.

Drug paraphernalia. Items that are possessed for the use of illegal drugs, including bongs, pipes, and other devices.

Due process. The guaranty that your life, liberty, and property are treated fairly under the law. It means that you have the right to be notified of any legal action taken against you, the right to be heard, and the right to confront the opposing side.

Equal protection. The principle that everyone in the same group or classification should be treated the same. One person shouldn't be singled out and treated differently.

Felony murder rule. When a person is involved in a crime (as a lookout, for example) that results in a murder, that person can be charged with murder even though he wasn't the one who pulled the trigger or caused the death of the victim.

Franchise. In politics, the right to vote.

Grand jury. A group of twelve to sixteen citizens who consider and investigate charges of criminal behavior. Their indictment, called a true bill, leads to a criminal trial of the person charged.

Guardian. A person who is appointed by a court to make legal decisions for someone else (a minor or an adult who has a disability).

Immunity. Legal immunity means being exempt or protected from a burden that applies to others: a person testifies against another in a criminal case in exchange for protection from being charged with related offenses.

Indictment. A formal, written accusation by a grand jury charging a person or business with a specific crime.

Initiative. A process whereby a citizen collects a required number of signatures on a petition to bring an issue before the public in an election.

In loco parentis. A Latin phrase meaning "in the place of a parent." It is a legal doctrine where an individual or school, for example, assumes parental rights, duties, and obligations without going through formal proceedings in court.

Interest groups. Groups of individuals who share a common interest and act to influence public opinion.

Jurisdiction. The legal authority of a court to hear and decide cases; the exercise of judicial power within certain geographic, monetary, or subject matter limits.

Juvenile. A person below the age of eighteen.

Magistrate. A local official who administers laws and has some of the powers of a judge.

Mandatory sentencing. A sentence that is required by state law. A trial judge or jury has no discretion when sentencing the offender.

Midterm elections. Elections held halfway through a president's four-year term, at which time all members of the House of Representatives are up for reelection, as are one-third of the 100 U.S. senators.

***Miranda* warnings.** These are the rights the police are required to tell a suspect in custody before questioning begins. They include the right to remain silent; the right to a lawyer and if you can't afford one, a lawyer will be appointed for you; and if you're under eighteen, the right to have a parent with you during questioning.

Misdemeanor. An offense that is less serious than a felony and is punishable by a sentence other than being sent to prison. Jail time up to one year is generally the maximum penalty for a misdemeanor.

Mootness. A doctrine in the law whereby a court will not decide an issue if there is no actual controversy.

Moratorium. A period of delay or a time when a particular activity is not allowed.

Naturalization. A legal process through which a citizen of one country becomes a citizen of another.

Neutrality. In the context of the Establishment Clause, neutrality is the idea that the government should not use religion or religious differences as a basis for action toward an individual, and that the government should neither encourage nor discourage religious beliefs or practices.

Opinion. A written statement from a court announcing its decision in a case.

Party. An individual, an organization, or a business that is named in a lawsuit as a plaintiff or defendant.

Plaintiff. In a civil action, the party who files the lawsuit. In a criminal case, the government is the plaintiff.

Primary. A primary election comes before the general election and is used to narrow the field of candidates. The winner goes on to compete in the general election.

Prior restraint. The restriction or prohibition of speech before it's made—for example, censoring newspaper articles before publication.

Probable cause. A legal standard requiring more evidence in favor of something than against. It is commonly used in law enforcement when deciding whether to arrest or charge someone with a crime, or in obtaining a search warrant.

Probation. A period of time when an adult or juvenile remains under the court's jurisdiction while performing specified duties such as community service, counseling, or drug testing. A violation of probation can result in prison or jail time.

Reasonable suspicion. When authorities have more than a hunch that you're up to something or are about to break a school rule or a law. Based on the totality of circumstances—time, place, activity, your school record, age, and source of information—a search by school officials or other authorities may pass the reasonable suspicion test without the need for a warrant.

Recidivism. Falling back into undesirable behavior such as criminal activity.

Referendum. The practice of referring a proposal or act of a legislature to the public for a full vote of the electorate for approval or rejection.

Rehabilitation. When speaking of the juvenile justice system, rehabilitation means addressing the juvenile's issues (personal and family) that brought him to the attention of law enforcement and the court through supervision, counseling, community service, and other appropriate services.

Restitution. The act of restoring a victim to the position he or she was in before suffering property damage or personal injury.

Settle. In the context of a lawsuit, this is when the parties involved reach an agreement acceptable to all parties before, or sometimes during, the trial of the case.

Standing. The requirement that a person have more than a mere interest in an issue to file a lawsuit. A plaintiff must have suffered a concrete and particularized injury in order for the court to determine that standing exists.

Stare decisis. The doctrine that judges should follow rules or principles announced in earlier cases. It is Latin for "let the decision stand."

Suffragist. A person advocating the extension of suffrage (the right to vote), especially to women.

Truancy. The failure to go to school when required unless you're excused by the school for a good reason, such as illness, a doctor's appointment, or a family emergency. Excessive tardies may also lead to a truancy charge. In some states, truancy is an offense that could land you in court.

Vacate. When speaking of lawsuits and appellate court decisions, to "vacate" a lower court's ruling means to set it aside as if it didn't exist in the first place. The court may then issue specific instructions to the lower court regarding the issues in the case.

Viewpoint discrimination. A form of discrimination against speech that is based on the content of the speech but as expressed by the speaker. Content is the subject matter while viewpoint is the speaker's position on the subject.

Warrant. A written order from a court directing law enforcement to arrest someone or search a specific place for evidence of a crime.

Notes

PART I

In re Burrus, 136 U.S. 586 (1890)

U.S. v. Butler, 297 U.S. 1 (1936)

Island Trees School District v. Pico, 457 U.S. 853 (1982)

U.S. v. Lovett, 328 U.S. 303 (1946)

Veasey v. Perry, 135 S.Ct. 9 (2014)

Frank v. Walker, 135 S.Ct. 1551 (2015)

PART II

Case 1

Miller v. Alabama, 132 S.Ct. 2455 (2012)

Jackson v. Hobbs, 132 S.Ct. 1733 (2012)

Roper v. Simmons, 543 U.S. 551 (2005)

Graham v. Florida, 130 S.Ct. 2011 (2010)

State v. Ragland, 812 N.W.2d 654 (Iowa 2012)

Stanford v. Kentucky, 492 U.S. 361 (1989)

Furman v. Georgia, 408 U.S. 238 (1972)

Kent v. United States, 383 U.S. 541 (1966)

Case 2

United States v. Antoine Jones, 132 S.Ct. 945 (2012)

Entick v. Carrington, 95 England Reporter 807 (1765)

Schmerber v. California, 384 U.S. 757, at page 767 (1966)

People v. Weaver, 12 N.Y.3d 433 (2009)

Riley v. California, 134 S.Ct. 2473 (2014)

Navarette v. California, 134 S.Ct. 1683 (2014)

State v. Alaniz, 815 N.W.2d 234 (2012)

Safford Unified School District v. Redding, 129 S.Ct. 2633 (2009)

New Jersey v. T.L.O., 469 U.S. 325 (1985)

Missouri v. McNeely, 133 S.Ct. 1552 (2013)

Maryland v. King, 133 S.Ct. 1958 (2013)

Florida v. Jardines, 133 S.Ct. 1409 (2013)

Olmstead v. United States, 277 U.S. 438 (1928)

Case 3

Camreta v. Greene, 131 S.Ct. 2020 (2011)

Forsyth v. Hammond, 17 S.Ct. 665 (1897)

Elk Grove Unified School District v. Newdow, 124 S.Ct. 2301 (2004)

In re Andre M., 207 Arizona 482, 88 P.3d 552 (2004)

New Jersey v. T.L.O., 469 U.S. 325 (1985)

Ohio v. Clark, 135 S.Ct. 2173 (2015)

Stone v. Farley, 877 F.Supp. 1246 (1995)

Case 4

Tinker v. Des Moines Independent Community School District, 393 U.S. 503 (1969)

Morse v. Frederick, 127 S.Ct. 2618 (2007)

Schenck v. U.S., 249 U.S. 47 (1919)

Jacobellis v. Ohio, 378 U.S. 184 (1964).

Bethel School District v. Fraser, 478 U.S. 675 (1986)

Hazelwood School District v. Kuhlmeier, 484 U.S. 260 (1988)

Wisniewski v. Weedsport Central School District, 552 U.S. 1296 (2008)

Kowalski v. Berkeley County Schools, 132 S.Ct. 1095 (2012)

Layshock v. Hermitage School District, 132 S.Ct. 1097 (2012)

Elonis v United States, 135 S.Ct. 2001 (2015)

Bethel School District v. Fraser, 106 S.Ct. 3159 (1986)

B.H. v. Easton Area School District, 725 F.3d 293 (2013)

Bivens v. Albuquerque Public Schools, 899 F.Supp. 556 (1995)

Case 5

McCreary County v. American Civil Liberties Union, 125 S.Ct. 2722 (2005)

Lemon v. Kurtzman, 91 S.Ct. 2105 (1971)

Van Orden v. Perry, 545 S.Ct. 2854 (2005)

Stone v. Graham, 101 S.Ct. 192 (1980)

Lee v. Weisman, 112 S.Ct. 2649 (1992)

Christian Legal Society v. Martinez, 130 S.Ct. 2971 (2010)

Good News Club v. Milford Central School, 121 S.Ct. 2093 (2001)

Westside Community Board of Education v. Mergens, 110 S.Ct. 2356 (1990)

Abington School District v. Schempp, 83 S.Ct. 1560 (1963)

Lynch v. Donnelly, 104 S.Ct. 1355 (1984)

Wallace v. Jaffree, 105 S.Ct. 2479 (1985)

Case 6

Board of Education v. Earls, 536 U.S. 822 (2002)

Camara v. Municipal Court of San Francisco, 387 U.S. 523 (1967)

Vernonia School District v. Acton, 515 U.S. 646 (1995)

Florida v. Harris, 133 S.Ct. 1050 (2013)

Treasury Employees v. Von Raab, 489 U.S. 656 (1989)

Skinner v. Railway Labor Executives' Association, 489 U.S. 602 (1989)

Case 7

Boy Scouts of America v. Dale, 530 U.S. 640 (2000)

National Socialist Party v. Skokie, 432 U.S. 43 (1977)

Village of Skokie v. National Socialist Party of America, 69 Illinois 2nd 605, 373 N.E.2d 21 (1978)

Brandenburg v. Ohio, 395 U.S. 444 (1969)

Hurley v. Irish-American Gay, Lesbian and Bisexual Group of Boston, Inc., 515 U.S. 557 (1995)

Roper v. Simmons, 543 U.S. 551 (2005)

Miller v. Alabama, 132 S.Ct. 2455 (2012)

Lawrence v. Texas, 539 U.S. 558 (2003)

Case 8

Texas v. Johnson, 491 U.S. 397 (1989)

Terminiello v. City of Chicago, 337 U.S. 1 (1949)

West Virginia Board of Education v. Barnette, 319 U.S. 624 (1943)

Walker v. Sons of Confederate Veterans, 135 S.Ct. 2239 (2015)

Barr v. Lafon, 538 F.3d 554 (Tennessee 2008)

Brown v. Entertainment Merchants Association, 131 S.Ct. 2729 (2011)

Spence v. Washington, 418 U.S. 405 (1974)

Smith v. Goguen, 415 U.S. 566 (1974)

Snyder v. Phelps, 131 S. Ct. 1207 (2011)

Case 9

Island Trees School District v. Pico, 457 U.S. 853 (1982)

Tinker v. Des Moines Independent Community School District, 393 U.S. 503 (1969)

Shelton v. Tucker, 364 U.S. 479, at page 487 (1960)

Hazelwood v. Kuhlmeier, 484 U.S. 260 (1988)

Julea Ward v. Polite, 667 F.3d 727 (Sixth Circuit Court of Appeals, 2012)

Boucher v. School Board of Greenfield, 134 F.3d 821 (Seventh Circuit Court of Appeals 1998)

R.O. v. Ithaca City School District, 645 F.3d 533 (New York, 2011)

Lange v. Diercks, 808 N.W.2d 754 (Iowa Court of Appeals, 2011)

Epperson v. Arkansas, 393 U.S. 97 (1968)

Meyer v. Nebraska, 262 U.S. 390 (1923)

Regents of the University of California v. Bakke, 438 U.S. 265 (1978)

Case 10

Plyler v. Doe, 457 U.S. 202 (1982)

Wong Wing v. U.S., 163 U.S. 228, at 242 (1896)

Brown v. Board of Education, 347 U.S. 483 (1954)

San Antonio School District v. Rodriguez, 411 U.S. 1 (1973)

Bonner v. Daniels, 907 N.E.2d 516 (Indiana 2009)

Case 11

Regents of the University of California v. Bakke, 438 U.S. 265 (1978)

Hirabayashi v. United States, 320 U.S. 81 (1943)

Grutter v. Bollinger, 539 U.S. 306 (2003)

Fisher v. University of Texas at Austin, 133 S.Ct. 2411 (2013)

Schuette v. Coalition to Defend Affirmative Action, 134 S.Ct. 1623 (2014)

EEOC v. Abercrombie & Fitch, 135 S.Ct. 2028 (2015)

Case 12

Ingraham v. Wright, 430 U.S. 651 (1977)

State of Iowa v. Rollins, 829 N.W.2d 589 (2013)

Simons v. State of North Dakota, 803 N.W.2d 587, 2011 ND 190 (2011)

Garcia v. Miera, 817 F.2d 650 (1987)

Brown v. Entertainment Merchants Association, 131 S.Ct. 2729 (2011)

In re Phillip B., 92 Cal. App.3d 796 (California, 1979)

Case 13

County of Sacramento v. Lewis, 523 U.S. 833 (1998)

Wolff v. McDonnell, 418 U.S. 539, 558 (1974)

Goss v. Lopez, 419 U.S. 565 (1975)

Lee v. Weisman, 112 S.Ct. 2649 (1992)

Couture v. Board of Education of Albuquerque Public Schools, 535 F.3d 1243 (10th Circuit Court of Appeals, 2008)

Laney v. Farley, 501 F.3d 577 (6th Circuit Court of Appeals, 2007)

D.C. v. School District of Philadelphia, 879 A.2 408 (2005)

Epperson v. Arkansas, 393 U.S. 97 (1968)

Case 14

Palmer v. Thompson, 403 U.S. 217 (1971)

Dred Scott v. John Sandford, 60 U.S. 393 (1857)

Plessy v. Ferguson, 163 U.S. 537 (1896)

Brown v. Board of Education of Topeka, 347 U.S. 483 (1954)

Brown v. Louisiana, 383 U.S. 131 (1966)

Loving v. Virginia, 388 U.S. 1 (1967)

Obergefell v. Hodges 135 S.Ct. 2584 (2015)

Case 15

Miranda v. Arizona, 384 U.S. 436 (1966)

In re Gault, 387 U.S. 1 (1967)

J.D.B. v. North Carolina, 131 S.Ct. 2394 (2011)

People v. T.C., 898 P.2d 20 (Colorado 1995)

New York v. Quarles, 467 U.S. 649 (1984)

Additional Supreme Court 5–4 Decisions

City of Los Angeles v. Patel (2015 WL 2473445)

Obergefell v. Hodges (2015 WL 2473451)

Burwell v. Hobby Lobby Stores, 134 S.Ct. 2751 (2014)

Hall v. Florida, 134 S.Ct. 1986 (2014)

Town of Greece v. Galloway, 134 S.Ct. 1811 (2014)

United States v. Windsor, 133 S.Ct. 2675 (2013)

Shelby County, Alabama v. Holder, 133 S.Ct. 2612 (2013)

Maetta Vance v. Ball State University, 133 S.Ct. 2434 (2013)

Salinas v. Texas, 133 S.Ct. 2174 (2013)

Maryland v. King, 133 S.Ct. 1958 (2013)

Smith v. United States, 324 F.2d 879 (1932)

National Federation of Independent Business v. Sebelius, 132 S.Ct. 2566 (2012)

Arizona Christian School Tuition Organization v. Winn, 131 S.Ct. 1436 (2011)

Citizens United v. Federal Election Commission, 130 S.Ct. 876 (2010)

District Attorney's Office v. Osborne, 129 S.Ct. 2308 (2009)

FCC v. Fox Television Stations, 129 S.Ct. 1800 (2009)

FCC v. Fox Television Stations, 132 S.Ct. 2307 (2012)

Corley v. United States, 556 U.S. 303 (2009)

District of Columbia v. Heller, 554 U.S. 570 (2008)

Kennedy v. Louisiana, 554 U.S. 407 (2008)

Kelo v. City of New London, 545 U.S. 469 (2005)

Bush v. Gore, 531 U.S. 98 (2000)

Bowers v. Hardwick, 478 U.S. 186 (1986)

Lawrence v. Texas, 539 U.S. 558 (2003)

Adkins v. Children's Hospital, 261 U.S. 525 (1923)

West Coast Hotel Company v. Parrish, 300 U.S. 379 (1937)

About the Authors

Thomas A. Jacobs, J.D., was an assistant Arizona Attorney General from 1972–1985, practicing criminal and child welfare law. He was appointed to the Maricopa County Superior Court in 1985, where he served as a judge pro tem and commissioner in the juvenile and family courts until his retirement in 2008. He also taught juvenile law for ten years as an adjunct professor at the Arizona State University School of Social Work. Judge Tom continues to write for teens, lawyers, and judges. Visit his website, AsktheJudge.info, for free interactive educational tools that provide current information regarding laws, court decisions, and national news affecting teens. It's the only site of its kind to provide legal questions and answers for teens and parents with the unique ability to interact with Judge Tom as well as with other teens.

Natalie C. Jacobs, J.D., works with her father, Judge Tom Jacobs, on the teen rights website AsktheJudge.info, which helps teens and their parents become better informed about youth rights and the laws affecting minors. Prior to joining her father in his work, Natalie worked as a criminal defense attorney. She has also volunteered with the Arizona Innocence Project, which investigates claims of innocence and works to exonerate people who have been wrongfully convicted. When she's not writing about youth-related issues or taking care of busy toddlers, Natalie enjoys relaxing evenings at home, cooking, reading, practicing yoga, hiking, traveling, having picnics, and just being outdoors with her family. She lives in the beautiful mountain town of Flagstaff, Arizona, with her husband Michael, her children Paige and Felix, and their beloved dogs.

Do you have lots of ideas and opinions? Have you ever seen a book or website and thought, "I'd do that differently"?

Then we want to hear from you! We're looking for teens to be part of the **Free Spirit Teen Advisory Council.** You'll help us keep our books and other products current and relevant by letting us know what you think about things like design, art, and content.

Go to www.freespirit.com/teens to learn more and get an application.

The Free Spirit Teens & the Law Series
Each book: paperback; 6" x 9"; ages 12 & up

Teen Cyberbullying Investigated
 Where Do Your Rights End and Consequences Begin?

by Thomas A. Jacobs, J.D.

Each chapter features a landmark cyberbullying court case and resulting decision, asks readers whether they agree with the decision, and urges them to think about how the decision affects their lives. 208 pp.

They Broke the Law—You Be the Judge
True Cases of Teen Crime
by Thomas A. Jacobs, J.D.

This book invites teens to preside over a variety of real-life cases to learn each defendant's background, the relevant facts, and the sentencing options available. After deciding on a sentence, readers learn what really happened and where each offender is today. 224 pp.

What Are My Rights?
Q&A About Teens and the Law
(Revised and Updated 3rd Edition)

by Thomas A. Jacobs, J.D.

To make informed decisions, teens need to know about the laws that affect them. This fascinating book helps teens understand the law, recognize their responsibilities, and appreciate their rights. 224 pp.

Every Vote Matters
The Power of Your Voice, from Student Elections to the Supreme Court
by Thomas A. Jacobs, J.D., and Natalie Jacobs, J.D.

This timely book focuses on Supreme Court decisions that came down to a single vote. As teens examine how the cases affect their lives and rights, the authors emphasize the power of an individual's vote in local, state, and national elections. 224 pp.

Interested in purchasing multiple quantities and receiving volume discounts? Contact edsales@freespirit.com or call 1.800.735.7323 and ask for Education Sales.

> **Many Free Spirit authors are available for speaking engagements, workshops, and keynotes.**
>
> Contact speakers@freespirit.com or call 1.800.735.7323.

For pricing information, to place an order, or to request a free catalog, contact:
Free Spirit Publishing Inc. 6325 Sandburg Road • Suite 100 • Golden Valley, MN 55427-3674 toll-free 800.735.7323 • local 612.338.2068 • fax 612.337.5050 help4kids@freespirit.com • www.freespirit.com

Index

A

Abercrombie & Fitch; Equal Employment Opportunity Commission (EEOC) v., *217, 219*
Abington School District v. Schempp, *113*
Abortion cases, *81*
Absentee ballots, *18, 27*
Absolutely True Diary of a Part-Time Indian, The (Alexie), *179*
Acton; Vernonia School District v., *127, 131*
Aetna Casualty & Surety Co.; Weber v., *196*
Affirmative action, *206, 207, 209, 211, 213, 215, 217, 219, 220, 221*
Age requirements,
　presidential candidates, *22*
　voting eligibility, *14, 17, 22, 24*
　young politicians, *22*
　See also Minors,
Alabama; Miller v., *34, 36, 38, 39, 41, 49, 151, 286*
Alaniz; State v., *60*
Alattar, Zana, *151*
Albuquerque Public Schools; Bivens v., *99*
Alexie, Sherman, *179*
Alito, Samuel,
　on Confrontation Clause, *77*
　on protection of minors from violent video games, *163*
Alternative schools, placement in, *249, 251*
American Association of University Women, *220*
American Civics Test, Arizona, *198*
American Civil Liberties Union (ACLU); McCreary County v., *103, 104, 106, 108, 118, 119*

American Library Association,
  Banned Books Week, *186*
  Office for Intellectual Freedom, *178, 188*
Amicus briefs, *6*
Andre M., In re, *75, 77*
Animal dissections, student action against, *29*
Anonymous tips, searches based on, *60*
Anthony, Susan B., *14*
Argentina, voting age, *24*
Arizona, civics test requirement for graduation, *198*
Arizona; Miranda v., *278, 280, 282, 284, 286*
Arkansas, religious test for public office, *118*
Arkansas; Epperson v., *183, 255*
Armbands, as symbolic speech, *83, 85, 160, 168*
AsktheJudge.info,
Association, freedom of, *138, 140, 141, 143, 145, 146, 148, 150, 151*
Athletes, drug testing of, *129, 131*
Attorneys,
  See Lawyers,
Australia, mandatory voting, *22*
Austria, voting age, *24*

B

Backpacks, searching, *58, 133, 135*
Bakke; Regents of the University of California v., *206, 207, 209, 211, 213, 221*
Ballots,
  absentee, *18, 27*
  languages used on, *18*
Banned Books Week, *186*
Barnette; West Virginia Board of Education v., *158*
Barr v. Lafon, *162*
Baskin, Morgan, *22*
Beeson, Ann, *9*
Belgium, mandatory voting, *22*
BensGuide.gpo.gov, *30*

Berkeley County Schools; Kowalski v., *92, 94*
Best Short Stories by Negro Writers, The (Hughes), *172*
Bethel School District v. Fraser, *88, 99, 160*
Bible clubs, *112, 113*
Bickel, Alexander M., *211*
Big Brother (television show), *51*
Bill of Rights,
    defined, *3*
    lack of protection for education, *198*
    See also Constitution,
Bivens v. Albuquerque Public Schools, *99*
Black, Jeremiah S., *11*
Black Boy (Wright), *172*
'Black Lives Matter' posters, *116*
Blackmun, Harry A.,
    on affirmative action, *221*
    on censorship, *174, 176*
    on desegregation, *259*
    on education for illegal immigrants, *196*
Bluhm, Julia, *27, 29*
Board of Education of Albuquerque Public Schools; Couture v., *247, 249*
Board of Education of Topeka; Brown v., *198*
Board of Education v. Earls, *121, 123, 125, 127, 129*
Bollinger; Grutter v., *215, 220, 221*
Bonner v. Daniels, *200, 201*
Book banning, *170, 172, 174, 176, 179*
Boucher v. School Board of Greenfield, *181*
Boy Scouts of America, policy changes, *148*
Boy Scouts of America v. Dale, *140, 141, 143*
Brandeis, Louis, on privacy rights, *64*
Brandenburg v. Ohio, *146*
Brattleboro, Vermont, *24*
Brazil, voting age, *24*

Brennan, William on,
    censorship, *174*
    on Equal Protection
    Clause, *194*
    on Fourth
    Amendment, *54*
    on freedom of
    expression, *158, 160*
    on illiteracy, *194*
Breyer, Stephen G., on
free speech, *88*
Bridges, Ruby, *268*
Brown v. Board of
Education of Topeka,
198, 261, 266, 268, 270, 271
Brown v. Entertainment
Merchants Association,
163, 237
Brown v. Louisiana, *268, 270*
Bullying,
    cyberbullying, *92, 94, 125*
    Day of Silence events, *166*
Burger, Warren,
    on education for illegal
    immigrants, *196*
    on free speech in
    schools, *99*

Burr, Aaron, *9*
Burrus, In re, *4*
Bush, George W., *11*
Butler; United States v., *4*

C

California; Navarette v., *60*
California; Riley v., *54, 58, 127*
California; Schmerber v., *54*
Camara v. Municipal
Court of San Francisco, *123*
Campaign finance rules, *27*
Campos, Santiago E., *99*
Camreta v. Greene, *68, 70, 72, 73*
Canada, ban on corporal
punishment in schools, *227*
Canine drug searches,
131, 132, 133, 135
CanIVote.org, *30*
Capital punishment,

See Death penalty;
Executions,
Carrington; Entick v., *53*
Car searches, *125, 131, 132*
Cell phones,
   police searches of, *54, 58, 127*
   school searches, *58, 125, 127*
   use of in class, *249*
Censorship,
   book banning, *170, 172, 174, 176, 179*
   school curriculum, *183, 185*
   student newspapers, *179, 181, 183*
   student theater productions, *186*
Certiorari, granting, *3, 4, 68, 70, 72, 73, 80, 81*
Change.org, *48*
Cheek swabs, *61, 302, 304*
Cheerleading, Sparkle Effect, *202*
Chicago, City of;
Terminiello v., *156*
Chicago-Kent College of Law, *31*

Child abuse,
   corporal punishment and, *228, 230, 232, 233, 235, 238*
   questioning of children about, *70, 72, 73, 77*
Children,
   See Minors,
Childress, Alice, *172*
China, protests against government, *24*
Christian Legal Society v. Martinez, *112, 113*
Christmas, observance of, *115*
Citizenship requirement for voting, *26*
Civics test requirement for graduation, *198*
Civil Rights Act of 1964, *206, 207, 266*
Civil War, *14*
Clark; Ohio v., *77*
Cleaver, Eldridge, *172*
Clubs,
   freedom of association, *150, 151*
   religious, *112, 113, 118*

Coalition to Defend Affirmative Action; Schuette v., *217*
Colleges and universities,
   affirmative action, *206, 207, 209, 211, 213, 215, 217, 220, 221*
   religious clubs and organizations, *112, 113*
College students, voting rights, *18*
Colorado, voter registration, *26*
Compulsory school attendance laws, *240*
Compulsory voting, *20, 22*
Confederate flags, *158, 162, 163*
Confessions,
   false confessions, *286*
   by juveniles, *75, 77, 79*
   Miranda v. Arizona, *280, 282, 284, 286*
Confrontation Clause, *77*
Constitution,
   amendments, *14, 17*
   authorization of Supreme Court, *70, 72*
   Bill of Rights, *3*
   Confrontation Clause, *77*
   differences in interpretation of, *170, 172, 174, 176, 178, 179, 181, 183, 185, 186, 188*
   Due Process Clause, *246*
   Equal Protection Clause, *190, 192, 194, 196, 198, 200, 203, 211, 259, 266*
   Establishment Clause, *103, 104, 108, 110, 112, 119*
   fluidity of interpretation, *270, 271, 276, 317*
   lack of protection for education, *198*
   See also specific amendments,
Corporal punishment,
   by parents, *228, 230, 232, 233, 237, 238*
   in schools, *223, 225, 227, 228, 230, 233, 235, 237, 238*

Couture v. Board of Education of Albuquerque Public Schools, *247, 249*
Criminal rights and issues,
   education in detention, *202*
   Fifth Amendment protection, *278, 280, 282, 284, 286*
   lawyers, access to, *284*
   school-to-prison pipeline, *254*
   sentencing for juveniles, *34, 36, 38, 39, 41, 43, 44, 46, 48, 49, 79*
   solitary confinement of juveniles, *237*
   voting, *20*
   wrongful convictions, *286*
Curriculum, censorship of, *183, 185*
Custodial interrogations, *278, 280, 282, 284, 286*
Cyberbullying, *92, 94, 125*

D

Dale; Boy Scouts of America v., *140, 141, 143*
Dance squads, Sparkle Effect, *202*
Daniels; Bonner v., *200, 201*
Day of Silence events, *166*
D.C. v. School District of Philadelphia, *249, 251*
Death penalty,
   for juveniles, *38, 43, 44, 151*
   for minorities, *44, 46*
   number of executions, *46*
Department of Motor Vehicles, voter registration, *17, 26*
Desegregation of schools, *261, 266, 268, 270, 271*
Des Moines Independent Community School District; Tinker v., *83, 85, 88, 92, 110, 168, 174, 176, 185*

Development, Relief, and Education for Alien Minors (DREAM) Act, *201*
Diercks; Lange v., *179*
Disabilities, individuals with,
 due process rights in schools, *247, 249*
 right to public education, *202*
 voter registration, *17*
Disciplinary actions by schools,
 for online expression, *251, 252, 254*
 physical punishment, *223, 225, 227, 228, 230, 233, 235, 237, 238*
 suspensions and expulsions, *240, 242, 244, 246, 247, 249, 251, 252, 254, 255*
Discrimination,
 based on religious beliefs, *217, 219*
 based on sexual orientation, *140, 141, 143, 148*
 based on wealth, *200*
 desegregation of schools, *261, 266, 268, 270, 271*
 determining intent of, *261*
 public accommodations laws, *140*
 by public libraries, *268, 270*
 by public swimming pools, *274*
 reverse discrimination, *206, 207, 209, 211, 213, 215, 217*
 student protests against, *29, 30*
 at swimming pools, *257, 259, 261*
 voting laws and, *18, 20, 300*
Disenfranchisement, *18, 20*
District of Columbia, ban on corporal punishment in schools, *227*
Diversity,

affirmative action and, *207, 209, 211, 213, 215, 217, 220, 221*
of Supreme Court justices, *6*
DNA evidence, *61, 286, 302, 304, 308*
Doe; Plyler v., *190, 192, 194, 196, 203*
DOMA, See Defense of Marriage Act (DOMA),
Domestic relations cases, *4*
Donnelly; Lynch v., *118*
Dorset, Minnesota, mayoral election, *22*
Dos Santos, Jilly, *29*
Douglas, William O.,
on desegregation, *261*
on free speech, *156*
Douglass, Frederick, *18*
Down These Mean Streets (Thomas), *172*
DREAM (Development, Relief, and Education for Alien Minors) Act, *201*

Dred Scott case, *14, 261, 264*
Dress codes, *162, 163, 165*
Driver's license, voter registration and, *17, 26*
Drugs,
canine alerts as basis for searches, *131, 132*
drug testing for extracurricular activities, *121, 123, 125, 127, 129, 131*
drug use statistics, *129*
marijuana legalization, *99*
promoting as free speech, *83, 85, 87, 88, 90, 92*
Dubois, W.E.B., *24*
Due process for school disciplinary actions, *225, 240, 242, 244, 246, 247, 249, 251, 252, 254, 255*

E

Earls; Board of Education v., *121, 123, 125, 127, 129*
Eighth Amendment,

corporal punishment, *225, 228*
sentencing for juveniles, *34, 36, 38, 39, 41, 43, 44, 46, 48, 49*

Elections,
endorsement of candidates, *12*
languages on ballots, *18*
midterm, *306*
presidential, *8, 9, 11, 313, 315*
primaries, *14, 26*
recounts, *11, 313, 315*
student participation in, *11, 165, 166*
voter registration, *14, 17, 20, 24, 26*
voter turnout, *12, 14*
See also Voting,

Electoral votes, *8, 9, 11*
Elk Grove Unified School District v. Newdow, *72*
Elonis v. United States, *97, 99*
Email, searches of accounts, *125*
Emancipation laws for minors, *293*
Emancipation Proclamation, *14*
Employers,
discrimination by, *217, 219*
drug testing by, *132, 133*
minimum wage laws, *220, 315, 316*

Ending Corporal Punishment in Schools Act of 2014 (H.R.5005), *230*
Entertainment Merchants Association; Brown v., *163, 237*
Entick v. Carrington, *53*
Epperson v. Arkansas, *183, 255*
Equal Access Act of 1984, *118*
Equal Employment Opportunity Commission (EEOC) v. Abercrombie & Fitch, *217, 219*

Equal Protection Clause, *190, 192, 194, 196, 198, 200, 203, 211, 259, 266*

Establishment Clause, *103, 104, 108, 110, 112, 119*

Evolution, teaching about, *183*

Executions,
 botched, *48, 49*
 number of, *46*

Expression, freedom of, See Free speech; Symbolic speech,

Extracurricular activities,
 drug testing and, *121, 123, 125, 127, 129, 131*
 getting involved in, religious organizations and clubs, *112, 113, 118*
 sports, *129, 131*

F

Facebook,
 free speech and, *97, 99*
 voter registration, *26*

Fair Labor Standards Act of 1938, *220, 316*

FairVote.org, *30*

Family Educational Rights and Privacy Act of 1974 (FERPA), *136*

Family law cases, *4*

Farley; Laney v., *249*

Farley; Stone v., *79*

Federal Post Card Application, *27*

Federal Voting Assistance Program, *27*

Ferguson; Plessy v., *264, 266, 271*

Fifteenth Amendment, *14*

Fifth Amendment, *75, 278, 280, 282, 284, 286, 287, 302*

'Fighting words' concept, *156, 158, 163*

Financial contributions, *27*

First Amendment,
 activities in violation of, *115*
 censorship, *170, 172, 174, 176, 178, 179, 181, 183, 185, 186, 188*

freedom of association, *138, 140, 141, 143, 145, 146, 148, 150, 151*
freedom of expression, *156, 158, 160, 162, 163, 165, 166, 168*
free speech, *83, 85, 87, 88, 90, 92, 94, 96, 97, 99, 100, 145, 146*
religious freedom, *103, 104, 106, 108, 110, 112, 113, 115, 116, 118, 119*
Tinker disruption test, *85, 88, 92, 110*
First Amendment Center, *188*
Fisher v. University of Texas, *215, 217, 221*
Flags,
    burning, *154, 156, 158, 160*
    Confederate, *158, 162, 163*
    as self-expression, *163, 165*
Florida; Graham v., *38, 39*
Florida v. Harris, *131, 132*
Florida v. Jardines, *61*
Foreign languages,
    on ballots, *18*
    ban on teaching, *183, 185*
Forsyth v. Hammond, *73*
Fortas, Abe, on student rights, *174*
Fourteenth Amendment,
    due process rights, *225, 244, 246*
    Equal Protection Clause, *190, 192, 194, 196, 198, 200, 203, 211, 259, 266*
    freedom for slaves, *264*
    ratification, *14*
Fourth Amendment,
    global-positioning systems, monitoring, *51, 53, 54, 56*
    interrogations and interviews, *70, 72, 73, 75, 77, 79, 80, 133*
    searches and seizures, *58, 60, 61, 63, 64, 66, 125, 133*
Francis, Pope, *220*
Frankfurter, Felix, *4*
Frank v. Walker, *20*
Fraser; Bethel School District v., *88, 99, 160*

Frederick; Morse v., *83, 85, 87, 88, 90, 92*
Free speech,
  controversial speech, *145, 146*
  'fighting words' concept, *156, 158, 163*
  hate speech, *146*
  in schools, *83, 85, 87, 88, 90, 99, 100*
  on social media, *92, 94, 97, 99*
  Tinker disruption test, *85, 88, 92, 110*
  vanity license plates, *97, 162*
  See also Symbolic speech,
Friend of court briefs, *6*
Furman v. Georgia, *44, 46*

G

Garcia v. Miera, *233, 235*
Gates, Robert M., *148*
Gault, In re, *287*
Gay and Lesbian Student Rights Law of 1993, *29*
Gay and lesbian students, See LGBTQ students,
Gay-Straight Alliance (GSA) Network, *151, 152*
Gender issues,
  voting rights and, *14, 17*
  wage gap, *220*
Georgia, voter registration, *17*
Georgia; Furman v., *44, 46*
Germany, voting age, *24*
Global-positioning systems, in criminal investigations, *51, 53, 54, 56*
Go Ask Alice (anonymous), *172*
Goguen; Smith v., *165*
Good News Club v. Milford Central School, *113*
Gore, Al, *11*
Goss v. Lopez, *240, 242, 244, 246*
GPS, in criminal investigations, *51, 53, 54, 56*
Graham; Stone v., *110, 112*
Graham v. Florida, *38, 39*
Greene; Camreta v., *68, 70, 72, 73*

Grutter v. Bollinger, *215, 220, 221*

H

Hairstyles, as self-expression, *160*
Hammond; Forsyth v., *73*
Harlan, John Marshall,
   on Fifth Amendment privilege, *284, 286*
   on separate but equal policy, *266*
Harris; Florida v., *131, 132*
Hate speech, *146*
Hayes, Rutherford B., *9*
Hazelwood School District v. Kuhlmeier, *88, 99, 100, 179, 181*
Headscarves, discrimination based on, *217, 219*
Hearings, for school disciplinary actions, *240, 242, 244, 246, 247, 249, 251, 252, 254, 255*
Henry, Barbara, *268*
Hermitage School District; Layshock v., *94*
Hero Ain't Nuthin' But a Sandwich, A (Childress), *172*
High schools,
   civics test requirement for graduation, *198*
   graduation, importance of, *244*
   religious clubs, *113*
   voter registration days, *27*
   See also Schools,
Hirabayashi v. United States, *213*
HIV-positive students, right to public education, *202*
Hobbs; Jackson v., *36*
Hodges; Obergefell v., *6, 270, 297*
Homosexuality,
   See LGBTQ students,
Hong Kong, *24*
House of Representatives, *9*
Hughes, Langston, *172*
Huntington Valley Swim Club, *274*

Hurley v. Irish-American Gay, Lesbian and Bisexual Group of Boston, Inc., *148*
Hyattsville, Maryland, *24*

I

I Am Jazz (television show), *30*
Identification, voter, *18, 20, 26*
Illegal drugs, See Drugs,
Illegal immigrants,
    deportation of noncitizen veterans, *201, 202*
    DREAMers, *201*
    education for children of, *190, 192, 194, 196, 198, 200, 201, 202, 203*
    number of, *198*
Illiteracy,
    literacy tests, for voting, *17, 18*
    provision of education and, *194*
Immunity, granting, *70, 72*

Independents, primary voting and, *26*
Ingraham v. Wright, *223, 225, 227, 228*
In loco parentis doctrine, *85, 129*
Innocence Project, *286*
Interracial marriage, *270, 274*
Interrogations and interviews,
    of minors versus adults, *79*
    by teachers, *77*
    without parental permission, *70, 72, 73, 75, 77*
Iowa, ban on corporal punishment in schools, *227*
Iowa, State of, v. Rollins, *230, 232*
Irish-American Gay, Lesbian and Bisexual Group of Boston, Inc.; Hurley v., *148*
Island Trees School District v. Pico, *4, 170, 172, 174, 176*

Isom, DeQuan, *22*
Ithaca City School District; R.O. v., *183*

J

Jackson, Robert H., on freedom of expression, *158*
Jackson v. Hobbs, *36*
Jacobellis v. Ohio, *88*
Jaffree; Wallace v., *119*
Jardines; Florida v., *61*
Jefferson, Thomas, *9*
Jennings, Jazz, *29, 30*
Johnson, Lyndon B., on voting, *17*
Johnson; Texas v., *154, 156, 158, 160*
Jones; United States v., *51, 53, 54, 56, 64*
Journalism,
  free expression laws for, *178, 179*
  school newspaper censorship, *179, 181, 183*
Judiciary Act of,
Jurisdiction of courts, *4*
Juvenile justice system,
  confessions by juveniles, *75, 77, 79*
  Miranda warnings, *75, 287, 289*
  right to education in detention, *202*
  sentencing and prison terms, *34, 36, 38, 39, 41, 43, 44, 46, 48, 49, 79*
  solitary confinement, *237*
  See also Minors,

K

Kagan, Elena,
  on canine alerts as basis for drug searches, *132*
  on granting certiorari, *73*
  on sentencing for juveniles, *39, 41*
Kennedy, Anthony M.,
  on First Amendment, *112*
  on flag desecration, *160*
  on free expression, *162*

on high school graduation, *244*
on sentencing for juveniles, *44*
Kennedy, John F., on racial discrimination, *206*
on right to vote, *17*
Kentucky, Ten Commandments displays, *104, 106, 108*
Kentucky; Stanford v., *43*
Kent v. United States, *46*
King; Maryland v., *61*
Kowalski v. Berkeley County Schools, *92, 94*
Kuhlmeier; Hazelwood School District v., *88, 99, 100, 179, 181*
Kurtzman; Lemon v., *106, 110*

L

La Farge, Oliver, *172*
Lafon; Barr v., *162*
L'Amour, Louis, *14*
Laney v. Farley, *249*
Lange v. Diercks, *179*
Languages, on ballots, *18*
Laughing Boy (La Farge), *172*
Lawrence v. Texas, *151, 315*
Law school admissions, reverse discrimination, *215*
Lawyers, right to, *284*
Layshock v. Hermitage School District, *94*
Lee v. Weisman, *112, 244*
Lemon v. Kurtzman, *106, 110*
Lewis, John, *17*
Lewis; County of Sacramento v., *240*
LGBTQ students,
Day of Silence of events, *166*
discrimination protests, *29*
exclusion from activities, *138, 140, 141, 143, 148, 150*
freedom of association, *140, 141, 143*

right to nonconforming dress, *273*
right to public education, *202*
transgender rights, *29, 30*
Libraries,
  Banned Books Week, *186*
  discrimination by, *268, 270*
License plates, free speech and, *97, 162*
Life sentences,
  for juveniles, *34, 36, 38, 39, 41, 43, 44, 46, 48, 49, 79*
  number serving, *38*
Lincoln, Abraham,
  on education, *200*
  Emancipation Proclamation, *14*
Literacy tests, for voting, *17, 18*
LoMonte, Frank, *181*
Lopez; Goss v., *240, 242, 244, 246*
Louisiana; Brown v., *268, 270*
Louisiana; Montgomery v., *41*
Lovett; United States v., *4*
Loving v. Virginia, *270*
Lynch v. Donnelly, *118*

M
Madison, James, *104*
Mail, voting by, *27*
Mandatory sentencing, *34, 36, 38, 39, 41*
Mandatory voting, *20, 22*
Marriage,
  interracial, *270, 274*
  same-sex, *6, 148, 270, 297, 300, 306*
Marshall, Thurgood,
  on racial discrimination, *209*
  Supreme Court appointment and service, *6*
Martinez; Christian Legal Society v., *112, 113*
Maryland,
  religious test for public office, *118*
  voting age, *22, 24*

Maryland v. King, *61, 302, 304*
Massachusetts, discrimination, protests against, *29*
Matthews, Stanley, *11*
McCreary County v. American Civil Liberties Union (ACLU), *103, 104, 106, 108, 118, 119*
McDonnell; Wolff v., *240*
McNeely; Missouri v., *61*
Mergens; Westside Community Board of Education v., *113*
Mexico, migrants from, *151*
Meyer v. Nebraska, *183, 185*
Michigan, ban on affirmative action, *217*
Midterm elections,
Miera; Garcia v., *233, 235*
Milford Central School; Good News Club v., *113*
Military funerals, protests at, *166*
Military personnel, absentee voting, *27*

deportation of noncitizen veterans, *201, 202*
Miller v. Alabama, *34, 36, 38, 39, 41, 49, 151, 286*
Minimum wage laws, *220, 315, 316*
Minorities,
  affirmative action, *206, 207, 209, 211, 213, 215, 217, 220, 221*
  death penalty bias, *44, 46*
  disenfranchisement, *18*
  See also Discrimination,
Minors,
  emancipation laws, *293*
  interviewing without parental permission, *70, 72, 73, 75, 77*
  legal rights and responsibilities, *292, 293*
  lying about age, *79*
  Miranda rights applied to, *75, 287, 289*
  protection from violent video games, *163*

search and seizure issues, *58, 60, 61, 63, 66*
sentencing, *34, 36, 38, 39, 41, 43, 44, 46, 48, 49, 79*
solitary confinement of, *237*
Miranda rights,
   for juveniles, *75, 287, 289*
   public safety exception, *289*
Miranda v. Arizona, *278, 280, 282, 284, 286*
Mississippi, religious test for public office, *118*
Missouri v. McNeely, *61*
Mock trials, *48*
Montgomery v. Louisiana, *41*
Morality of Consent, The (Bickel), *211*
Morris, Desmond, *172*
Morse v. Frederick, *83, 85, 87, 88, 90, 92*
Motor Voter Law, *17*

N

Naked Ape, The (Morris), *172*
National Institute on Drug Abuse, *129*
Nationalmocktrial.org, *48*
National Socialist Party of America; Village of Skokie v., *145, 146*
National Socialist Party v. Skokie, *145, 146*
National Voter Registration Act (Motor Voter Law), *17*
National Youth Rights Association (NYRA), *22, 290*
Native Americans, voter identification, *20*
Navarette v. California, *60*
Nazi symbolism, *145, 146*
Nebraska; Meyer v., *183, 185*
Newdow; Elk Grove Unified School District v., *72*
New Jersey, ban on corporal punishment in schools, *227*

New Jersey v. T.L.O., *60, 61, 63, 77, 127*
Newspapers, censorship by schools, *179, 181, 183*
Nicaragua, voting age, *24*
Nineteen Eighty-Four (Orwell), *51*
Nineteenth Amendment, *14, 17*
No Más Muertes (No More Deaths) organization, *151*
Nonverbal actions, See Symbolic speech,
North Carolina,
   religious test for public office, *118*
   school district rezoning, *261*
North Dakota, State of; Simons v., *232, 233*
NYRA,
   See National Youth Rights Association (NYRA),

O

Obama, Barack,
   deferred action for immigrant students, *201*
   on Rosa Parks, *266*
   on student privacy rights, *136*
   on voting, *14*
Obergefell v. Hodges, *6, 270, 297*
O'Connor, Sandra Day,
   on affirmative action, *215, 220, 221*
   on religious freedom, *119*
   Supreme Court appointment and service, *6, 11*
   on Ten Commandments displays, *106*
Ohio; Brandenburg v., *146*
Ohio; Jacobellis v., *88*
Ohio v. Clark, *77*
Olmstead v. United States, *64*
Online expression, disciplinary actions for, *251, 252, 254*

free speech and, *92, 94, 97, 99*
positive messages, *97*
social media contracts, *135*
Oregon, voter registration, *26*
Orwell, George, *51*
@OsseoNiceThings, *97*
OurTime.org, *30*
Oyez Project, *31*

P

Paddling,
See Corporal punishment,
Palmer v. Thompson, *257, 259, 261*
Parents,
permission to interview students, *70, 72, 73, 75, 77*
physical punishment by, *228, 230, 232, 233, 237, 238*
Parks, Rosa, *266*
Patton, Paul, *43*
People v. T.C., *287, 289*
People v. Weaver, *56*
Perry, Tyler, *274*
Perry; Veasey v., *20*
Phelps; Snyder v., *166*
Philadelphia, School District of; D.C. v., *249, 251*
Phillip B., In re, *237*
Pico; Island Trees School District v., *4, 170, 172, 174, 176*
Pildes, Rick, *20, 22*
Pipeline to prison, schools as, *254*
Pledge of Allegiance, *72, 115, 116*
Plessy v. Ferguson, *264, 266, 271*
Plyler v. Doe, *190, 192, 194, 196, 203*
Political contributions, *27*
Poll taxes, *17, 18*
Popular vote, presidential elections, *8*
Post Card Application, *27*
Poverty,
as barrier to voting, *18*
discrimination based on, *200*

Powell, Lewis, Jr.,
  on affirmative action, *211*
  on Fourteenth Amendment, *213*
  on freedom of expression, *186*
  on school discipline, *228*
Powell, William,
  on affirmative action, *207*
  on education for illegal immigrants, *196*
  on school discipline, *223, 227, 246*
Prayer,
  in schools, *112, 113, 115*
Pregnant students, right to public education, *202*
President, U.S.,
  age requirement, *22*
Presidential elections,
  election process, *8, 9, 11, 24, 26, 27*
  recount of ballots, *11, 313, 315*
  voter turnout, *12, 14*
Primaries, voting in, *14, 26*
Prison terms for juveniles, *34, 36, 38, 39, 41, 49*
Privacy rights, *51, 53, 54, 56, 58, 60, 61, 63, 64, 66, 123, 125, 127, 129, 131, 132, 133, 135, 136, 295, 297*
Private schools, corporal punishment in, *227*
Probable cause standard, *123*
Property taxes, school district funding, *200*
Public libraries, discrimination by, *268, 270*
Public swimming pools,
  racial discrimination, *274*
  segregation of, *257, 259, 261, 274*
Puerto Rico, ban on corporal punishment in schools, *227*

Q

Quota systems for college admissions, *206, 207, 209, 211, 213, 215, 217*

R

Racial issues,
  affirmative action, *206, 207, 209, 211, 213, 215, 217*
  Confederate flag displays, *158, 162, 163*
  death penalty bias, *44, 46*
  desegregation of schools, *261, 266, 268, 270, 271*
  disenfranchisement, *18*
  segregation, *257, 259, 261*
  See also Discrimination,
Ragland; State v., *39, 41*
Railway Labor Executives' Association; Skinner v., *132*
Real Kids, Real Stories, Real Change (Sundem), *31*
Reasonable suspicion test for school searches, *58, 66, 123, 125, 136*
Redding; Safford Unified School District v., *61, 63*
Regents of the University of California v. Bakke, *188, 206, 207, 209, 211, 213, 221*
RegisterToVote.org, *26*
Registration,
  See Voter registration
Rehnquist, William,
  on exclusionary rights of private organizations, *141, 143*
  on selection of cases, *4*
Religious freedom,
  belief in God as test for public office, *118*
  clubs and organizations, *112, 113, 118*
  headscarves, wearing, *217, 219*
  prayer, *112, 113, 115, 299*

separation of church and state, *103, 104, 118, 119*
    Ten Commandments displays, *103, 104, 106, 108, 110, 112*
Rent, *186*
Rikers Island, *237*
Riley v. California, *54, 58, 127*
Roberts, John, on free speech at school events, *87, 88*
RocktheVote.com, *18, 31*
Rodriguez; San Antonio School District v., *200*
Roe v. Wade, *81*
Rollins; State of Iowa v., *230, 232*
Roper v. Simmons, *38, 43, 44, 151*
R.O. v. Ithaca City School District, *183*

S

Sacagawea, *14*
Sacramento, County of, v. Lewis, *240*
Safford Unified School District v. Redding, *61, 63*
Same-day voter registration, *17, 20*
Same-sex marriage, constitutionality of, *270, 297, 300*
    support for, *6, 148*
San Antonio School District v. Rodriguez, *200*
Sandford; Scott v., *261, 264*
San Francisco, Municipal Court of; Camara v., *123*
Scalia, Antonin,
    on affirmative action, *217*
    on searches and seizures, *53*
    on Ten Commandments displays, *108*
Schempp; Abington School District v., *113*
Schmerber v. California, *54*
School Board of Greenfield; Boucher v., *181*

School District of Philadelphia; D.C. v., *249, 251*
School elections, involvement in, *11*
Schools,
   alternative schools, placement in, *249, 251*
   censorship by, *170, 172, 174, 176, 178, 179, 181, 183, 185, 186, 188*
   clustered schools, *261*
   compulsory attendance laws, *240*
   corporal punishment, *223, 225, 227, 228, 230, 233, 235, 237, 238*
   curriculum censorship, *183, 185*
   desegregation, *261, 266, 268, 270, 271*
   dress codes, *162, 163, 165*
   drug testing, *123, 125, 127, 129, 131*
   due process for disciplinary actions, *240, 242, 244, 246, 247, 249, 251, 252, 254, 255*
   free speech, *83, 85, 87, 88, 90, 99, 100*
   funding via property taxes, *200*
   illegal immigrants, education for children of, *190, 192, 194, 196, 198, 200, 201, 202, 203*
   interrogations and interviews, *77*
   in loco parentis doctrine, *85, 129*
   obligation to protect students, *127, 129*
   prayer in, *112, 113, 115*
   quality of education, *200, 201*
   right to search, *58, 60, 61, 63, 66, 123, 125, 127*
   separate but equal policy, *261, 266, 268, 270, 271*
   social media policies, *135*
   suspensions and expulsions, *240, 242, 244, 246, 247, 249, 251, 252, 254, 255*

Tinker disruption test, *85, 88, 92, 110*
zero-tolerance policies, *92, 94, 129, 254*
School start times, student action and, *29*
School-to-prison pipeline, *254*
Schuette v. Coalition to Defend Affirmative Action, *217*
Scotland, voting age, *24*
Scott v. Sandford, *14, 261, 264*
SCOTUSblog, *31*
Searches and seizures,
  based on anonymous tips, *60*
  car searches, *131, 132*
  cell phones, *54, 58*
  drug testing, *121, 123, 125, 127, 129, 131*
  global-positioning systems, monitoring, *51, 53, 54, 56*
  interviews as, *70, 72, 73*
  reasonable suspicion test, *58, 66*
  by school officials, *60, 61, 63*
  strip searches, *61, 63, 135*
Segregation,
  public swimming pools, *257, 259, 261, 276*
  public transportation, *264, 266*
Self-incrimination, protection from, *75, 278, 280, 282, 284, 286, 287*
Sentencing for juveniles, *34, 36, 38, 39, 41, 43, 44, 46, 48, 49, 79*
Separate but equal policy,
  education, *266, 268, 270, 271*
  public swimming pools, *257, 259, 261, 276*
  public transportation, *264, 266, 276*
Seventeen magazine, *27, 29*
Shelton v. Tucker, *176*
Signs and posters, as symbolic speech, *83, 85, 87, 88, 90, 92, 116, 160*

Simmons; Roper v., *38, 43, 44, 151*
Simons v. State of North Dakota, *232, 233*
Sixth Amendment, Confrontation Clause, *77*
Skinner v. Railway Labor Executives' Association, *132*
Skokie; National Socialist Party v., *145, 146*
Slaughterhouse Five (Vonnegut), *172*
Slavery,
    Dred Scott case, *14, 264*
    voting rights of slaves, *14, 20*
Smith, Heather, *18*
Smith v. Goguen, *165*
Snyder v. Phelps, *166*
Social media,
    cyberbullying, *92, 94*
    free speech and, *92, 94, 97, 99*
    positive messages on, *97*
    school policies, *135*
    searches of accounts, *125*
Solitary confinement of minors, *237*
Sons of Confederate Veterans; Walker v., *162*
Sotomayor, Sonia,
    appointment to Supreme Court, *6*
    on GPS monitoring, *56*
Soul on Ice (Cleaver), *172*
Souter, David,
    on due process, *240*
    on Establishment Clause, *108*
South Carolina, religious test for public office, *118*
Spanking,
    See Corporal punishment,
Sparkle Effect, *202*
Special needs,
    See Disabilities, individuals with,
Speech, freedom of,
    See Free speech,
Spence v. Washington, *163*

Sports, involvement in, *129, 131*
Stanford v. Kentucky, *43*
State laws,
   bans on affirmative action, *217*
   free expression for students, *178, 179*
   minimum wage, *220*
   provision of public education, *200*
   See also specific states and specific cases,
State of Iowa v. Rollins, *230, 232*
State v. Alaniz, *60*
State v. Ragland, *39, 41*
Stevens, John Paul,
   on free speech at school events, *88, 90*
   on power of government, *77*
   on racial discrimination, *207*
Stewart, Potter,
   on pornography, *88*
   on schools, freedom in, *176*
Stone, Harlan,
   on racial discrimination, *213*
   on selection of cases, *4*
Stone v. Farley, *79*
Stone v. Graham, *110, 112*
Strip searches, *61, 63, 135*
Studen Press Law Center, *188*
Student Digital Privacy Act (proposed), *136*
Students, ID cards as voter identification, *18, 20*
Students Organize for Syria (SOS), *151*
Sundem, Garth, *31*
Supreme Court,
   amicus briefs, *6*
   diversity of, *6*
   on formulas for voting procedures, *17*
   history of, *3*
   jurisdiction, *4*
   justices, nomination and confirmation, *11*
   oral argument process, *4*
   qualifications for justices, *6*

ranking system, *8*
reversal of decisions, *270, 271*
roles and responsibilities of, *3, 4, 6, 8*
selection of cases, *3, 4, 68, 70, 72, 73, 80, 81*
size and composition of, *3*
yearly schedule, *3*
See also specific cases,
Suspensions from school, *240, 242, 244, 246, 247, 249, 251, 252, 254, 255*
Swastika, as symbolic speech, *145, 146*
Swimming pools, discrimination at, *257, 259, 261, 276*
Switzerland, voting age, *24*
Symbolic speech,
    armbands, *83, 85, 160, 168*
    Confederate flags, *158, 162, 163*
    'fighting words' concept, *156, 158, 163*
    flag burning, *154, 156, 158, 160*
    hairstyles, *160*
    signs and posters, *83, 85, 87, 88, 90, 92, 116*
    swastikas, *145, 146*
    tattoos, *166*
    T-shirts, *160, 162, 163*
Syria, student support for, *151*

T

Takoma Park, Maryland, *22, 24*
Taney, Roger B., on slavery, *264*
Tattoos, as self-expression, *166*
Taxes,
    poll taxes, *17, 18*
    property taxes for school district funding, *200*
T.C.; People v., *287, 289*
Teachers,
    interrogations and interviews by, *77*
    mandatory reporting of child abuse, *77*

Teen courts, *8, 48, 254*
Television,
Ten Commandments, display of, *103, 104, 106, 108, 110, 112*
Tennessee, religious test for public office, *118*
Terminiello v. City of Chicago, *156*
Texas,
   religious test for public office, *118*
   school district rezoning, *261*
   Ten Commandments displays, *110*
   voter identification, *20*
Texas; Lawrence v., *151*
Texas v. Johnson, *154, 156, 158, 160*
Thirteenth Amendment, *14*
Thomas, Clarence,
   on affirmative action, *217*
   on drug testing, *125*
   on free speech in schools, *90*
   on in loco parentis doctrine, *85*
   on punishment by parents, *237*
   on Tinker disruption test, *92*
Thomas, Piri, *172*
Thompson; Palmer v., *257, 259, 261*
Tilden, Samuel, *9*
Tinker v. Des Moines Independent Community School District, *83, 85, 88, 92, 110, 168, 174, 176, 185*
T.L.O.; New Jersey v., *60, 61, 63, 77, 127*
Toronto mayoral election, *22*
Transgender rights, student action for, *29, 30*
   See also LGBTQ students,
Transportation, as barrier to voting, *18*
Treasury Employees v. Von Raab, *132*
Trevor Project, *152*
Tsarnaev, Dzhokhar, *289*

T-shirts, as symbolic speech, *160, 162, 163*
Tucker; Shelton v., *176*
Tufts, Bobby, *22*
Twenty-Fourth Amendment, *17*
Twenty-Sixth Amendment, *22*

U

Underground newspaper, censorship of, *181*
Undocumented residents,
　See Illegal immigrants,
United Nations Committee on the Rights of the Child, *225*
United States; Elonis v., *97, 99*
United States; Hirabayashi v., *213*
United States; Kent v., *46*
United States; Olmstead v., *64*
United States v. Butler, *4*
United States v. Jones, *51, 53, 54, 56, 64*
United States v. Lovett, *4*
United States; Wong Wing v., *192*
Universities,
　See Colleges and universities,
University of Texas; Fisher v., *215, 217, 221*
U.S. Constitution,
　See Constitution,
U.S. House of Representatives, *9*

V

Veasey v. Perry, *20*
Vernonia School District v. Acton, *127, 131*
Video games, *163*
Village of Skokie v. National Socialist Party of America, *145, 146*
Virginia; Loving v., *270*
VolunTEEN Nation, *31*
Volunteer opportunities, community involvement, *186*

election campaigns, *11, 165, 166*
   importance of, *14*
   teen courts, *8*
   voting rights organizations, *12*
Vonnegut, Kurt, *172*
Von Raab; Treasury Employees v., *132*
Voter Empowerment Act (H.R.12), *17*
Voter identification laws, *18, 20, 26*
Voter registration,
   eligibility requirements, *14, 24, 26*
   online, *17*
   same-day, *17, 20*
Voting,
   age requirements, *14, 17, 22, 24*
   barriers to, *18, 20*
   historical perspective, *14, 17*
   importance of, *14, 317*
   mandatory, *20, 22*
   power of one vote, *9, 11, 316*
   racial discrimination, *14, 18, 300*
   rights and responsibilities, *12, 14*
   women's rights, *14, 17*
Voting Assistance Program, *27*
Voting Rights Act Amendment of 1975, *18*
Voting Rights Act of 1965, *17, 266, 300*

W

Wade; Roe v., *81*
Walker; Frank v., *20*
Walker v. Sons of Confederate Veterans, *162*
Wallace v. Jaffree, *119*
Warren, Earl,
   on enforcement of criminal law, *280*
   on Miranda v. Arizona, *284*
   on segregation, *266, 268*
Washington, George, *9*
Washington; Spence v., *163*

Washington state, voter registration, *26*
Weapons,
   school searches and policy, *92, 133*
Weaver; People v., *56*
Webber, Diane, *31*
Weber v. Aetna Casualty & Surety Co., *196*
Weisman; Lee v., *112, 244*
Westboro Baptist Church of Topeka, Kansas, *166*
Westside Community Board of Education v. Mergens, *113*
West Virginia Board of Education v. Barnette, *158*
White, Byron,
   on desegregation, *261*
   on student newspaper editorial control, *181*
   on suspensions from school, *244, 246*
Wisconsin, voter identification, *20*
Wolff, Laurie, *29*

Wolff v. McDonnell, *240*
Women,
   Supreme Court appointment and service, *6, 11*
   voting rights, *14, 17*
   See also Gender issues,
Wong, Joshua, *24*
Wong Wing v. United States, *192*
Wong Wing v. U.S., *192*
Workplace discrimination, *217, 219, 300, 302*
Wright, Richard, *172*
Wright; Ingraham v., *223, 225, 227, 228*

Y

York (slave), *14*
Your Voice Your Vote (Webber), *31*
Yousafzai, Malala, *178*
YouthActivismProject.org, *31*

Z

Zero-tolerance policies, *92, 94, 129, 254*

www.ingramcontent.com/pod-product-compliance
Lightning Source LLC
Chambersburg PA
CBHW011747220426
43667CB00020B/2926